# Women of Fashion

# WOMEN OF FASHION

## TWENTIETH-CENTURY DESIGNERS

746.92

## VALERIE STEELE

RIZZOLI
NEW YORK

FOR MY PARENTS

First published in the United States of America in 1991 by
Rizzoli International Publications, Inc.
300 Park Avenue South
New York, NY 10010

Library of Congress Cataloging-in-Publication Data

Steele, Valerie

   Women of fashion / by Valerie Steele
      p.   cm.
   Includes bibliographical references and index
   ISBN 0-8478-1394-0
   1. Costume design — History.  2. Women costume designers — History.
   3. Fashion — History.  I. Title.
   TT504.S74   1991                                91-2168
   746.9′2 — dc20                                  CIP

PAGE 1: Backstage at the Carolyne Roehm fashion show, Autumn 1990. Photograph
by Roxanne Lowit.
FRONTISPIECE: Madame Grès, Day dress, 1959. Photographer unknown. Photograph courtesy of The Costume Institute, The Metropolitan Museum of Art, New York.
PAGE 6: Vivienne Westwood, Mini-crini, Spring/Summer 1986 collection. Photograph
courtesy of Vivienne Westwood.

Designed by Mary McBride
Set in type by Graphic Composition, Inc., Athens, GA
Printed and bound by Dai Nippon, Tokyo, Japan

# CONTENTS

Acknowledgments    7
Introduction: Men Do Dominate    9
 1 The Rise of the Bearded Couturier    19
 2 Mothers of Invention    27
 3 Chanel: *"L'Elégance, C'est Moi"*    39
 4 Vionnet: "I Loved Women"    54
 5 Schiaparelli: Joke or Genius?    65
 6 Regiment of Women    70
 7 Spinach versus Mink    90
 8 All-American    103
 9 Wife-Dressing for Success    114
10 Think Pink!    124
11 Fashion Liberation    133
12 London: Feminine Not Feminist    147
13 Paris: La Vraie Femme    162
14 Milan: Angels Have No Sex    171
15 Madrid: Wild Child    178
16 Tokyo: Like the Boys    183
17 New York: Closing the Gender Gap    190
Postscript    212
Notes    213
Bibliography    218
Index    222

# ACKNOWLEDGMENTS

First of all, I wish to thank the designers who consented to be interviewed for this book and/or contributed illustrative material: Anne Marie Beretta, Laura Biagiotti, Carven, Bonnie Cashin, Patricia Clyne, the Fendi Sisters, Agnès de Fleurieu, Jennifer George, Carolina Herrera, Barbara Hulanicki, Jacqueline Jacobson, Betsey Johnson, Norma Kamali, Donna Karan (and Arnell/Bickford Associates), Rei Kawakubo of Comme des Garçons, Mary McFadden, Mariuccia Mandelli of Krizia, Nicole Miller, Rebecca Moses, Hanae Mori, Jean Muir, Charlotte Neuville, Diane Pernet, Zandra Rhodes, Carolyne Roehm, Sybilla, Chantal Thomass, Isabel Toledo, Pauline Trigère, Patricia Underwood, Joan Vass, Adrienne Vittadini, and Vivienne Westwood.

Thanks also to the following institutions and individuals: The Art Institute of Chicago, The Artists Rights Society, Laura Ashley, Inc., The Bettmann Photo Archives, The Brooklyn Museum, The Center for Creative Photography at the University of Arizona, The Centro Studi e Archivo della Communicazione, Università di Parma, The Chicago Historical Society, The Cincinnati Museum of Art, Mark Contratto, The Costume Institute of The Metropolitan Museum of Art (Robert Kaufman), The Edward C. Blum Design Laboratory of The Fashion Institute of Technology (Irving Solero), The Fashion Institute of Technology Library's Special Collections, J. Henry Fair, Stephen Gan, Joshua Greene, The Harvard Theatre Collection of The Harvard University Library, Horst P. Horst, Scott Hyde, The Kobal Collection, Alexander Lavrentier, Roxanne Lowit, Sheila Metzner, The Musée de la Mode et du Costume (Chantal Fribourg), The Neal Peters Collection, Nina Ricci, The Union Française des Arts du Costume, Maria Chandoha Valentino, The Victoria & Albert Museum, and Warner Brothers Pictures.

This book could not have been completed without the assistance of Leora Kahn, who did much of the picture research. Other essential players were my agent, John Wright, and at Rizzoli, Robert Janjigian, Jennifer Condon, and Mary McBride. Thanks also to Holly Brubach, John Carins, Marianne Carlano, Xavier Chaumette, Ann Coleman, Arlene Cooper, Kitty d'Alessio, Fred Davis, Jean Dreusedow, Diana Edkins, Bill Ewing, Fabienne Falluel, Marion Greenberg, Maris Heller, Catherine Johnson, Susan Kaiser, Betty Kirke, Harold Koda, Lynn Kutsche, Corinne LaBalme, Katel Le Bourhis, Freddy Lieba, Ruth Lynam, Richard Martin, Marjorie Miller, Florence Müller, Joane Olian, Amy Osaki, Janet Ozzard, Marie-Hélène Poix, Jan Reeder, Barbara Schreier, Marzena Szczeniowska, Otto Thieme, Katie Valgenti, Michel Voyski, Innocenta Wäjdowicz, Linda Weltners, Palmer White, Elizabeth Wilson, and all my students. Most of all, thanks to my husband, John Major.

# INTRODUCTION: MEN DO DOMINATE

I t's true: *Men do dominate women's fashion.* A recent study found that approximately 65 percent of famous twentieth-century fashion designers have been male, and only 35 percent female. Admittedly, the number of women appears to be growing: The 1988 edition of *Who's Who in Fashion* lists 42 percent female and 58 percent male designers.[1]

But it remains true that *almost all the big names are male*: Calvin, Ralph, and Oscar in America, Yves, Karl, and Giorgio in Europe. A recent poll in *W* asking "top international designers to name their favorite colleagues" produced a scorecard of twenty-one designers, only two of whom (Vivienne Westwood and Donna Karan) were women.[2]

At the same time, fashion headlines increasingly proclaim that a new generation of "designing women" is "closing the gender gap."[3] According to one French magazine:

Never before have women designers been so powerful. From Japan's Rei Kawakubo to Donna Karan in the United States and England's saucy Vivienne Westwood — it's women now who are offering the challenge, provocation, and innovation to push fashion forward. . . . Chanel, Schiaparelli, and Vionnet would be proud.[4]

Today, when women designers are in the news but still make up only a minority of the most successful fashion designers, it is time for a new look at the history of women in fashion. This is especially important because many popular beliefs about the subject need to be reassessed.

*What are the reasons for male fashion dominance?* "Man-and-woman-on-

ABOVE: *Vivienne Westwood, Minidress, Spring/Summer 1989 collection. Women play an important and highly visible role on the British fashion scene. Photograph courtesy of Vivienne Westwood.*

OPPOSITE: *Donna Karan for DKNY, Rayon-and-acetate jacket and pants, denim bodysuit, cotton tank bodysuit (left), and Wool jacket and pleated trousers, linen bodysuit, and silk scarf, Spring 1990 collection. Photograph by Peter Arnell, courtesy of Arnell/Bickford Associates and Donna Karan.*

ABOVE: *Rei Kawakubo for Comme des Garçons, Bonded, double-faced jacket, triple-layered nylon knit T-shirt, and bonded, double-faced estelle georgette pants, Autumn/Winter 1990–1991 collection. This Japanese designer says that her clothes are made for modern women "who do not need to assure their happiness by looking sexy to men, by emphasizing their figures, but who attract them with their minds." Photograph by Brian Griffin for* Six 6, *1990, published by Comme des Garçons Co., Ltd.*

the-street" interviews conducted in the late 1980s by writer Dianne T. Meranus reveal a number of possible reasons for continuing male dominance. Many people, for example, believe that men design clothes that are more "flattering" to women, either because "men know how they like women to look" or because "men don't like the way women look, so they work at changing their appearance." Other theories focus on the psychology of the wearer: "Women dress to please men" and therefore prefer to be dressed by a man, whose "taste and expertise [they] respect . . . more than a woman's."[5]

Oscar de la Renta has suggested that women designers tend to be less "objective" than men designers, because the women design first and foremost for themselves.[6] This psychological explanation for male fashion dominance is, in fact, very commonly believed — and not only among male designers! Men are more successful because they do not impose their "personal design restrictions on their product," suggested Sharon Tate in *Inside Fashion Design*.[7]

Another popular explanation for male dominance emphasizes the role of sexism: "Men get easier entrée to the field because of prejudice toward women."[8] In some cases, of course, sexism may play a role, as we shall see. But the conspiratorial view of fashion history is problematic, as are explanations that focus on the psychology of the designer and/or the wearer. Such explanations rely too heavily on assumptions about unchanging human nature.

Yet if we look at the history and sociology of women's participation in the world of fashion, we find important changes over time, as well as significant variations between different cultures.

Coco Chanel is always mentioned as the exceptional woman in the male-dominated history of fashion. Many people assume that Chanel was one of the first women fashion designers and that the number of women in the fashion industry has risen slowly but steadily as women have become increasingly liberated.

In reality, however, women's participation in the world of fashion has fluctuated considerably over time. From 1675 until well into the nineteenth century, the vast majority of dressmakers were women. In fact, when a handful of male dressmakers began to appear in Paris during the Second Empire (in the mid-nineteenth century), people were shocked that "real men" were professionally employed dressing and undressing ladies.

Yet within only a few years, men like Charles Frederick Worth had established a new stereotype: the male fashion dictator. *How and why did a few "bearded couturiers" come to overshadow the "queens of the needle?"* This is not merely an interesting historical question but one that bears on the situation in fashion today. Because the same thing happened again after World War II.

Meanwhile, in the early twentieth century, women designers made a comeback. As renowned fashion photographer Cecil Beaton observed, "sandwiched between two world wars, between Poiret's harem and Dior's New Look, two women dominated the field of haute couture."[9] The two women were Chanel and her arch-rival, Schiaparelli. Great as these two were, however, they were hardly atypical. The feminine leaders of Paris fashion also included Alix (later known as Mme Grès), Sonia Delaunay, Jeanne Lanvin (whom Karl Lagerfeld calls "a great, great designer"), Nina Ricci, the incomparable Madeleine Vionnet (whom Diana Vreeland called "the most important dressmaker of the twentieth century"), and many others.

Obviously, there were male designers, too, in the years between the wars, but "the excitement lay among the regiment of women."[10] *Why did women dominate Paris fashion during the 1920s and 1930s?* To understand women's leading role, we will look carefully at the careers of these *femmes créatrices*. Without neglecting the overall pattern, we will also focus on three women who stand out as exceptional creators: Chanel, Vionnet, and Schiaparelli. They were not merely successful in their day but continue to exert

an enormous influence on contemporary fashion. Moreover, they epitomize three very distinct creative types.

Chanel represents the woman of style. *"L'Elégance, c'est moi,"* she declared. Or as *Vogue* put it, "The essence of the Chanel Look was Chanel herself." But who was Chanel? To understand her style, we must go beyond the Chanel mythology to the woman herself — as demimondaine and dandy. Motivated by the iconoclasm of the sexual outsider, Chanel destroyed traditional feminine fashion, replacing it with an austere elegance, hitherto associated with the male dandy.[11] Thus, while Chanel's is very much a *woman's style,* it is based on a male model of power.

LEFT: *Claire McCardell, Bloomer playsuit in plaid cotton, 1942. The Costume Institute, The Metropolitan Museum of Art, New York. Courtesy of the photographer, Joshua Greene*

OPPOSITE: *Madeleine Vionnet, Empire-style evening dress, 1937. Photograph from Femina, courtesy of Special Collections, Fashion Institute of Technology Library, New York.*

Vionnet, by contrast, represents the professional dressmaker. Apprenticed at the age of eleven, she was typical of the army of women in the "needle trades." Among fashion connoisseurs, Vionnet is famous for her amazing technical skills. Yet her unique creative genius also had a more personal significance. Unlike many women in fashion, she never designed for herself but only for women whose physical beauty inspired her. Vionnet's clothes revealed the beauty of the female body, because she loved women.

Schiaparelli provides a third model. Still smarting because Vionnet had dismissed her as "a milliner," Chanel asserted that she was a real dressmaker when she described the upper-class divorcée Schiaparelli as "that Italian artist who makes clothes." Schiap (as she was commonly known) is important, not only because she represents an early version of the "socialite" designer but because she linked fashion and art and because her subversive wit continues to inspire avant-garde designers.

World War II ended the golden age of the Parisian couturière. Of the many women who flourished prior to World War II, only a handful (most notably Chanel and Alix Grès) were successful in the postwar period. But in the United States, American women became a significant force during the 1940s and even the 1950s.

"Women designers set new fashions," declared *Life* in 1946. Claire McCardell, in particular, became famous for making clothes that gave women the "maximum freedom of action." Tina Leser and Carolyn

Schnurer also designed innovative sportswear that idealized "the long-legged, tennis-playing, swimming girl."[12]

In light of this success, the question naturally arises: *Why did men like Dior dominate international fashion after 1945?* Part of the answer no doubt lies in the changing structure of the couture and the reassertion of French fashion leadership. The French couturier Jacques Fath argued that men were simply "the best designers" because fashion was art and men were innately more "creative" than women.

This book will analyze not only the history of women's participation in fashion but also the current status and influence of women designers throughout the world. Why do women designers today seem to be more important in London than in Paris, for example? Though broad in scope, the book is selective rather than encyclopedic in design and intention. Many good designers are mentioned only briefly; this is no reflection on their talent. It should be an encouraging sign that there are today so many women fashion designers that only an encyclopedia would suffice to describe them all.

The chapters dealing with contemporary fashion have been arranged loosely in cultural and geographical clusters. The chapter on London, for example, includes sections on Zandra Rhodes, Jean Muir, Vivienne Westwood, and Katharine Hamnett. The chapter on New York has been loosely subdivided into the categories Seventh Avenue, Uptown, and Downtown — to emphasize how women are working in a variety of different milieus and styles.

Any format that sets women apart is controversial, because it may seem to place women in a sort of cultural ghetto. Some of the fashion designers with whom I spoke expressed concern over just this type of ghettoization. Similarly, women who are painters often resist being categorized as "women painters" — rather than simply painters who happen to be women. The fact of being female may be an important, even fundamental, aspect of an individual's creativity, without necessarily having significance for her art as such.

Nevertheless, it is also true that feminism's search for neglected "heroines" has led to the rediscovery and reevaluation of important women artists, such as Frida Kahlo, who were previously regarded as, at best, marginal figures. The same might be accomplished for women working in fashion. It is *not*, however, the purpose of this book to rewrite fashion history by implying that women have been the best designers. Rather, I hope to call attention to the significant contributions that women have made — contributions that have often been overlooked or misunderstood.

Is there a distinctively female sensibility in fashion design? If the phenomenon exists, there are certainly limits to its general applicability. There are no clear female tracks marching through fashion history, nor can we automatically identify any given dress as designed by a woman. What criteria would we look for? Comfort? Practicality? But certainly there are men who have designed comfortable, practical clothes — just as there have been women designers who have created physically restrictive and overtly sexual styles.

ABOVE: *Adrienne Vittadini,
Red tartan linen sheath,
Spring 1990 collection.
Photograph courtesy of
Adrienne Vittadini.*

OPPOSITE: *Barbara
Hulanicki, Mother-
and-daughter, bias-cut floral
crepe dresses for Biba, 1969.
Photograph courtesy of
Barbara Hulanicki*

If a female designer like Jhane Barnes can successfully design mens-wear, why should the reverse not be true as well? Through the power of imagination, a male designer like Saint Laurent may think himself into a woman's situation. An individual's sense of gender, like his or her sense of self, is multifaceted. Virgina Woolf believed that the greatest artists were "androgynous," in that they could, through empathy and imagination, express the insights and experiences of both men and women. Chanel designed as a woman, but she also clearly identified herself with powerful male figures, and her style represents a brilliant union of male and female principles.

Significantly, contemporary women designers have differing perceptions of women's influence — *as women* — on fashion. "I am a woman," says Sonia Rykiel, "consequently I design as a woman." But Mariucci Mandelli of Krizia insists, "Creative people are like angels: They do not have a sexual identification." Clearly, there is no simple yes-or-no answer to the question, "Does the fact of being a woman influence the fashions that a woman designer creates?"

Nevertheless, although the notion of a female design sensibility is controversial, it may still have some validity. At least some women designers (perhaps a minority) seem to have brought to their work an authenticity of female experience, while others (at least on occasion) have also expressed a uniquely female perspective. Perhaps the most important reason to address the issue, however, is the simple fact that many people *already* assume that there are certain differences between male and female designers, but they tend not to analyze their assumptions, which may rest on premises to which they would object.

# 1
# THE RISE OF THE BEARDED COUTURIER

**W**eaving and sewing have been women's work throughout most of world history. Anthropologists claim that textiles often symbolize women's role in society, just as weapons symbolize the role of men. Among the Iban of Borneo, for example, the laying out of warp threads for the loom is called "the warpath of women."[1] In the West, also, terms such as *the distaff side* and *spinster* associate femininity with cloth production. We might infer from this that, historically, most fashion designers have been women. But we would be wrong.

When the production of clothing gradually ceased to be a home industry and became a profession, the business of making clothes fell into the hands of men. With the rise of capitalism in the medieval cities of Europe, the professionalization of clothing production effectively excluded women. Legally, only men could belong to the guild of tailors.

There was, however, considerable clandestine female competition, as many women illegally made clothes for sale. In 1675, during the reign of Louis XIV, a royal edict recognized the de facto existence of female dressmakers, arguing that for many women "this work was the only means of honestly making a living." The edict further announced that the "modesty of women and girls" required that they be "dressed by persons of their own sex."[2]

Louis XIV may have been motivated more by the desire for public order (and for additional tax revenue) than by sincere concerns about morality. But religious imperatives and socio-political reasons converged, and a law was passed in Paris permitting women to serve a three-year apprenticeship in cutting and dressmaking, after which they could go into business

ABOVE: *A young woman at work in Guatemala. Weaving and sewing were traditionally woman's work. Photograph by J. Bird, (Negative number 127632), courtesy of the Department of Library Services, American Museum of Natural History, New York.*

OPPOSITE: *François Boucher,* La Marchande de Modes, *1746. Reproduced by permission of the Trustees, The Wallace Collection, London.*

as couturières, making clothes for women and children.[3]

"The Couturière is a woman *authorized* to make various clothes, in her capacity as a member of a community established in Paris in 1675," declared the *Dictionnaire raisonné universel des Arts et Métiers*. "Couturières make dresses for women, skirts, jackets, etc. The scissors, needle and thimble are the equipment that couturières use to work the fabrics which serve to dress women in an elegant manner."[4]

The basic gender division between tailors (who were men) and dress-makers (who tended to be women) marked the first step toward "the victory of the couturières in the Grande Siècle."[5] There were only a handful of tailoresses, the male tailors retaining a monopoly on menswear and on tailored garments for ladies.[6] But the number of couturières grew rapidly, and their field of activity expanded. By 1773 there were some 1700 official couturières in Paris.

Since the fashion industry was still organized into guilds, there were many rules delineating who was allowed to produce or sell particular fashion items. Mercers sold textiles, couturières sewed dresses, and *marchandes de mode* (usually translated as milliners) decorated these dresses. Yet ambitious individuals constantly exceeded their official "job descriptions."

Rose Bertin, *marchande de modes de la reine*, became notorious as Marie-Antoinette's "Minister of Fashion." In many popular fashion history texts she is described as the "first" fashion designer. This is an oversimplification, but she certainly had a flair for publicity and made the most of her responsibility for "styling" many of Marie-Antoinette's clothes.

"Mademoiselle Bertin seemed to me an extraordinary person, full of her own importance and treating princesses as equals," recalled the fashionable aristocrat Baroness d'Oberkirch in her memoirs. Bertin's "jargon" was "amusing," but it "came very near impertinence if one did not hold her at arm's length, and degenerated into insolence when one did not nail her to her place."[7] Oberkirch also patronized the couturier Baulard's, explaining that "he and Alexandrine used to be the most celebrated, but Bertin has dethroned them." One wonders if she was amused or annoyed when M Baulard kept her "for more than an hour while he held forth against Mademoiselle Bertin, who put on the airs of a Duchess, and was not even a *bourgeoise*." Bertin may have been vulgar and insolent, constantly boasting about her "latest work" for the queen, but the Baroness admitted that her clothes and bonnets were "original" and "of rare perception."[8]

A recent scholarly history of the clothing of Ancien Régime France by Daniel Roche argues that not only were women able to compete successfully with male fashion professionals, but the importance of the female labor force was in large part responsible for the success of the fashion industry in the eighteenth century. The women, more than the men, adventurously directed the transformation of modes and manners.

Moreover, the new corporations of *couturières*, *lingères*, and *marchandes de mode* helped give fashion "a female identity" that was professional, social, and sexual. The milliners' guild, for example, was an offshoot of the mercers' guild, and contemporaries described milliners as having been "working under the shadow of their husbands" [i.e., under the mercers]. But then

the women broke away to form their own organization — a show of female independence that Roche calls "a family and sexual rupture."[9]

A handful of men were also encroaching on the preserve of the couturières. By the Napoleonic period, Louis Hippolyte Leroy, a tailor and former hairdresser, was the preeminent creator of ladies' dresses. On his way up, Leroy went into business with at least two female dressmakers. Apparently his partner, Mme Bonneau, was "only an average dressmaker" but wore his clothes with considerable chic and thus served as a "living advertisement" for Leroy's skill. His next partner, however, Mme Raimbault, was described in contemporary fashion journals as the "Michelangelo of fashion."

After using her money to open a shop on the rue de Richelieu, Leroy "threw her out unceremoniously, keeping her employees and her designs."[10] He also conducted a campaign of ridicule against the fashionable dress-maker, Mme Germond, whom he displaced as the Empress Josephine's favorite designer — just as Worth would replace Mme Palmyre as the Empress Eugènie's favorite.

Satirized as the "King of fashion" and *le Dieu des chiffons,* Leroy was one of the first men to achieve fame in the field of women's fashion. He was not alone, however. As one fashion magazine put it in 1806: "Our tailors today despise tailoring and only busy themselves with what they call the design of clothes."[11]

As early as 1814 the *Almanach des Modes* reported: "Millinery and dress-making were always women's occupations. When one sees how men have invaded the feminine domain this confusion of taste makes one wonder whether Nature has not made some sort of mistake in them."[12] This was almost certainly *not* a reference to homosexuality. Rather, the idea of Nature's "mistake" probably alluded to the belief that men and women were *by nature* different and that therefore they had different roles to play in society.

Most people believed that women were uniquely well suited to create clothes because fashion was an important part of every woman's life. The couturière and, even more, her sister the milliner, were recognized female types and, indeed, romantic figures in the popular imagination. They were even regarded as "artists" and sexy "aristocrats" among working-class women, because they spent their days creating beautiful, feminine adornments. Among the many nineteenth-century images of milliners, Degas's paintings stand out, because he actually showed the milliners making hats, instead of flirting with male customers.

In the mid-nineteenth century about 50,000 women in Paris were employed in the "needle trades," ranging from humble seamstresses to well-known couturières, such as Mmes Camille, Vignon, Palmyre, and Victorine. The poet Alfred de Musset praised Palmyre's ball gowns, and the novelist Stendhal mentioned Victorine's "ravishing" dresses. By and large, the names of these nineteenth-century couturières have today been forgotten — obliterated by the spectacular rise of the male couturier.

The number and prominence of male couturiers increased in the mid-nineteenth century, however, disrupting the by-then traditional distinction between female dressmakers and male tailors. "The *métiers* which have through all eternity belonged to women have been taken up by . . . men," complained journalist Jules Janin.[13] A tailors' periodical fretted that "these bearded couturiers" were beginning to replace female dressmakers. It was

ABOVE: *Charles Frederick Worth, the first great male couturier. Caricature by Bertall from* La Comédie de notre temps, *1874.*

BELOW: *Edgar Degas,* The Millinery Shop, *1879–1884, oil on canvas. Courtesy of The Art Institute of Chicago, Mr. and Mrs. Lewis Larned Coburn Memorial Collection. Photograph © 1990 The Art Institute of Chicago. All rights reserved.*

ABOVE: *Mary Cassat*, The Fitting, *1891. Courtesy of The Art Institute of Chicago, Mr. and Mrs. Martin A. Ryerson Collection. Photograph © 1990 The Art Institute of Chicago. All rights reserved.*

not right that "men dress women today." Not only did they lack feminine "innate taste," they also encroached on the "arts and industries" that provided a living for so many women.[14]

How and why did a handful of "bearded couturiers" come to overshadow the "queens of the needle"? To begin with, the men's very peculiarity gave them notoriety. Charles Frederick Worth (1825–95) was the most famous of the new couturiers, and almost all contemporary descriptions emphasize the astonishing fact that he was a man. Many Victorians were shocked that men, *real men*, were employed in dressing and undressing ladies. Journalists even hinted at the existence of a subliminally sexual relationship between male couturiers and their female clients.

"Would you believe that in the latter half of the nineteenth century there are bearded milliners," wrote Charles Dickens, "authentic men . . . who with their solid fingers, take the exact dimensions of the highest titled women in Paris — robe them, unrobe them, and make them turn backward and foreward before them."[15]

The stereotype of the male fashion "dictator" dates from this time, because men not only entered the fashion industry, they profoundly altered it. Couturières like Mmes Vignon and Palmyre collaborated with individual clients to create one-of-a-kind dresses. But however skillful she was, the dressmaker was essentially a hireling, who deferred to her client's wishes. By contrast, Worth made a series of models, which he then presented to his clients.

Worth professionalized the craft of fashion, transforming it into "big business." By insisting on his creative "genius," Worth also redefined dressmaking as "high art." Thus, he was simultaneously artist and industrialist — two roles that women were unaccustomed to playing. He helped establish a new and powerful image of the couturier as fashion dictator, which contrasted with the subordinate position of the traditional female dressmaker.

Contemporary accounts emphasize (and probably exaggerate) Worth's dictatorial methods. The writer Hippolyte Taine, for example, describes Worth demanding of a woman, "Madame, who has recommended me to you? In order to be dressed by me you have to be introduced. I am an artist." To another client he said, "Move about, turn around . . . come back in eight days. By that time I will have composed a dress suitable for you."[16]

According to a report on the Paris Exhibition of 1867: "The biggest dressmaker of society and the demi-monde is a man — and a man who knows how to treat courtesans and duchesses disdainfully, one might almost say with unparallelled rudeness." Another reporter expanded the complaint: "Now men dictate ladies' dresses and are arbiters of fashion, a custom which we hope will not become general."[17]

Would "great ladies" have consented to be dictated to had the dressmaker been another woman? In the fairly rigid class hierarchy that characterized nineteenth-century society, ladies were used to dictating to their working-class dressmakers. It was upsetting enough that Worth had risen from humble origins, but as a man he could still plausibly tell women what to wear — especially since women were supposed to dress to please the men in their life.

"One must be a man in order to be able to dress women," declared Ernest Feydeau in his book *L'Art de plaire* (1871).[18] Women were described by Feydeau as smiling seductively and pleading with the couturier to make them beautiful.

The old stereotype of women as "fashion's slaves" expanded to include the belief that they were, in particular, the willing slaves of Worth. The fact that Worth was an Englishman was also forgotten, as a new international stereotype developed that "fashion originated with Frenchmen."[19]

The reasons for the rise of the "bearded couturier" have much to do with general socioeconomic trends that affected nonfashion industries as well. As the organization of work became more clearly professionalized, larger in scale, and more industrialized, men came to dominate the upper ranks of even hitherto female professions: Midwives were replaced by obstetricians, for example — and only a handful of women were able to receive the new medical training.

Meanwhile, women filled the ranks of unskilled or semi-skilled labor: Skilled male weavers were replaced on the new power looms by women and even children. In offices, female secretaries replaced male clerks, but the actual duties of these female workers became far more circumscribed and routine.

The development of capitalism meant, in practice, the feminization and proletarianization of much of the labor force. The vast majority of those in the fashion industry were women. Owners and business managers tended to be men, but below this the hierarchy within any dressmaking establishment was largely female, from the saleswomen and forewomen to the humble seamstresses and apprentices. Those in the ateliers were often young, unmarried women, but married women were also employed, doing piecework at home. The design influence of the skilled female workers must have been considerable, although they labored anonymously.

Occasionally a woman could exploit her hands-on skill. In the United States, Mrs. Ellen Curtis Demorest recognized that American women had difficulty making attractive clothes, so she invented the sized paper dress pattern. According to writer Caroline Milbank, Madame Demorest (as she was known professionally) was "as important to American nineteenth-century fashion as Charles Frederick Worth was to the development of the Paris couture."[20]

The stereotype of men as creative geniuses had as its corollary the denigration of women as "mere" technicians. But despite the notoriety of male couturiers, there were also many women designers. Indeed, by the early twentieth century, male and female fashion designers shared the spotlight. Jacques Doucet was successful, for example, but so were the Callot sisters. The House of Worth continued under the direction of Worth's two sons, but its greatest competitor was Jeanne Paquin, whose couture house was right next door on the rue de la Paix.

# 2
# MOTHERS OF INVENTION

**W**orth's fame contrasts with the oblivion into which Jeanne Paquin has fallen—although in her heyday she was widely regarded as "the world's greatest fashion authority."[1] If anyone was Worth's successor, it was Paquin, and yet most fashion histories mention her briefly, if at all. Since her first name is rarely given, some writers have even assumed that she was a man or have thought that her husband was the real designer.

Why has she been forgotten? Perhaps because she was a woman, suggests fashion historian Jan Reeder.[2] Worth captured the popular imagination because he was a man in a predominantly female profession, whereas Paquin has tended to be regarded, in retrospect, as just one of many female dressmakers—on a par with Worth's predecessors and contemporaries, women like Clementine Bara, Rosalie Prost, and Eugènie Gaudry, whose names are remembered only by specialists.

Contemporary standards of female modesty meant that Paquin could not "blow her own horn" the way Worth and Poiret did—or the way Chanel was to do, only a few years hence. Thus, in the 1920s it was an advantage for Chanel to be a woman but in 1900 something of a disadvantage for Paquin, at least in terms of her historical reputation. As a respectable woman, Paquin only occasionally gave interviews, although she was renowned for her chic, and one of the mannequins at the Paris Universal Exhibition of 1900 was a sumptuously dressed wax figure of Paquin herself.

Not only were her dresses prominently featured at the Universal Exhibition, but Paquin was even elected president of the fashion section of the exhibition, demonstrating that she was highly respected by her peers. Moreover, the giant statue that towered over the entrance to the Universal

ABOVE: *Paquin, Avant-garde blue day dress, 1911. Illustration by Paul Iribe for* L'Eventail et la fourrure chez Paquin.

OPPOSITE: *Jeanne Paquin, Day dress, 1905. Photographed by Paul Boyer for* Figaro-Modes.

Exhibition (and that was nicknamed "La Parisienne") was dressed in clothes designed by Paquin. If we look back at her life and career, Paquin's importance comes into focus.

She was born Jeanne Marie Charlotte Beckers in 1869, the daughter of a physician. As a young girl she was apprenticed to a minor Parisian couturière, and then employed at the Maison Rouff, where she worked her way up to the position of première, the designer's right-hand, in charge of the atelier. In 1891 she married the businessman Isadore René Jacob *dit* Paquin, with whom she opened a *maison de couture* on the rue de la Paix. (Later, in the 1920s, another couturier, Joseph Paquin, also worked in Paris, but he was no relation, and it may be that historians have confused Jeanne and Joseph.)

Like the House of Worth, which at this time was run by Charles Worth's sons, that of Paquin employed more than 2,000 workers, at a time when most important fashion establishments employed from 50 to 400. A popular song, "The Revolutionary March of the Dressmakers," began with the lyrics:

> What does the little delivery girl demand
> Of the House of Worth or of Paquin?
> A little more salary,
> Less work to do.

One of Jean Béraud's paintings shows the dressmakers pouring out of Paquin's on a lunch break. Gervex's painting, *Paquin at 5 o'clock* (1905), shows Paquin in the center of her salon, surrounded by ladies busily shopping.

According to one contemporary account, "Madame Paquin is pretty, she is gifted, she is charming. Everyone is fond of Madame Paquin." M Paquin, also, is described as "handsome" and personable. Indeed, the house was said to owe its success to the "personality [of] this clever and ornamental young couple."[3] After her husband's untimely death in 1907, her brother helped with the business, but Jeanne Paquin remained the designer.

She rapidly developed a great reputation and was soon dressing some of the smartest and most aristocratic clients in Europe, such as the queens of Belgium, Portugal, and Spain, as well as famous courtesans like Liane de Pougy and La Belle Otéro. Paquin was also the first Parisian couturière to open foreign establishments — in London, and then in Buenos Aires and Madrid. She was the first woman decorated with the Legion of Honor for her contributions to the French economy, and toward the end of her career she presided over the *Chambre Syndicale de la Haute Couture*, the official organizing body of the Paris fashion industry.

AU JARDIN DES HESPÉRIDES
Tailleur de Paquin pour l'automne

ABOVE: *Paquin, Tailored suit, 1913. Illustration by Georges Barbier for* Gazette du Bon Ton.

Paquin was, however, undoubtedly overshadowed by the spectacular rise of avant-garde fashion designer Paul Poiret. In contrast to Poiret, Paquin did not introduce any startling innovations in fashion design. But it is not entirely fair that Poiret has received the lion's share of the credit for the prewar "revolution" in fashion design. Between 1908 and 1914 many other Parisian designers (including Paquin) also dramatically changed their style of dress and presentation.

But whereas Poiret relished each *succès de scandale* — such as making his "hobble skirts" so tight that they had to be slit — Paquin modified avant-garde styles. Her hobble skirt had ingenious hidden pleats, so that, although the skirt looked slim, "walking was a pleasure." There was "not the slightest sign of a slit or an opening" in Paquin's evening dresses, since she filled the openings with chiffon underskirts. According to the *Lady's Pictorial*, "It is, appropriately enough, a woman who has solved the great skirt problem of the day, and devised a style which, while exceedingly smart, is not in the least extreme."[4] Paquin's popularity was probably based, in part, on her ability to modify the new fashions, making them somewhat more practical and conventional. This practicality and sense of moderation was thought to be peculiarly "feminine."

But while making her more successful at the time, this tendency toward moderation has probably made her seem less significant in the eyes of history. Moreover, most fashion historians think of Paquin primarily in light of her turn-of-the-century dresses. Yet her style changed dramatically over the next few years.

Like Poiret, Paquin employed the most avant-garde Art Deco illustrators to portray her modern styles. Indeed, we receive an entirely different impression of her development if we look at these fashion illustrations by Barbier and Iribe than if we identify her solely with the more conventional fashion photographs.

In fact, Paquin advocated fashion innovation. As the designer Maggy Rouff wrote many years later: "I can still hear the crystal voice of Mme Paquin [saying that fashion] 'must constantly renew itself, without weakness or fear, even with audacity.'" In 1910, when avant-garde fashions seemed ugly to many people, Paquin declared that the first commandment of the couture was that fashion must be new, must correspond to the current standard of beauty and the current way of life. Yet, significantly, Paquin insisted that fashion designers did not dictate change but rather followed

Robe de foulard, garnie de plissés.

PAQUIN

ZUT!. IL PLEUT!!...

Petite robe de promenade de Cheruit

LA FONTAINE DE COQUILLAGES

Robe du soir de Paquin

the subtle changes in style initiated by "the women in the street."[5]

Paquin was not an innovator like Worth and Poiret, but from 1891 until her death in 1936, she ran a truly first-class house. Throughout the belle epoque, Madame Paquin's dictatorship in the empire of style impressed observers. According to Robert Forrest Wilson's *Paris on Parade* (1925), "Fashion once simply did not know what to wear until Madame Paquin brought out her season's models; and as for her competitors, their plight was pitiful."[6]

Moreover, as the *inspiratrice* and *animatrice* of a celebrated couture house, Paquin herself was an inspiration to young women designers. "With what joy I talked about fashion with Mme Paquin!" recalled Maggy Rouff, who regarded the elder couturière as her "guide" and "master."[7]

ABOVE: *Paquin, Evening wrap of rose silk faille and black velvet, 1912. The Costume Institute, The Metropolitan Museum of Art, New York. Courtesy of the photographer, Joshua Greene.*

In his novel *A la recherche du temps perdu*, Marcel Proust identified what he regarded as the four greatest couture houses of the time: In addition to Paquin "sometimes," he mentioned Callot, Doucet, and Chéruit. Three of these four houses were headed by women.

Mme Chéruit is now a rather shadowy figure, who is remembered mostly for having purchased several of Paul Poiret's early fashion sketches. Stylish and attractive, she was her own best mannequin. The day Poiret visited her, for example, she wore a deep-blue dress with a white ruff and invisible fastenings, a simple, rather daring style.

She apparently received her training in the 1880s at Raudnitz and opened her own house early in the twentieth century, but it is not clear to what extent she herself was a designer. She may have supervised her more technically skilled assistants. Louiseboulanger, for example, was employed as a designer for the House of Chéruit before launching her own business in 1923.[8]

The Callot sisters — Marie, Marthe, Régina and Joséphine — are generally acknowledged to have been among the greatest couturières of their day, "although they go in rather too freely for lace," Proust complained. The daughters of a painter and a lacemaker, perhaps they inherited both their artistry and their love of lace.

"Then, is there a vast difference between a Callot dress and one from any ordinary shop?" asked Proust's fictional alter ego, Marcel. To which his mistress, Albertine, replied: "Why, an enormous difference. . . . Only, alas! what you get for three hundred francs in an ordinary shop will cost two thousand there. But there can be no comparison; they look the same only to people who know nothing at all about it."[9]

Madeleine Vionnet was the Callots' most famous protégée, and she always regarded them as outstanding dressmakers — far superior to people like Poiret and Chanel. (Without her "apprenticeship" with the Callot sisters, Vionnet believed, she would never have been able to create her own greatest works.) By 1900 the House of Callot employed 600 workers and catered both to to the American fashion trade, which eagerly copied their simpler designs, and to individual clients, on whose dresses were lavished the most sumptuous ornamentation.

Lucille (1862–1935) was the first internationally famous English designer — if we exclude Worth, who had moved to France and become in most respects thoroughly Parisian. Like the Callot sisters, she created romantic dresses awash in lace and silk roses, although Lucille's were far less advanced in terms of design and technique. But whereas the Callot sisters were, in a sense, the ordinary — albeit excellent — products of an advanced fashion system, Lucille was a genuine trailblazer.

Her original name was Lucy Kennedy, and in the 1890s she and her mother worked as dressmakers out of their home in London. So did hundreds of other "little dressmakers," but Lucille's picturesque chiffon dresses and tea gowns gradually gained a reputation. It helped when she married Sir Cosimo Duff-Gordon, gaining access to a much more exalted clientele.

It also helped that she was a striking personality and a self-publicist. By 1909 Lucille was said to be making about the equivalent of $200,000 a year. "I had a message for women I dressed," she wrote later. "I was the first dressmaker to bring joy and romance into clothes. I was a pioneer."[10]

Like her sister, the novelist Elinor Glyn, Lucille was an advocate of the new eroticism. Glyn is said to have invented the term "It" (as in Clara Bow, the "It-Girl"), "It" being sexual magnetism, more powerful than mere beauty. Her "shocking" novels, like *Three Weeks*, inspired wags to quip: "Would you like to sin/with Elinor Glyn/On a tiger skin?/ Or would you prefer/ To err/ With her/ On some other fur?"

Lucille used sensuous language to describe her dresses: "For me there was a positive intoxication in taking yards of shimmering silks, laces airy as gossamer, and lengths of ribbons, delicate and rainbow-coloured, and fashioning of them garments so lovely that they might have been worn by some princess in a fairy tale."[11]

Her romanticism was expressed in the names that she gave her models, which she called "gowns of emotion." One dress was called "Do you love me?" Another was "Kiss me again," while a third carried the risqué title, "The sighing sound of lips unsatisfied."

In those innocent, pre-Freudian days, dresses named "The garden of love" and "The gap in the hedge" caused no shocked laughter, although everyone understood a name like "I paid the price." Equally typical of Lu-

cille's sensibility, however, were exotic names like *"Mille et une nuit"* (a pink
and silver tea gown) and the chinoiserie fantasy, "Chu-Chin-Chow." A
purple satin rain cape was named "Happy though damp."

As these names indicate, her clothes were always rather theatrical and,
in fact, she designed many stage costumes; in 1907, for example, she
dressed Lilie Elsie for her part in *The Merry Widow.* She was also an astute
businesswoman, opening branches of her couture house in New York and
Paris. Following Worth's lead, she held fashion shows, in which her statu-
esque mannequins displayed her gowns to clients. At least one of her model-
girls caught an aristocratic husband this way.

Like Poiret, and unlike Paquin, Lucille promoted the delightfully
shocking, boasting that in the prewar years she had "loosed upon a startled
London . . . draped skirts which opened to reveal slender legs."[12]

Jeanne Lanvin was "a great, great designer," says Karl Lagerfeld, but she
has been unjustly neglected, because by the 1920s "she was a nice old
lady" — and not a fashion personality like Chanel.[13] Like Chanel, Lanvin
created her own style based on her own experiences. Lanvin's style expressed the idealized image of youthful motherhood and happy girlhood.

"What an admirable and pretty story is that of Mme Lanvin," wrote a
French journalist in 1925. "By touching the miracle of maternal love, a
young and talented milliner becomes a couturier of genius."[14]

She was most famous for her mother-daughter ensembles, which were

characterized by youthful romanticism and unabashed femininity. Already a *grande couturière* before World War I, Lanvin became even more successful in the 1920s, despite the fact that her pretty *jeune fille* style contrasted markedly with the dominant look of streamlined androgyny.

The eldest of ten children in a poor family, Lanvin was orphaned at an early age and had to act as a second mother to her siblings. Later she would create a veritable fashion cult devoted to her beloved daughter, Marie-Blanche. Appropriately, the *griffe* (symbol) that Paul Iribe designed for the House of Lanvin shows a mother leaning toward her daughter.

Motherhood is the one aspect of female sexuality that has *not* played a significant role in twentieth-century fashion, which is one reason why Lanvin has been relatively forgotten. Yet Lanvin herself certainly led an independent life. In 1880, when she was thirteen, she was apprenticed to the milliner Suzanne Talbot and steadily worked her way up, from errand-girl to head milliner.

In 1886, with about 40 francs saved and credit for 300 francs, Lanvin opened her own millinery establishment in a two-room apartment at 22 rue de Faubourg Saint-Honoré.

According to legend, one day at Longchamps she met a "gentleman rider," an Italian named Di Pietro. Their daughter, Marie-Blanche, was born in 1897, but Lanvin was left to support her alone. This child changed her mother's life. According to her friend and contemporary Louise de Vilmorin, Marie-Blanche was "the unique and inexhaustible" focus of Jeanne

SI ON RENTRAIT GOUTER...
Tailleur et Robes d'enfant, de Jeanne Lanvin

TU DIRAS BONJOUR...
Robes de jeunes filles et d'enfant pour l'après-midi de Jeanne Lanvin

LES CHEVAUX DE BOIS
ROBE D'APRÈS-MIDI ET ROBE D'ENFANT, DE JEANNE LANVIN

Lanvin's love, her inspiration, the source of her ambition, the reason why she worked so hard.[15]

The clothes that Lanvin made for her beloved daughter were much admired, and soon she began to design dresses for the children of her clients — and then dresses for their mothers. Marie-Blanche has said that it was sometimes tiring, being her mother's little mannequin, changing clothes four times a day, but she always admired her mother's talent.

By 1909 there existed the nucleus of a couture house over which Jeanne Lanvin presided for fifty years. One of Lanvin's specialties was the *robe de style*, a dress with a long full skirt, inspired by the styles of the eighteenth century, which was especially suited to girls and young women. Lanvin's clothes were prominently featured in the 1925 "Art Deco" exhibition, where her famous embroideries were especially admired.

Other designers emphasized the aesthetic of the Machine Age, but Lanvin was one of the best of the romantic Art Deco designers. "Modern clothes need some sort of romantic quality," she insisted in 1929; they should not be "too prosaic and practical."[16]

Lanvin was a modern thinker, however, and by the 1920s she also sold sportswear, furs — and even menswear, which was designed by her nephew. "Her studio is a real workroom," reported a journalist, "full of photographs, antique jewelry, old Breton vests, and Chinese dragon robes . . . marvellous things which she turns into fashion."[17]

Lanvin also pioneered the creation of designer perfumes like "My Sin" (1925) and "Arpège" (1927). She commissioned deluxe perfume bottles from Lalique and Sèvres, which were veritable *objets d'art.*

In the 1930s she continued to design long romantic garden party dresses in organdy or broderie anglaise, which echo the earlier *robes de style.* By reviving full skirts, panniers, crinolines, and bustle effects, Lanvin influenced many later designers, such as Schiaparelli and Balenciaga. At the same time, she was known for her neoclassical evening dresses, which *Vogue* called "the most seductive modernization of the antique."[18]

Lanvin met with her staff every morning to share the ideas that she had jotted down in her little Hermès notebook.[19] Although she was not a "hands-on" dressmaker like Vionnet, she was respected by her peers, who repeatedly elected her head of the couture section of various international exhibitions. Most importantly, she created a very personal style: romantic, lyrical, even theatrical, and immensely appealing to many women.

Although definitely not a modernist, Jeanne Lanvin was one of the first modern "career women," who singlehandedly built an enormous fashion empire based on the love she felt for her daughter.

The House of Lanvin has existed for a century, but after Madame's death the house went into something of an eclipse. In 1980 Jeanne Lanvin's great-nephew, Bernard Lanvin, assumed control, and his wife, Maryll Lanvin, a former model, became head designer. Neither the critics nor the public rallied to her designs, and in 1990 the Midland Bank bought a 34 percent interest in Lanvin, launching a major reorganization of the house, including the search for a new designer.

Claude Montana, a young designer who first rocketed to fame in 1978 with a collection that combined Punk and militarism, became the new couturier at Lanvin in 1990. Both display an obsession with perfectionism, and both of them have been partial to the color blue. But in other respects, it is hard to imagine a designer more different from Jeanne Lanvin, who was neither a rebel nor a modernist. Montana, however, is an extremely creative figure who will almost certainly bring new fame to the House of Lanvin, so we may have occasion more often to recall Jeanne Lanvin's great talent.

"Bearded couturiers" like Worth and Poiret did not sweep women designers aside. At the turn of the century there were a number of talented and successful women designers, who provided a crucial link between the dressmakers of the nineteenth century and the generation of more famous couturières who flourished during the 1920s and 1930s.

ABOVE: *Jeanne Lanvin, "a great, great designer," according to Karl Lagerfeld. Photograph by Gremela, courtesy of the Union Française des Arts du Costume, Paris.*

# 3
# CHANEL: "L'ELÉGANCE, C'EST MOI"

"*L'Elégance, c'est moi,*" said Chanel — unless the quotation is apocryphal, like so much else in the Chanel legend. "I invented my life," she once said. The journalist Ernestine Carter put it more bluntly: "During her long life Chanel wove such an elaborate tissue of lies about herself . . . that hard facts are . . . hard to come by."[1] Chanel's most recent biographer more tactfully began his book with the words, "She made up things."[2]

Chanel lied both to conceal a bitter past and to create a brilliant new persona. Yet we must know the truth about her life if we are to understand her style, because, as *Vogue* wrote about her in 1954, "the essence of the Chanel Look was Chanel herself."[3] Ironically, the legend that she did so much to create has obscured the true nature of her genius.

Gabrielle Chanel was born in poverty in 1883. Her parents married a year later. When she was a young girl and her mother died, her father abandoned her. This first betrayal must have hurt her deeply, because to conceal the fact that she had spent her youth in an orphanage, Chanel later concocted the story that her father had left her with relatives when he went to seek his fortune in America.

If she lied naively about her childhood, she deliberately shrouded the next period of her life in mystery. "How old was she when she was twenty?" her biographer Marcel Haedrich wondered.[4] And what was she doing? At this point in French history many women worked in the needle trades, and it would have been quite normal for a working-class girl like Gabrielle to have become a seamstress. Instead, after a brief stint as a shopgirl, she next had an abortive career as a café singer, during which time she seems to have adopted the nickname "Coco."

ABOVE: *Chanel in a suit of her own design, 1929. Although she did not singlehandedly invent the style of the 1920s, in retrospect it is the Chanel Look that epitomizes the era. Photograph courtesy of Bettmann/Hulton.*

OPPOSITE: *Gabrielle "Coco" Chanel in basic black with costume jewelry, 1937. Chanel is the most famous woman in the history of fashion. Photograph courtesy of the Union Française des Arts du Costume, Paris.*

Chanel claimed that Coco had been her father's pet name for her, but, in fact, the name was probably taken from a café-concert song, such as "Ko Ko Ri Ko" or "Qui a vu Coco?" Years later, her friend Misia Sert wondered why Chanel used such a "vulgar" name, but like the names Olympia and Nana, Coco was the sort of sobriquet found among the belle-epoque courtesans.

Already possibly a part-time prostitute, as was common in the milieu of the café-concert, Chanel seized the best opportunity for advancement available to a poor girl, becoming the mistress of a series of wealthy men. Chanel's early years as a demimondaine were crucial to her development, since they enabled her to enter a much higher social realm, at the expense of suffering all the humiliations of the kept woman.

## DEMIMONDAINE AND DANDY

As the *irrégulière* of the wealthy playboy Etienne Balsan, Chanel probably had a difficult life. Balsan's nephews presume that Coco "amused" Uncle Etienne; she was his "playmate-mistress," the "charming provincial." They deny that she ever had to eat with the servants in the kitchen, but admit that when Balsan had respectable guests Coco was probably not permitted to dine with them. When Balsan's official mistress, the actress Emilienne d'Alençon, came to visit, Chanel was expected to accept the situation.[5]

Courtesans and actresses were among the most fashionable women of the belle epoque. Unconstrained by issues of modesty or propriety, their clothes were always "in the fashion of the day after tomorrow": luxurious, decorative, and, above all, seductive. Sometimes they even broke the taboo against women wearing trousers or going without a corset.

"The fact that the *demi-monde* is so frequently a pioneer in matters of fashion is due to its peculiarly uprooted form of life," wrote sociologist George Simmel. "The pariah existence to which society condemns the *demi-monde* produces an open or latent hatred against everything that has the sanction of the law, of every permanent institution, a hatred that finds its . . . most innocent and aesthetic manifestation in striving for ever new forms of appearance. In this continual striving . . . there lurks an aesthetic expression of the desire for destruction."[6]

Chanel's close friend, Paul Morand, certainly saw in her an example of "that advanced guard of country girls . . . who go out, confront the dangers of the city, and triumph, doing so with that solid appetite for vengeance that revolutions are made of."[7]

Yet — significantly — Chanel chose not to imitate the ostentatious and overtly sexual fashions characteristic of the courtesan. The typical demimondaine dressed seductively to attract attention, and her clothing became even more splendid after she acquired a wealthy protector. Men who formed liaisons with a famous *grande horizontale*, in the words of one contemporary writer, "keep a woman as they keep a yacht, a stud, or a sporting estate, and they require of her everything that can augment the reputation of their fortune and . . . their celebrity as *viveurs*."[8]

Chanel's fashion iconoclasm took a different form: She invented her own personal style, based on the attire of her male protectors — clothing that represented the masculine power and aristocratic independence that she craved.[9] In the process she ruthlessly destroyed many of the traditions of feminine fashion, while forcing high society to accept her as a power in her own right.

Speaking of herself in the third person, Chanel later told her friend Salvador Dali, "She took the English masculine and made it feminine. All her life, all she did was change men's clothing into women's: jackets, hair, neckties, wrists. Coco Chanel always dressed like the strong independent male she had dreamed of being. She set women free because she had suffered too long from not being free herself."[10]

ABOVE: *Chanel, Woman's hat, 1913. Chanel was a milliner before she became a couturière. Photograph from* Les Modes, *courtesy of Special Collections, The Fashion Institute of Technology Library, New York.*

But Chanel was no middle-class feminist in a man-tailored business suit. If she appropriated the masculine model it was not merely because men's clothes were more functional, but because of their symbolic power. The style of the English gentleman (including his sporting clothes) had influenced women's tailored suits since the nineteenth century, although the French had always laughed at the stereotypical Englishwoman in her practical tweeds. Chanel was not the first, then, to adapt the features of menswear to feminine dress. Rather, her genius lay in doing for women's clothes what the dandies had done for menswear a century before.

Dandyism is a "cult of the self," wrote the poet Charles Baudelaire. The dandy is "in love with *distinction* above all things, [and] the perfection of his toilet will consist of absolute simplicity," which is symbolic of his "aristocratic superiority of mind."[11]

Baudelaire's insistence on black clothing also prefigured Chanel's "little black dress." Theirs was not the black of bourgeois respectability or conventional mourning, however, but something far more subversive. The dandy was "the Black Prince of Elegance."[12]

Like the nineteenth-century dandy, Chanel designed clothes that redefined the concept of elegance. A disciplined, refined and austere elegance replaced old-fashioned, ostentatious luxury, while also modifying the anonymity of the modern masculine uniform. Chanel's dandiacal style asserted that while any nouveau-riche social climber or high-priced prostitute could appreciate rich, elaborate dress, it took a sophisticated, modern sensibility to see that less was truly more. Elegance, for Chanel, was the rejection of anything extraneous.

Chanel also rejected sartorial decoration, because it was associated with feminine sexuality. Her philosophy of style was closely related to a strand in the modernist aesthetic that emphasized minimalism and the exaltation of form, while eschewing extraneous ornamentation as "feminine," "barbaric," even "criminal." Modernists like the Viennese architect Adolf Loos regarded ornament and decoration as symptomatic of degenerate eroticism, and they frequently framed the issue "in terms of an opposition between *male* and *female* styles. . . . In their call for a simple, functionalist, modern aesthetic, advocates saw themselves as champions of an orderly masculinity, as cultural saviors from the feminized depravity marked by ornamentation."[13] Reformers also attacked the dress of "women and sav-

ABOVE TOP: *"Le vrai chic,"* *a drawing by Sem for* L'Illustration, *1914, is said to portray one of Chanel's early suit designs.*

ABOVE: *Chanel, Three jersey costumes, 1916, from* Les Elégances Parisiennes. *Photograph courtesy of the Union Française des Arts du Costume, Paris.*

ages," arguing that only inferior, childish humans would be attracted to bright colors and ornamentation. Although Chanel later reintroduced "barbaric" ornamentation in the form of costume jewelry, her initial move toward simplicity was motivated by an aversion to anything associated with "inferior" and "promiscuous" female sexuality.

## FROM MILLINER TO COUTURIÈRE

But Chanel was as yet still only a kept woman who had a certain style. Her professional career began in 1910, when she started designing hats. In belle-epoque Paris, it was almost a cliché for men to set their mistresses up as milliners. Chanel was financed by Etienne Balsan (and initially sold her hats from his Paris apartment). She was also funded by Balsan's friend, the Englishman Arthur "Boy" Capel. Indeed, for a while, the three of them seem to have had an uneasy ménage à trois.

"I was able to open a high-fashion shop," said Chanel, "because two gentlemen were outbidding each other for my hot little body."[14]

The cartoonist Sem portrayed Capel as a sporting centaur, carrying one of Chanel's hats like a trophy on the end of his polo mallet, with Mademoiselle Chanel clinging to his neck. Soon, however, she would achieve the independence that she craved.

In 1913 Capel financed a clothing shop in the fashionable seaside resort town of Deauville, where, in addition to hats, Chanel sold simple sportswear. It was in Deauville, among the vacationing rich, that Chanel first pioneered the use of humble fabrics like jersey and comfortable garments like sweaters and sailor blouses. In 1916 she opened a *maison de couture* in a sumptuous villa facing the casino in Biarritz, another very fashionable resort town, far from the ravages of the First World War.

From the very beginning, Chanel created casual sportswear, priced extravagantly high. A Chanel dress cost anywhere from 3,000 to 7,000 francs in 1915; if we use the higher figure, that would be $350, or in today's money, $2,100.

But it was not merely that her clothes were expensive. Chanel deliberately used "poor" fabrics, like jersey, which had hitherto been used primarily for men's underwear. She was enchanted by the American who saw her clothes and exclaimed, "Imagine having spent so much money without it showing!" Rich fabrics were too easy, she said. "Jersey is something else!" And she added, "By inventing jersey, I liberated the body."[15]

The Americans were among the first to appreciate Chanel's style. Both *Vogue* and *Harper's Bazaar* featured clothes from Chanel's Biarritz collections in 1916. "Chanel is master of her art, and her art resides in jersey," declared *Vogue.* And: "Jersey and chic are synonymous."[16]

The French were a little slower to appreciate Chanel — or at least to spell her name correctly. In March 1916 *Les Elégances Parisiennes*, a publicity organ for the French couture, printed an illustration of three *costumes de jersey* (jacket-and-skirt ensembles) by *Gabrielle Channel.*

Vionnet, an expert dressmaker, was always contemptuous of Chanel,

dismissing her as "a milliner." "The dressmakers didn't take me seriously," Chanel recalled years later, "and they were right. I knew nothing about the business. In the beginning I had my milliners making my dresses; I didn't know that specialized workers existed. But this was just as well, because I learned everything for myself." And she added, defiantly, "Besides, it isn't all that complicated."[17] Her claim to fame was conceptual, not manual.

## THE TWENTIES

"Chanel had only to appear in order to make the whole prewar mode fade away, causing Worth and Paquin to wither and die," wrote Chanel's friend, Paul Morand, many years later.[18] But he exaggerates. After the war, Chanel was finally able to open her *salon de couture* in Paris at 31 rue Cambon, but it was not until the mid–1920s that she really became famous as a designer.

Those who exaggerate Chanel's role at this time conveniently forget that Vionnet was also quietly changing fashion, as was the fashion revolutionary Paul Poiret. It was Poiret who eclipsed traditional couturiers like the Worth brothers, the Callot sisters, and Jeanne Paquin — women fashion designers as well as men. Almost a decade before Chanel began designing clothes professionally, Poiret created exotic, brilliantly colored clothes that were intended to be worn *without a corset.* He even designed trousers for women. Although Poiret had a liberating impact on fashion, his emphasis on originality and exoticism was becoming *démodé* by the 1920s.

"Eccentricity was dying," Chanel recalled. "I hope to have had a part in killing it."[19] She professed to be nauseated by Poiret's "barbaric" reds, greens, and electric blues. "These colors are impossible," declared Chanel, who became famous for her black and beige clothing. One must be "suspicious of originality," she insisted, because couture could all too easily become costume. "Schéhérezade is easy. A little black dress is difficult."[20]

"What has Chanel invented?" demanded Poiret. "Poverty deluxe." "Simplicity does not mean poverty," countered Chanel. Certainly, no one ever looked poor in a Chanel suit, and no one poor could ever have bought one. As *Harper's Bazaar* observed in 1922, "Chanel has succeeded in making simplicity, costly simplicity, the keynote of the fashion of the day."[21]

Chanel did not invent the look of the twenties by herself. She did not singlehandedly "liberate the leg," for example. In the twenties, almost everyone designed short dresses, especially for daytime. But as British *Vogue* noted in 1923, "The very short skirt at once suggests that the lady is dressed by Chanel, who makes all her skirts short, whether for morning, afternoon, or evening." In 1929, however, when Patou lowered the hemline, Chanel "hit the deck but seconds behind the Great Innovator."[22]

Chanel's famous little black dress of 1926 was rightly praised by *Vogue* as a "fashion Ford." But, again, others were thinking along the same lines. In 1922 Premet's designer turned out "a plain boyish-looking little slip of a frock — black satin with white collar and cuffs," which was named "La Garçonne" after the best-selling novel of the same name. According to a book written in 1924, Premet's "Garçonne" achieved "probably the most sensational success reached by any individual dress model of recent years . . . counting both licenced and illegitimate reproduction, a million "Garçonnes" were sold over the earth."[23]

During the 1920s many designers, both male and female, were creating simple, comfortable, boyish clothes. Jean Patou, for example, designed modern sportswear very much like Chanel's, but he had the misfortune of dying early, and his contributions have been largely forgotten — or credited to Chanel.

"A man cannot leave the same image that a woman can," Karl Lagerfeld insists. Even the other women designers of the period fade in comparison with Chanel. While Lagerfeld is a great admirer of Lanvin, for example, he admits that "her image was not as strong as Chanel's, because she was a nice old lady and not a fashion plate."[24] If we look through old fashion magazines, we see that Vionnet, Lanvin, even the sportswear designer — and sportswoman — Jane Régny received as much or more press coverage in the twenties than Chanel.

But Chanel *herself* looked modern. Even before she became well known as a designer, she was already famous as a personality in Parisian society. "Chanel had flair and she was a supersaleswoman, if not a creator in the sense that Poiret was, and she was by no means an artist to equal Vionnet," recalled *Vogue* editor Edna Woolman Chase in the 1950s. "Chanel's success was due as much to her personality as to her skill and hard work."[25] In retrospect, it is the Chanel Look that seems to epitomize the era, because Chanel herself seemed to be the quintessential modern woman.

Her relationships with men also contributed to her personal legend. As one American writer admitted in 1961, "Her spectacular love affairs, her luxurious mansions, her gorgeous jewels, . . . her flashing wit, her dashing looks, her teeth-rattling temper, and the whole extravagantly colored pat-

tern of her life have been every bit as fascinating to the public as the styles that she has set during the course of her extraordinary career."[26]

It has been argued that Chanel "made it chic to look poverty-stricken," because her relationship with "the poverty-stricken Grand Duke Dmitri" gave her an understanding of economic realities.[27] But Chanel already had an all-too-intimate understanding of poverty — and gambler that he was, Dmitri was an expensive accessory, even for a rich woman like Chanel. The opera singer Marthe Davelli allegedly told Chanel, "If you're interested you can have him. He really is a little expensive for me."[28]

If anything, Dmitri influenced Chanel to design more luxurious clothes, using fur and embroidery. Chanel's Russian peasant look was a passing phase, but the influence of menswear, especially English sportswear, was of lasting significance.

And here, too, Chanel's private life influenced her fashions. "Her romance with the Duke of Westminster became notorious," recalled Cecil Beaton. The duke not only gave her "a gold-mine in jewels" but also "a mill where she designed her particular brand of English tweeds. . . . She was seen in the hunting field with rows of pearls swinging on her habit."[29]

The Duke of Westminster was a "big hunk of a man," floridly handsome, easily bored and prone to sudden rages. But his rather difficult character seems to have meshed with Chanel's, for although they often fought savagely, Chanel looked back on her ten years with him with pleasure.[30] In a photograph from 1925, Chanel appears to be wearing a jacket taken directly from his wardrobe.

Whether or not Chanel ever had an affair with French businessman Pierre Wertheimer, her relationship with this man was one of the most significant in her life. To understand why, we must go back to 1921, when "Chanel Number 5" perfume was developed. Contrary to popular belief, it was not the first designer perfume (Poiret had created several), but it *was* the first to bear the designer's name, and it remains popular today. Romantic stories were embroidered around this scent: that five was Chanel's lucky number, for example, or that the scent was the fifth one that she developed.

Recently, however, *Forbes* magazine published an article, "The Billionaires Behind Chanel," which revealed some much more interesting business realities behind Chanel's fashion and perfume empire.[31] Apparently, in 1924 Wertheimer helped establish Parfums Chanel to produce and market "Chanel Number 5." Eventually "he came to own the entire business built on her name." Chanel retained only the couture business, which was a separate (and far less profitable) company. Thus, the authors note, "without quite realizing the long-term implications of what she was doing, Coco Chanel had signed away the most profitable potential of her business for a relative pittance." By 1935 she saw what she had done and launched the first of many legal actions aimed at renegotiating their agreement.

Meanwhile, as the twenties gave way to the thirties, the *garçonne* look gave way to greater femininity, and Chanel's relationship to fashion underwent a subtle change.

## THE 1930s

Photographs of Chanel *herself* during the 1930s have a familiar, iconic power. She appears in navy or beige suits or in black dresses, drenched in jewelry, both real and fake. When the Duke of Westminster's fiancée, Miss Loelia Ponsonby, met Chanel, the designer was wearing a dark blue suit, a white blouse, and light stockings. "Described in this way she sounds like a high-school girl," wrote the future duchess, "but actually the effect was one of extreme sophistication."[32]

Photographs of Chanel's clothes in fashion magazines tell another story, however. During the 1930s she was known primarily for her long, romantic evening dresses—precisely the belle-epoque styles that she had rejected back in her youth. Dresses in white lace or tulle, which reminded French buyers unpleasantly of Hollywood, are not at all what we associate with the Chanel Look. A typical mention in the May 1934 *Harper's Bazaar* praised Chanel's "innocent chiffon with pleated baby frills." She even designed tea gowns. And her suits were not what we think of as Chanel suits, being rather tightly fitted and with long skirts.

The thirties also saw the rise of a new media star: Elsa Schiaparelli. Although Chanel was much richer than Schiaparelli, the Italian received more attention in the press, and Chanel was furiously jealous. Chanel's fashions began to seem safe, even bourgeois, in comparison with Schiap's witty creations.

Although costume jewelry was certainly sold in Chanel's boutique (and she wears it in her photographs), we seldom see it in her collections — except in her gypsy collection. In time, Chanel's famous costume jewelry would radically subvert standards of taste, but her revolution was always ambiguous, since these "fakes" were based on her own collection of real jewels. Certainly during the 1930s, Schiaparelli's peculiar Surrealist jewelry was more fashionable.

Schiaparelli was not Chanel's only problem. In May 1936, Chanel's workers went out on strike. Furious, Chanel refused to negotiate. Instead, she fired 300 women. They refused to leave; the Maison Chanel was "occupied." Although Chanel had risen from poverty herself, she did not identify at all with her workers. It was only in July that she reluctantly agreed to wage increases and vacations.

Even years later, Chanel described the strike as "a farce," and the workers as "sick in the head." She ranted: "A sit-down strike. Graceful, wouldn't you say? Attractive to think of women in such a position, on their behinds. I mean, what idiots those girls were!"[33]

To her friends, of course, Chanel showed a different face. Her charm, loquacity, and generosity were legendary. Mean as she was to her workers, Chanel lavished a fortune on Diaghilev's Ballets Russes. Indeed, she encouraged and sometimes secretly funded many artists. When the young photographer Horst refused to accept payment for his now-famous portrait of Chanel, she subtly assessed his tastes and needs, then sent over a truckload of admired antique furniture for his apartment.

Years later she wrote to Horst, complaining, "People make me sick. . . . They steal from my pocket what I offer them with my hands." It was a statement, Horst concluded, that exemplified "her characteristic wit, with its mixture of generosity and contempt, sentiment and bitterness."[34]

Horst was fascinated and impressed by Chanel, observing that most people were afraid of her. Certainly, she insisted on dominating her little circle of wealthy and/or artistic friends. According to Horst, when Salvador Dali (another indefatigable talker) came to dinner, Chanel put an alarm clock on the table: Dali had ten minutes until it was again her turn to speak.

While in her fifties, Chanel had a brief affair with the twenty-nine-year-old Italian count, Luchino Visconti. Her home on the Riviera, La Pausa, was "a golden world," he recalled, with gardens in which she was "the first to cultivate 'poor' plants like lavender and olive trees," rather than "roses and lilies." But even her lover had to admit that Chanel was a hard woman. The future film director called her "*La Belle Dame sans Merci*" (after the cruel femme fatale in Swinburne's fin-de-siècle poem). Later he would remember "her sufferings, her pleasure in hurting, her need to punish, her pride, her rigor, her sarcasm, her destructive rage, the singlemindedness of a character who goes from hot to cold, her inventive genius."[35]

Horst recognized that Chanel was a consummate actress, and one of her favorite roles was to appear to be "just a working woman."[36] And, in addition to everything else, she was that — at least until 1939.

ABOVE: *Chanel, Blue linen summer suit, 1937 (left), displayed with a red afternoon dress of the same period by Mainbocher. The Costume Institute, The Metropolitan Museum of Art, New York. Courtesy of the photographer, Joshua Greene.*

In 1939, with the outbreak of war, Chanel closed her couture house. According to a recent scholarly study on fashion under the Occupation, Chanel fled Paris and took refuge in the South of France. Then, though her colleagues and friends pleaded that she reopen her salon, she obstinately refused. Chanel herself wrote to Horst: "What an explosion of fury that I am not making a Spring Collection! My answer is that I am tired! Naturally it's a lie. I am well and full of ideas for making things in the future. But at the moment one must keep still. . . ."[37]

If Chanel's career had ended then (as many couturières' did), she would be remembered today only as one of a number of successful women designers from the period between the wars. Her revival in 1954 was something of a miracle, especially considering her behavior during the occupation of Paris. To put it bluntly, Chanel collaborated with the Nazis and, as a result, for many years after the war, she was treated as a pariah.

Already an ardent supporter of the right-wing Vichy regime, Chanel, when the Germans occupied Paris, took a Nazi officer as a lover. When she was arrested by the Allied forces after the liberation of Paris, Chanel supposedly said, "At my age, when a man wants to sleep with one, one doesn't ask to see his passport."

But her crime was not merely that she had slept with a German, or practiced the kind of passive collaboration that was common during the dark years. According to recently declassified British intelligence archives, Chanel was denounced as a German agent as early as 1943, when she took part in "Operation *Modellhut*," a scheme to use Chanel to influence the Duke of Westminster's old friend, Winston Churchill. In April 1944, just before Germany collapsed, Chanel traveled to Berlin to meet with high Nazi functionaries.[38] In other words, it appears that Chanel actively worked with and for the Nazis.

Although she was arrested by the forces liberating Paris, Chanel was soon released — probably because she could have revealed embarrassing information about high-born British friends who had been too cozy with the Nazis. Chanel then ingratiated herself with the American soldiers by distributing bottles of "Chanel Number 5" at her boutique (which, unlike the salon, had always remained open).

The story of "Chanel Number 5" has, however, an ugly wartime twist. When the Nazis occupied Paris, Jewish-owned businesses were seized. Chanel approached the Commission of Jewish Affairs, arguing that since the Wertheimers were Jewish and had fled the country, the company should be transferred to her control. But the Wertheimers had outwitted her by transferring their ownership of Parfums Chanel to an "Aryan" friend, Félix Amiot. And since Amiot supplied arms to the Germans, the Nazis decided against Chanel. After the war, Amiot gave his shares back to the Wertheimers, who still own Chanel today.

For almost ten years after the war, Chanel lived in self-imposed exile in Switzerland. Even after she quietly returned to France, her reputation as a collaborator remained damaging. Her old friend Bébé Bérard described her as an "arch offender." When Cecil Beaton tried to look her up, he found that "[other] French friends seemed vague about whether or not Chanel still existed. . . . Certainly, she had long since given up making clothes." In his diary, Beaton described Chanel as being obsessed with her "disgrace": "She wished to rehabilitate herself in the eyes of the . . . Parisians . . . who, because of her 'collabo' reputation, had dropped her cold."[39]

## THE FIFTIES AND SIXTIES

Yet, significantly, Beaton also recorded that "although she had not designed clothes for many years, she appeared today to be ahead of fashion, so incredibly spruce was she, in a Beau Brummell way — yet totally French — in navy blue serge over white linen blouse. . . . The simplicity of her perfectly tailored suit was paradoxically overwhelmed by a fantastic array of jewels, strings of pearls hanging in cascades among chains of rubies and emeralds and gold links. . . ."[40]

In a sense, Chanel only really discovered the essence of her style late in her life. All the elements of her style had existed before the war, but it was only in the 1950s that she pulled them together. According to Lagerfeld, "It was only then that she invented the 'petit tailleur Chanel,' the way we know this concept now, making believe it had been this way always."[41]

Of course, she had designed jersey cardigan suits in the 1920s (as had Patou and others), but these early styles looked more like sweaters than suits, while her suits of the 1930s were crisply fitted. The suits of the 1950s, which were comfortable and slightly boxy, marked a significant step forward. At the time, though, this was not immediately apparent.

In 1954, at the age of seventy, Chanel reopened her couture house. Although cynics said that she did so just to promote flagging sales of her perfume, the public was "whipped to a frenzy of expectation by the extraordinary advance publicity."[42] "Her opening was mobbed," *Life* observed — but afterwards the press called it "a fiasco." The French press contemptuously dismissed her first collection as "ghosts of her 1930s gowns."[43]

Chanel was not one to take defeat quietly. "Once I helped liberate women. I'll do it again," she defiantly told a journalist for *France-Soir.* In private, also, she insisted that women would be too smart to stay away for long. She blamed her bad reviews on the journalists and others "under the sway of the 'little queers,' as she called Dior and the other male designers."[44]

It was the era of the New Look, when male designers like Dior and Balenciaga were creating innovative fashions. The press was filled with news about the Y-Line, the A-Line, the H-Line. Hemlines went down, skirts became full, then they narrowed. The press loved it, and so did a large segment of the public. And yet it would become clear that there were a number of women (especially in America) who were confused by the changes.

Always combative, Chanel angrily dismissed the extravagances of "those gentlemen." Of Dior's New Look, she said, "Was he mad, this man? Was he making fun of women? How, dressed in that thing [a Dior dress], could they come and go, live or anything?"[45] If one of them used a boned bodice, she demanded to know how the wearer could bend over. "And that other fellow with his 'Velázquez style'!" Didn't his customers look like brocaded armchairs?

The sight of women in New Look styles acted on her as "a red flag to a bull," recalled Franco Zeffirelli. In his autobiography, he describes Chanel loudly and angrily hissing at two girls: "Look at them. Fools, dressed by queens living out their fantasies. They dream of being women, so they make real women look like transvestites. . . . They can barely walk. I made clothes for the new woman. She could move and live naturally in my clothes. Now look what those creatures have done. They don't know women. They've never *had* a woman!"[46]

"Fashion is now in the hands of American Seventh Avenue and the pederasts," she tactlessly told Cecil Beaton.[47] Accustomed to a fashion world filled with other successful women designers (whom, admittedly, she disliked), she was unpleasantly surprised when this world became increasingly populated by gay male designers.

Or perhaps she simply saw the propaganda value of proclaiming herself the one woman in a fashion world increasingly dominated by men.

"Ah no, definitely no, men were not meant to design for women," Chanel insisted. "Men make dresses in which one can't move."[48] She conveniently forgot the era of the twenties and early thirties, when male designers like Patou created the kind of loose, comfortable clothes that she revived with such success in the fifties.

But the Americans were increasingly fascinated by the original Chanel Look. By the time she brought out her third collection, *Life* proclaimed, "She is already influencing everything. . . . Chanel is creating more than a fashion: a revolution."[49] As Karl Lagerfeld notes, Chanel's genius was in doing the right thing at the right time.

Toward the end of her life, however, Chanel wanted to freeze fashion. Although her dresses had once been the shortest in Paris, she angrily attacked the miniskirt, calling it "disgusting" and making fun of the "old little girls" who wore it. Although she had pioneered the wearing of trousers, she never made pantsuits. (Yves Saint Laurent pioneered pantsuits, as did André Courrèges.)

Her style became associated with older women of the haute bourgeoisie. "Coco became too refined, too distinguished at the end of her time," says Lagerfeld. "When she lectured on elegance, she was *so* boring. It was more fun when she was young and cruised around being a kept woman."[50]

After Chanel's death, her style became almost totally fossilized and began to fade in significance. Then in 1980 Karl Lagerfeld was brought in, and the Chanel Look became modern again and more popular than ever. Journalist Javier Arroyello credits Karl Lagerfeld with being "the man who broke the spell of the Chanel mummy. He likes to picture himself as an emergency doctor who . . . rejuvenated the famous Chanel suit, the exausted uniform of the *grandes bourgeoises,* through repeated shock treatments (he brought leather and even denim to the kingdom of gold-trimmed tweed) and intensive corrective surgery (wider shoulders, roomier jackets, a sharper silhouette that includes even pants)."[51]

Anyone who suggests, simplistically, that Chanel created not fashion but eternal *style*, needs to think more carefully: "All the stuff pre-Karl was so-o-o square," says Caroline Kellett, an English fashion editor. "Putting it on, I just felt a frump."[52] Yet ultimately there is something about Chanel's concept of fashion — about Chanel herself — that keeps inspiring designers decade after decade.

## CHANEL'S PLACE IN HISTORY

Over the years, naive admirers have happily repeated even the most implausible stories about "the fiery peasant girl from Auvergne."

One day she felt chilly, so she put on her boyfriend's polo sweater and — *voila!* Chanel invented sportswear.

One night at the Ritz a heater exploded, setting her long hair on fire,

so she chopped it off and launched the new fashion for short hair.

No matter that these stories are patently false. Because Chanel lived so long and repeated her claims so vehemently, almost everyone believed her version of fashion history. Few of her old friends were still alive who remembered the Duke of Westminster saying with exasperation, "Gabrielle, why do you lie so much?"

Of course, in some ways mythology is much more satisfying than historical accuracy. In the film *Chanel Solitaire*, Coco tells another woman, "I don't wear corsets. You shouldn't either." We see the young Coco wearing boy's clothes to a fancy dress party. Suddenly women abandon corsets and wear trousers.

Mademoiselle abolished "oppressive corsets" and long "cumbersome skirts," proclaimed press releases from the House of Chanel; she "liberated women from all constraints." And she supposedly invented everything from designer perfume to short skirts.

"We sometimes have to laugh at the whole Coco Chanel mythology," confessed Inès de la Fressange (back when she was Lagerfeld's muse and the number-one Chanel model). "I don't think that Coco herself had so much humour."[53]

Because Chanel talked constantly, journalists have been able to quote her in support of any position they wish. For example, Chanel did say that fashion must go down into the street, it cannot remain in the drawing room — and this has rightly been cited as evidence of her modern attitude. But in the 1960s she also said, "Fashion cannot come up from the street; it can only go down into the street."[54] And this, of course, was no longer true, if it ever had been.

Each successive generation reinterpreted her (heavily fictionalized) life story. In the 1950s and 1960s, it was the romantic side of her life that captured the popular imagination, while in the 1970s and 1980s she was reincarnated as a feminist heroine. "I am on the side of women," Chanel said just before her death in 1971.[55] And women responded, regarding her as "the great emancipator," the first designer to liberate women's bodies.

"While male designers sought to control or expose the female form, Chanel and the host of women designers who have followed her have simply unleashed it," argued the feminist periodical *Ms.* in 1986. "The great question that plagued Freud was answered easily by Chanel: She knew what women wanted."[56]

BELOW: *Karl Lagerfeld for Chanel, The Chanel suit and look rejuvenated, Spring/ Summer 1991. Photograph by Maria Chandoha Valentino.*

But it is wrong to think of Chanel as a feminist, although she was, in her way, a liberated woman, and her success owed much to the emancipation of women. Chanel always believed that women dressed to please men and that they could not trust other women. She talked constantly about the importance of love in a woman's life, and her relationships with men profoundly influenced the style that she created. While Chanel's concept of style is very much a woman's style, it is based on a male model of power. We have wanted Chanel to be a heroine, and so Americans especially have become accustomed to a saccharine, fairy-tale version of Chanel's life and work. The French, always more realistic about human nature, admit that she was a kind of "sacred monster," brilliant and awe-ful.

Coco Chanel is probably the most important fashion designer of the twentieth century. Although not the first woman designer, she is certainly the most famous *woman* in the history of fashion. Chanel did not "invent" the little black dress, designer perfume, costume jewelry or trousers for women. Indeed, to focus on such phenomena trivializes her true significance, which involves an *attitude* toward style.

The real secret of Chanel's success was not that her clothes were simple or even comfortable but that they were casually elegant. As the former Chanel model Inès de la Fressange recently put it, "Chanel invented casual chic: the opposite of uptight French women with poodles."[57] Just as, today, Giorgio Armani's "unstructured" jacket is actually a very complicated construction, so also did Chanel create an extremely expensive look, produced with consummate artistry and deceptive simplicity. Chanel first became famous at a time when to appear to pay too much attention to clothes was *démodé*, while to wear one's clothes *avec desinvolture*, in a free and easy manner, was the look of modernity. Because this remains true today, we still admire Chanel.

Chanel was the woman that other women wanted to look like. In this sense she represented a new type of fashion designer who combined in her person the hitherto masculine role of the fashion genius with the feminine role of fashion leader. She was not the dressmaker, but the woman of style.

# 4
# VIONNET: "I LOVED WOMEN"

ABOVE: *Madeleine Vionnet, "Costume pour tourisme aérien" (Ensemble for air travel), 1922. Illustration by Thayaht for* Gazette du Bon Ton.

OPPOSITE: *Vionnet, Evening dress, 1938. Photograph courtesy of the Union Française des Arts du Costume, Paris.*

adeleine Vionnet was born in 1876 (seven years before Chanel) and died in 1975 (four years after her). Vionnet had none of Chanel's glamour. She looked like a governess, but she made other women look like goddesses.

If Chanel epitomizes the woman of style, Vionnet represents the professional dressmaker. Whereas everyone has heard of Chanel, the name Vionnet is legendary only within the world of fashion, where connoisseurs like Diana Vreeland have long regarded her as "the most important dressmaker of the twentieth century."[1]

Vionnet is best known as the "inventor" of the bias cut, and she has usually been analyzed solely in terms of her amazing technical innovations. Yet Vionnet's body-worshipping designs were not merely the product of a skilled seamstress. Her creative genius also had a more personal significance, which led her to evolve a uniquely "female" style that forever changed the relationship between body and clothes.

The secret of Vionnet's art arose from her life, just as surely as it did for Chanel. But whereas Chanel spent her young womanhood as a kind of courtesan, Vionnet's youth was in many ways typical of the army of women in the "needle trades." On one level, her life and career epitomize the historic importance of women in the Paris fashion world.

When Madeleine was only three, her mother ran off with another man. Her beloved father was an ordinary working-class Frenchman, and although he was proud that Madeleine excelled at school, a woman friend convinced him that the little girl should not spend years studying to become a teacher.

A BIARRITZ, CHEZ MADELEINE VIONNET

Modèles déposés. Reproduction interdite.

Thus, at the age of eleven, Madeleine was apprenticed to Mme Bourgueil, a dressmaker in the suburbs of Paris, near Aubervilliers. As an old woman, Vionnet recalled, bitterly, how she had to leave school "in the middle of the year. . . . I was going to get the prize for excellence. I have never forgotten it."[2]

Further disappointments were in store for Madeleine, since in belle-epoque France there were virtually no labor protection laws: "One time we had to make a dress bodice in two pieces," recalled Vionnet. "A woman worker made one and I made the other. They were ready at the same time, and each piece was as good as the other. She received three francs, and I only ten sous. That has always vexed me."[3] Such injustices, however, had a significant effect on Vionnet: Throughout her life, she always identified with the working girl.

Vionnet married at eighteen, but after the death of her baby daughter she obtained a divorce and set off for London. She remained there five years. She first worked for the English branch of Paquin's couture house. Then she directed the tailors' workshop for an English dressmaker, Kate Reilly. Because she spoke English well, Vionnet also dealt with clients, and she frequently traveled to Paris to buy French dresses, which Reilly copied.

By 1901 Vionnet was back in Paris, because of her father. She had gone to see him every month, which was expensive, and she had never liked crossing the Channel.[4] When the Callot sisters offered her a position in Paris, she accepted. It was at Callot that she began to create her first designs.[5]

Throughout her life Vionnet emphasized how much she learned as *première* in the personal atelier of Mme Gerber, the eldest of the celebrated Callot sisters. "I have made Rolls Royces," Vionnet declared, "and without Madame Gerber, I probably would have made Fords."[6]

Mme Gerber was "a great lady totally occupied with a profession that consists of adorning women . . . not constructing a costume." She was "a true dressmaker," Vionnet insisted, "not a decorator or a painter like those of today."[7]

Vionnet was quite capable of sincere admiration for skillful dressmakers, so it was not egotism that led her to dismiss Chanel as "a milliner," an insult that threw Chanel into a rage. Vionnet also wrote off Paul Poiret as a *costumier*, not a *couturier*. In her old age Vionnet admitted that Chanel was "a woman of taste,"[8] but she could never accept that a stylish woman (like Chanel) or a clever man (like Poiret) could be the equals of a professional who understood exactly how to construct a dress.

In 1907 Vionnet was offered the position of designer at Doucet, Poiret's former employer. "To compare Mme Gerber with Doucet is to compare magnificent pomp with a pretty little trifle," insisted Vionnet. But Jacques Doucet offered her an irresistible opportunity to launch her own line: "Create a young house in the old house of Doucet," he said, "and do whatever you want."[9]

Vionnet always claimed that she abolished corsets as early as 1907 — before Poiret and Chanel. "I have never been able to tolerate corsets myself," recalled Vionnet. "Why should I have inflicted them on other women?

ABOVE: *Jeanne Hallée, Emerald green evening gown, circa 1913, and Callot sisters, pink silk tea gown, 1910. The Costume Institute, The Metropolitan Museum of Art, New York. Photograph courtesy of the photographer, Joshua Greene.*

OPPOSITE TOP LEFT: *Vionnet, "Pendant les modèles" (Draping the models), 1922. Diana Vreeland regarded Vionnet as "the most important dressmaker of the twentieth century." Illustration by Thayaht for* Gazette du Bon Ton.

OPPOSITE TOP RIGHT: *Vionnet, "De la fumée" (Of the smoke), 1922. Illustration by Thayaht for* Gazette du Bon Ton.

OPPOSITE BOTTOM: *"A Biarritz, chez Madeleine Vionnet" (The House of Vionnet, Biarritz), 1924–1925. Illustration by Thayaht for* Gazette du Bon Ton.

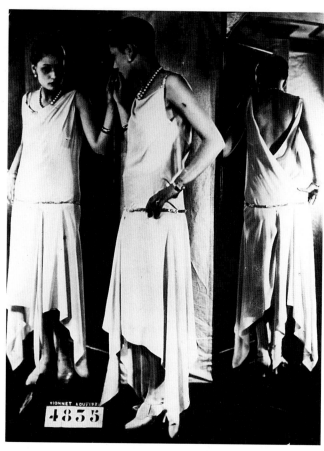

ABOVE: *Vionnet, Day dress, 1935. Photograph courtesy of the Union Française des Arts du Costume, Paris.*

ABOVE RIGHT: *Vionnet, Evening dress, 1928. Photograph courtesy of the Union Française des Arts du Costume, Paris.*

*Le corset, c'est une chose orthopédique.*"[10] Of course, no one person was responsible for the demise of the corset, but it is true that Vionnet's clothes could not be worn over ordinary foundation garments. A photograph of one of her dresses in a 1932 edition of *Vogue* even shows the outline of a nipple underneath the fabric.

Many of her early designs were intimate clothes for *déshabillé*, and she applied to evening wear the same lingerie techniques: pin-tucking, fagoting, rolled hems — which allowed her to eliminate interfacing and keep the fabric pliant. By experimenting with the diagonal bias cut and applying lingerie techniques, Vionnet was able to create dresses that gently, sensuously followed the lines of the figure.

Yet Vionnet's dresses were not necessarily easy to wear: "Comfort . . . in clothing is a mental rather than a physical condition," observed fashion historian Anne Hollander. "Old sartorial difficulties [like corsets] were exchanged for new ones. . . . [A] bad figure had no hiding place, and the need for a good one was never more obvious."[11] Vionnet's dresses were "so glamorous, but you couldn't have hips."[12]

Vionnet herself said that she wanted to impose on all her clients a respect for their bodies. She advocated the practice of exercise instead of a reliance on "deforming armor." As she told a journalist for *Marie-Claire* in 1937, "I have sought all my life to be the doctor of line."[13]

Just as Poiret's early designs had scandalized his employer's more conservative clients, so also were Vionnet's designs controversial. "I made a revolution all by myself!" she boasted later. Unfortunately, the personnel of the House of Doucet boycotted Vionnet's reforms en masse. The saleswomen, in particular, discouraged clients from even looking at Vionnet's dresses. They said her dresses looked like negligées.

But Vionnet's avant-garde clothes soon had at least a small following, especially among the younger and more adventurous demimondaines such as Eve Lavallière. The actress Lantelme, in particular, urged Vionnet to leave Doucet and open her own establishment. She was small "and very pretty," recalled Vionnet, "and she loved what I made." Lantelme's lover reluctantly agreed to provide 400,000 francs if Vionnet could come up with an equal amount. Unfortunately, Lantelme drowned before the arrangements were completed.

Nevertheless, by 1912 Vionnet had saved 100,000 francs and borrowed another 200,000 — enough to open her own small *salon de couture*. But with the outbreak of war in 1914, she closed her shop. Because she had made a point of helping her workers find new jobs, many of them returned to her in 1919, when she was able to reopen. Mme Martinez de Hoz, the loveliest of Vionnet's Argentine clients, helped find the necessary capital.

Although she lived for almost a century, Vionnet designed under her own name for only twenty years, during which time she created some of the most beautiful dresses ever made. "My head is a real work-box," Vionnet once said. "It has always held needle, scissors and thread. Even when I'm walking down the street I can't stop myself looking to see how the clothes of passers-by are made, even men's clothes! I say to myself: 'Suppose one were to put a tuck there, to give more breadth to the shoulder. . . .'"[14] And yet the source of her inspiration was not merely in needle and thread.

LEFT: *Vionnet and her wooden mannequin, circa 1935. Photograph courtesy of the Union Française des Arts du Costume, Paris.*

Vionnet herself said that she always sought "to dress a body . . . not to construct a dress."[15] The psychology behind her body-worshiping designs was simple and profound: Vionnet loved the beautiful bodies of women.

It is the great strength — and the great weakness — of women designers that so many of them essentially create clothes *for themselves* and for women who resemble them. But this was never true of Vionnet, whose feminine ideal, the tall, slender woman with a long neck, was definitely not based on her own body.

"I was short . . . and I hate short women," she said.[16] "I was dumpy," she confessed in another interview, adding that both her triumphs and her disappointments ended by bringing her to a good restaurant. "I have never made dresses for myself, except sack dresses. 'Mme Madeleine looks like a country priest,' said my workers."[17]

She enjoyed dressing beautiful women, such as the actress Lantelme and the Duchess de Gramont, but only reluctantly created designs to be copied by foreign buyers for women whom she would never see. And she seldom appeared in her salon to fit ordinary clients, because she claimed that "if I saw a woman who was ugly or short or fat, I would show her the door. . . . *Je dirai Va-t'en!*"[18] Vionnet worked directly in the material, without going through the stage of preparatory sketches, in contrast to many designers, who begin with a sketch and then let their assistants attempt to turn a drawing on paper into a three-dimensional dress. She said once, "I do not know how to draw. But if I did know, I would try to force myself to forget at the moment of creation. In my opinion, drawing hinders research, while appearing to facilitate it."[19] Existing sketches of Vionnet designs were all drawn *after* the dresses themselves had been created.

Vionnet's technique was unusual and highly significant. She created her designs on a small wooden mannequin (about two feet tall) with a jointed body, on which she draped and pinned the fabric. This allowed her to concentrate on the abstract, architectural properties of a dress. Then she would enlarge the dress and try it on a real woman, such as the Duchess de Gramont.

"Ah, she was a real model," Vionnet recalled. "Tall and lovely. When I was designing a dress, I had only to ask her to come and try it on . . . and I knew *exactly* where it was wrong."[20]

Because she worked in three dimensions and understood the properties of fabric, Vionnet was able to revolutionize the art of dressmaking. "She had something close to genius in her use of fabrics," wrote Cecil Beaton.[21] She studied the way fabric drapes differently depending on the way it is cut — with, against, or across the weave.

She is most famous for "inventing" the bias cut — fabric cut diagonally across the weave. Elizabeth de Gramont recounts the story: "One day, while draping material, Vionnet noticed that, cut along the bias, it fell much better and moulded the body to perfection. . . . Vionnet affirms that without her particular style of working, she would never have found the bias."[22]

Unfortunately, this pretty story needs to be modified slightly, as the late brilliant fashion historian Guillaume Garnier pointed out: "In fact, the use of fabric on the bias is already present in the clothing of the nineteenth

OPPOSITE: *Vionnet, Two designs for déshabillé, circa 1936. The designer's body-worshipping fashions sensuously followed the lines of the figure. Photograph courtesy of the Musée de la Mode et du Costume, Paris, and the photographer, Chantal Fribourg.*

61

century, for example, for collars and cuffs. But the use of the bias, limited to certain well-defined parts of the costume, had not yet surrendered all its possibilities." Garnier also noted that while couturiers such as Poiret had shown an interest in cutting on the bias, "it is certainly to Vionnet that we can trace the systematic use of the bias in the architecture of the dress."[23]

Although Vionnet is most famous for her bias-cut evening dresses, she also made discreet day clothes. Her tailoring was not masculine, however, since she tried to avoid cutting the material, whenever it was possible to *mold* the fabric instead. Her emphasis was always on precision, proportion, and the plasticity of the material — all of which she contrasted with the changes of fashion and with the decorator's "flounces and fiddle-faddle."

"I never made fashion," Vionnet insisted. "I never saw fashion. I don't know what fashion is. I made the clothes I believe in."[24] Her contemporaries agreed. In 1924 the *Gazette du Bon Ton* declared:

Madeleine Vionnet is above fashion. Not that she is out of fashion, but she announces the fashion of tomorrow. She has resisted the current religion for the ultra-flat woman, for ridiculous silhouettes which escape the laws of three dimensions. Madeleine Vionnet encourages women to take pride in harmonious proportions, [in] the fine outline of a chest which is firm and not shameful, and [in] fine shapely legs.[25]

This is not to say, however, that Vionnet never changed her style. In the autumn of 1934 she scrapped an entire collection two weeks before her opening. *Vogue* noted that "as a result Vionnet stands today . . . not for self-effacing crêpe de chine but for conspicuous stiff bustles, picture dresses and triumphs in taffeta." Yet (as Madeleine Ginsburg points out), Vionnet achieved this without recourse to stiffening materials, simply through skillful construction.[26]

"Either you *can* or you *cannot* wear a Vionnet, just as you *will* or will *not* wear a Poiret!" warned the authors of a 1929 guide to shopping in Paris.[27] "Much has been written about the clothes of Vionnet," they continued. "But it may interest you to know that Madeleine Vionnet is a woman with the interests of a woman, reflecting them outside her rôle as a designer. She has planned the most hygienic ateliers for her hundreds of girls; she has installed a gymnasium, dental and medical clinics, and a hospital; she arranges all the details of the *accouchements* of the women who work for her. . . . Many have followed her in carrying out these ideas, but none has surpassed her . . . because Vionnet is a self-made woman with intimate knowledge of the problems of the working girl."[28]

At the height of her empire, in 1928, Vionnet employed more than a thousand workers, whom she provided with health benefits (as did Jeanne Lanvin), good working conditions, and professional training, "according to new technical methods." In this way she hoped "to raise the moral level of the profession" and to create "the workers of the future."[29]

What was it like, working for Vionnet? "Splendid!" recalled Palmyre Bouvard. "Madame Vionnet had installed airy new workshops just for us. One never saw that in the couture! There were big work tables, chairs instead of stools, and even electric light, a great novelty in 1921. Furthermore, she gave us good salaries, paid vacations, and a refectory where the workers ate for free!" Jeanne Mardon was even more enthusiastic: "When I began working at Vionnet, I came from the house of Chanel, where we worked on stools. I entered Vionnet's workroom, and what did I see: Chairs! I said to myself: 'This is the Ritz here!' which made everyone laugh."[30] Even after she retired, Vionnet actively encouraged improved working conditions in the couture, especially for apprentices. Moreover, her concern for the working woman was related to her concern for the liberated female body.

The sight of Vionnet's dresses on exhibit in 1987 at the Fashion Institute of Technology moved journalist Jeff Weinstein to ask, "Did Vionnet sexualize and liberate the rich '20s matron?" Weinstein speculates that if male designers exploited the visual appeal of erogenous zones like the legs and the breasts, perhaps, with Vionnet's designs, "sexuality [was] directed in, toward the body," rather than outward, toward the eye of the (male) beholder.[31]

Vionnet married for the second time in the 1920s, to a White Russian military officer, Dmitri Netchvolodoff. He was eighteen years younger than Vionnet, who was then at the height of her career. Apparently, "Netch" benefited financially from their short-lived relationship, but she seems, nevertheless, to have been fond of him.

By contrast, she claimed to have forgotten the name of her first husband! "I only know that he had magnificent teeth," she recalled, "but the rest of him was not too good." Fundamentally, she insisted, "I cannot live with a man. I cannot bear to have a master, and in those days, within a marriage, it was the husband who dominated."[32] Her true family seems to have been her colleagues and collaborators.

She was always faithful to the female body. "One must examine the anatomy of every customer," Vionnet said. "The dress must not hang on the body but follow its lines. It must accompany its wearer and when a woman smiles the dress must smile with her."[33]

The anatomy of beautiful women inspired her, as she revealed in an interview with Bruce Chatwin. She recalled, for example, that many of her clients were South American, including the wives of Cuban sugar millionaires. "They were not intelligent, those Cubans!" said Vionnet. "But they were properly made. They moved well, and you could do something with them." Then there were the Argentine women — "with undulating buttocks like carnivores (avec leurs fesses ondoyantes des carnivores)." At this point in her interview with Chatwin, Vionnet sank "her white head back onto the pillow and, in a moment of unguarded reverie, sigh[ed], 'They always said I loved women too much!'"[34]

If Vionnet's apparent lesbianism were merely a matter of biographical interest, it would hardly be worth mentioning, except as a footnote to the period. After all, in the 1920s and 1930s, many women in Paris were lesbians or experimented with bisexuality. (Chanel, for example, probably had an affair with her friend Misia Sert.) But Vionnet's love for women is worth our attention, because it inspired designs that glorified their bodies.

# 5
# SCHIAPARELLI, JOKE OR GENIUS?

Elsa Schiaparelli was born in 1890 in the Palazzo Corsini in Rome. Her distinguished family was both aristocratic and intellectual. Their attitude toward women was conservative, and Schiaparelli was rebellious. When in her youth she published a volume of erotic poetry, her family promptly packed her off to a convent — and only released her when she went on a hunger strike.

A misfit in upper-class Roman society, she traveled to London, where she met and immediately married a bizarre Theosophist, the Comte de Kerlor. This inappropriate marriage presumably stemmed from the same rebellious nature. The couple moved to New York in 1919 and had a daughter, "Gogo," whereupon Kerlor faded from the picture. Abandoned by her husband and with her father recently dead, Schiaparelli found herself stranded, virtually penniless, in a foreign country with a child to support. To earn money in New York she took a variety of jobs, including selling Nicole Groult's dresses; then, in 1922, she returned to Paris, where she acted as a cultural guide for wealthy American women.

"Poverty forced me to work, and Paris gave me a liking for it," Schiaparelli said later.[1] Her first attempts to design dresses met with little success, however. (Maggy Rouff told her that she would be better off planting potatoes.) Then one day, leading a shopping tour to Poiret's *maison de couture*, Schiaparelli impulsively tried on a magnificent evening coat. Poiret not only generously offered to give her the coat, he encouraged her to continue to design clothes herself.

Poiret was her first mentor — "He was the Leonardo of fashion," recalled Schiaparelli in her autobiography — and throughout her career she

ABOVE: *Elsa Schiaparelli, circa 1938. Photograph by Corsaint-Dorvyne, courtesy of the Union Française des Arts du Costume, Paris.*

OPPOSITE: *Schiaparelli, Shoe hat (designed with Salvador Dali) and cocktail suit with lip appliqué pockets, 1937. Photograph courtesy of Special Collections, The Fashion Institute of Technology Library, New York.*

was influenced by his sense of theater and color. "For colors, she is the feminine Poiret," declared *Harper's Bazaar* in 1934.[2] Certainly, the man who launched "barbaric" colors and harem trousers had a great deal in common with the woman who created shocking pink and a hat shaped like a shoe!

The mutual antipathy that Chanel and Poiret had felt broke out again between Chanel and Schiaparelli. Their styles were absolutely antithetical: Chanel created casually elegant clothes, inspired by menswear. In their apparent simplicity and functionalism, they implied that *progress* in women's clothes had occurred. By contrast, Schiaparelli emphasized a traditionally "feminine" wealth of ornamentation, color, and fantasy.

Yet the aesthetic debate between the two women was by no means simply a repetition of Chanel's old feud with Poiret. Poiret's costume fantasies were not those of Schiaparelli. Whereas Poiret's woman was an exotic, erotic odalisque, Schiap's style combined masculine and feminine imagery for a very different effect.

Schiaparelli's day suits were characterized by a "hard" chic, featuring broad, often padded, shoulders that tapered to a narrow waist and hips. As *Vogue* put it in 1931, ". . . clothes carpenter that she is, Schiaparelli builds up the shoulders, planes them off, and carves a decisive line from under the arms to the hip-bone, gouging in the waist."[3] On top of this hard, masculine silhouette, however, she lavished a wealth of trimmings, brilliant colors, and outrageous accessories.

Chanel described Schiaparelli as "that Italian artist who makes clothes." Schiaparelli, in turn, referred to Chanel as "that dreary little bourgeoise."[4] Their insults are revealing.

It was not merely that Schiaparelli was "artistic," however, although she certainly moved in avant-garde artistic and intellectual circles in New York and Paris. Nor is her fame based primarily on the fact that she collaborated with artists like Salvador Dali, Jean Cocteau, Bébé Bérard, and Vertès — although working with them made her feel "supported and understood beyond the crude and boring reality of merely making a dress to sell."[5] The point is that Schiap regarded fashion as *art*. She wrote in her autobiography, *Shocking Life*, "Once or twice I had thought that instead of painting or sculpture, both of which I did fairly well, I could invent dresses or costumes. Dress designing, incidentally, is to me not a profession but an art."[6] Notice that Schiaparelli did not distinguish between "dresses" and "costumes," whereas Chanel distinguished sharply between costume design (an art, like drama) and fashion (an aspect of contemporary life). For Schiaparelli, all clothing (and body decoration) was a form of *masquerade*. It was playful.

Schiaparelli's impeccable social credentials gave her instant entrée into the high society that largely rejected Chanel (even during her association with the Duke of Westminster). More significantly, Schiap's innate sense of self-worth provided a base from which to rebel and to be deliberately frivolous. By contrast, Chanel, who had to work and fight so hard and so long, could only be serious.

At no time in her autobiography does Schiaparelli display much interest in the *technique* of the couturier — the way one cuts, drapes, and sews.

She employed fine craftspeople, like the embroiderers at Lesage, but she herself was much less of a craftswoman than Chanel, to say nothing of a real dressmaker, like Vionnet.

Schiaparelli saw dress design in terms of artistic inspiration — "wild ideas."[7] Artistic never meant "pretty." But what, exactly, did she create that made her work seem so shocking? Although her career spanned a quarter of a century, Schiaparelli is remembered primarily for her 1928 trompe l'oeil sweaters and for her Surrealist fashions and accessories of the late 1930s.

And it is in the artistic movement known as Surrealism that we find the essence of her style. As Salvador Dali wrote in his autobiography, "new morphological phenomena occurred" at Schiaparelli's dressmaking establishment; "here the essence of things was going to be transubstantiated."[8]

There were relatively few women artists in the Surrealist movement, and they tended to be ambivalent about the male artists' language of erotic desire, which often focused on erotic violence. Although they did not ignore the connections between sexuality (and sexual repression) and violence, some of the women also explored questions of feminine disguise and masquerade. This was right up Schiap's alley. Furthermore, like Freud, the much-exploited patron saint of the Surrealists, Schiaparelli realized that the entire relationship between body and clothes was fraught with eroticism — both perverse and playful.

Schiaparelli often deliberately "confused" body and clothing imagery.

ABOVE: *Schiaparelli, Sketch for the lobster dress, designed in collaboration with Salvador Dali, 1937. Photograph courtesy of the Union Française des Arts du Costume, Paris.*

For example, she collaborated with Jean Cocteau on a jacket decorated with embroidered hands that seem to clasp the wearer's body. She used see-through cellophane for her famous "glass" cape.

More profoundly, she and Dali created the famous "Tear Dress"—an evening gown with a printed tromp l'oeil design of ripped fabric. "The imagery of violence is counterposed by the elegance of the dress," wrote Caroline Evans and Minna Thornton. "The way in which the dress acts to displace sexual meanings from the body is brilliantly exploited."[9] The "Tear Dress" was a precursor both of Vivienne Westwood's clothes, which actually were ripped, and Rei Kawakubo's clothes, which were specially woven with tears in the fabric.

In an era of amusing and often outrageous hats, Schiaparelli and Dali created the ultimate Surrealist accessory: the hat in the shape of an upside-down shoe. Certainly it is absurd to wear a foot covering on the head, but the "Shoe Hat" was not "merely" a joke—or only in the sense that Freud meant when he wrote *Jokes and Their Relation to the Unconscious*.

In the unconscious mind, the sexual appeal of the body may be displaced onto clothes. Not only is the sexual symbolism of a high-heeled shoe blatantly phallic (in one suggestive version, the heel of the shoe was pink), but the hat itself is also a phallic symbol. Moreover, the "Shoe Hat" was intended to be worn with a black tailored suit that had pink lips appliquéd around the pockets, implicitly suggesting a connection between the pocket, the mouth, and the vagina. Obviously, this type of association is usually only made unconsciously, in dream imagery, for example. But Schiaparelli and Dali brought the image of the phallic woman at least to the verge of consciousness by means of a joke. "By keeping men off, you keep them," declared Schiaparelli.[10]

Schiaparelli also made a "Lamb-chop Hat"; an evening dress (worn by the Duchess of Windsor) featuring the image of a giant cooked lobster decorated with parsley; a purse in the shape of a telephone; a necklace made of aspirins; buttons in the form of safety pins; gloves with appliquéd fingernails—a host of unsettling images that made women's high fashion look as bizarre as anything discovered by anthropologists or uncovered by psychopathologists. At the very least, they seem to presage the most radical Punk anti-fashion of the 1970s.

"Curiously enough," she recounted in her autobiography, speaking of herself in the third person, "in spite of Schiap's apparent craziness and love of fun and gags, her greatest fans were the ultra-smart and conservative women, wives of diplomats and bankers, millionaires and artists, who liked severe suits and plain black dresses."[11]

The subversive goals of the Surrealists were to some extent simply co-opted or domesticated by the world of high fashion. André Breton, the high priest of Surrealism, might declare that beauty must be "convulsive," but society women favored Surrealist fashion because it was chic. Moreover, like Poiret, Schiaparelli had a keen sense of the publicity value of "shocking" innovations. For her new perfume, "Shocking," Schiaparelli commissioned a perfume bottle in the shape of a woman's torso by the artist Leonor Fini, who was best known for her erotica.

Yet there was something genuinely subversive in Schiaparelli's contribution to fashion. Her irreverence and her eccentric wit continue to influence many avant-garde designers. Jean-Paul Gaultier says that he is inspired by her "humorous irony." The jewelry designer Billy Boy boastfully insists, "I have never, *never*, said that I was the reincarnation of Elsa Schiaparelli."[12] And Christian Lacroix praises Schiaparelli for being "the first to open couture to contemporary artistic currents and give it a sense of the ludicrous. The joy and dynamism, the variety and mix of colors and shape, the lack of prejudice — in short, freedom — are most inspiring in her fashion work."[13]

"Madame Schiaparelli has taken literally the expression: the theatre of the mode," wrote Jean Cocteau in *Harper's Bazaar*. He continued,

Whereas in other times only a few mysterious and privileged women dressed themselves with great individuality and by the violence of their style destroyed the "moderne" style, in 1937 a woman like Schiaparelli can invent for all women . . . that violence which was once the privilege of very few, of those who might be called the actresses in this drama-outside-theatre which is the World.

Schiaparelli is above all the dressmaker of eccentricity. Has she not the air of a young demon who tempts women, who leads the mad carnival in a burst of laughter? Her establishment in the Place Vendome is a devil's laboratory. Women who go in there fall into a trap, and come out masked. . . .[14]

When World War II broke out, the party was over. Schiaparelli fled to America. But before moving on to the war years, when American women came to the fore, or the postwar decades, when men dominated the world of fashion, let us take one last look at the golden age of the couturière.

LEFT: *Schiaparelli, Evening suit in pale pink silk crepe with embroidery designed by Jean Cocteau, 1937. The Chicago Historical Society, gift of The Art Institute of Chicago.*

# 6
# REGIMENT OF WOMEN

ABOVE: *Mme de Wagner and Mlle Madeleine designed the fashions at Drécoll, illustrated in* Art, Goût, Beauté, *1925.*

OPPOSITE: *Louiseboulanger, Evening dress, circa 1935. Photograph by Man Ray, courtesy of Scott Hyde,* © *1991 Artists Rights Society.*

There were male designers, too, in the years between the wars, but "the excitement lay among the regiment of women."[1] In addition to Chanel, Lanvin, Vionnet, and Schiaparelli, the feminine leaders of Paris fashion included Alix (later known as Mme Grès), Augustabernard, the Callot sisters, Mme Cheruit, Sonia Delaunay, Nicole Groult (who was Poiret's sister), Jenny, Louiseboulanger, Lucile Paray, Madeleine de Rauch, Jane Régny, Nina Ricci, and many others.

To understand why there were so many successful couturières in the period between the wars, we need to recognize that this was *not* a new phenomenon. Contrary to popular belief, it is not at all true that women only began to work after the First World War. The flourishing of female designers in the 1920s and 1930s was not the result of a newly liberated female work force. For the first time, however, middle-class and even upper-class women entered the work force in great numbers, and they often gravitated towards traditionally "feminine" fields, such as fashion.

These *"femmes créatrices"* may be divided into several categories, according to their professional backgrounds, social origins, and fashion specialties.[2]

There were those like Vionnet, who rose through the ranks of the couture hierarchy from simple *arpète* (apprentice) through *première* (forewoman) to found their own couture houses.

Then there were women who had a spectacular rise, like Chanel and, in some respects, Lanvin.

Thirdly, there were society women who went into fashion either because they needed the money or because the fashion business, hitherto der-

Créations Jane Régny
COUTURE - SPORT
11, Rue La Boëtie, Paris

ABOVE: *Mme Jenny,*
*Evening dresses, circa 1926,*
*illustrated in* Style Parisien.

ABOVE RIGHT: *Jane Régny,*
*Couture sport dresses, 1927,*
*illustrated in* Art, Goût,
Beauté. *Régny was a*
*well-known tennis player and*
*specialist in sportsclothes.*
*Photograph courtesy of Special*
*Collections, The Fashion*
*Institute of Technology*
*Library, New York.*

ogated as "trade," was in the process of becoming fashionable and "artistic."
The upper-class divorcée Schiaparelli was probably the most successful of
these mondaines. Many aristocratic Russian emigrées also opened couture
houses in Paris in the 1920s, as did a growing number of Frenchwomen of
good family. As one journalist put it in 1927, "To work has become a kind
of sport in *le grand monde*, at precisely the moment when the world of workers thinks only of amusing itself."[3] Today, of course, there are still a number
of "socialite" designers, such as Carolina Herrera and Jacqueline de Ribes.

A fourth category, also very common today, consisted of women who
played crucial artistic or technical roles in the fashion business without ever
opening their own businesses. However important they were in real life,
historically they were essentially anonymous. But even designers who had
their own businesses and were famous in their day have been forgotten or
neglected by subsequent generations — and are worth recalling.

A fifth category comprised the milliners, who were very numerous.

Before looking at these women designers, however, let us consider one
of the male minority. Jean Patou was a leading designer of both active
sportswear (such as tennis and golf costumes) and spectator sportswear. As
we have seen, he was one of Chanel's main competitors.

In an interview in the 1920s, the photographer Baron de Meyer asked
Patou whether women were better dressmakers. "I don't believe," said Patou, "that to belong to what is termed *le beau sexe* is an advantage for a
dressmaker, especially not for a *chef de maison*. Particularly so, when the
*patronne* is young, good-looking and chic." (This was probably a slap at Chanel.) "She will," Patou said, "as a matter of course, while designing her new
models, consider the effect she herself would produce in these same gowns.
To my way of thinking, this is detrimental to good dressmaking, for there is

more than one type of woman to consider. Women's styles and women's figures vary considerably and all of these should be taken care of. . . . The models designed by men seem to me to be more to the point and to fulfil their purpose better. After all, for whom do women dress? Isn't it men that women wish to please?"[4]

Patou's opinions were remarkably similar to those held by later generations of male designers. The defensive tone of his remarks, however, inadvertantly reveals his awareness that many of his contemporaries believed that women — *le beau sexe* — were, indeed, superior dressmakers. And yet why should they have assumed this?

Some people seem to have felt that female designers were more in touch with the changing needs of modern women. Sports, for example, were a major influence on the styles of the 1920s. And some sportswomen themselves designed clothes.

Jane Régny was a well-known tennis player who specialized in fashions for sport and travel. A shopping guide of the day described Régny as an attractive young woman from a good family who "saw the inevitable conquest of her world by the new idea of sports for women, of a freer life, with different demands on the couturiers." From the time she opened her couture house in 1922, her clothes received a great deal of attention in the fashion press.

Régny was "one of the first to realize the difference between the sport clothes that can be comfortably and appropriately worn by the participant, and those that can be worn by a spectator."[5] Although her brief foray into evening wear was not well received, her sweaters and simple sports suits were among the best of their kind.

Madeleine de Rauch and her three sisters were also avid semiprofessional sportswomen who opened a couture house in 1927. As Madeleine said, "We have adopted a sportive style without renouncing elegance."[6]

Jenny Sacerdote, known professionally as Mme Jenny, was also described as "a strictly modern woman." According to an observer in 1929, "She wears the uniform of the businesswoman, [one day] a two-piece dress, cleverly individualized, [the next] a pleated skirt with a charming sweater."

The clothes she designed were also characterized by "this new spirit that we call *modern*," since "she began to crash through the old routine of morning dress, afternoon dress, dinner gown, and evening gown, with models dedicated to *sport*," which made her especially popular with ever-sportive Americans.

Her clothes featured simple lines, fine fabrics, and colors like "rose Jenny" and turquoise blue. In addition to producing some 800 models a year, she also created "all the delicious accompaniments of a woman's lounging hours: *négligés*, pyjamas . . . lingerie." In 1928 she was awarded the Grand Prix d'Elégance.[7]

Although Sacerdote had served a brief period of apprenticeship as *première vendeuse* for Bechoff-David before she opened the House of Jenny in 1908, she was not a trained designer: Jenny was "the creator," her colleague, Mme Cosme, "the technician," according to one account.

Jenny was often painted by the artists of her day, especially by Van

ABOVE: *Jean Patou, Day dress, circa 1925, illustrated in* Art, Goût, Beauté. *Patou believed that men were better designers than women, but his was the minority opinion during the 1920s. Photograph courtesy of Special Collections, The Fashion Institute of Technology Library, New York.*

Dongen. Although she made a great deal of money, her husband was a gambler who spent it as fast as it came in. As a result, in 1938 her house merged with that of another woman designer, Lucile Paray.

Paray had originally intended to be a writer and fell into designing almost by accident, after creating a dress for a friend. She opened her couture house in 1930 and created a number of sophisticated ensembles.

The Russian-born Sonia Delaunay epitomized the new idea of the artist-couturier. An avant-garde painter, like her husband, Robert Delaunay, she also designed textiles featuring brilliant colors in abstract patterns. As early as 1911 she made a colorful patchwork quilt for her infant son. The quilt was inspired by Russian folklore, which was to have a great influence on both her art and her fasion.

Delaunay was born in the Ukraine in 1890. The daughter of a factory worker, she was adopted by a wealthy Jewish family, and in 1908 went to Paris where she came in contact with the most advanced artistic innovators. Soon she was creating what she called *Robes-Poèmes*, dress designs that juxtaposed geometric blocks of color and lines of poetry. Delaunay's friends were avant-garde painters and poets like Guillaume Apollinaire, who once wrote a poem to her entitled "On Her Dress She Wears her Body." Apollinaire also wrote a newspaper article in 1914 in which he described "Monsieur and Madame Delaunay, painters, who are launching the reform of costume." In cut their clothes followed the line of the day, he reported, but their use of color was intensely new. Robert Delaunay, for example, sometimes wore a green coat, sky-blue vest, and red velvet trousers, while Sonia wore even more strikingly colored dresses.[8]

As was the case with many other Russian expatriates, Delaunay's income had been wiped out by the Russian Revolution of 1917, and she needed money. In 1921 she sold textile designs to Agnès Drecoll; in 1922, when a Lyons textiles manufacturer saw the *Robes-Poèmes* and asked her to design patterns for fabrics, she accepted.

Her textile designs were a great success, and soon she was also collaborating with the couturier Jacques Heim, making sportswear, dresses, coats, and accessories, which they displayed at the 1925 Paris Exhibition. Her clothes were conventional in cut but the dress construction was intended to emphasize the textile design, which featured violent chromaticism and bold geometric patterns. Once, for a publicity photograph, she even painted a Citroën car to match the motoring coat that she had designed for Heim. "If painting has become part of our lives, it is because women have been wearing it," Delaunay declared.[9] She also cited the revolution in women's dress — the abandonment of corsets, long skirts, and collars — which she traced to the fact that women were now leading active lives. "I dressed the avant-garde and the intellectuals . . . the wives of painters and architects. Mme Gropius came to me. . . . I also designed for the ballet."

In 1966 an interviewer asked her when she became interested in fashion. "Never," Delaunay replied. "I closed my couture house in 1931, because everything was becoming too complicated. . . . And I saw that the future of fashion lay with industrial couture, what we call today 'ready-to-wear.'" She continued to design fabrics for couture houses such as Chanel

LEFT: *Jane Régny, Daytime dress; hat by Agnès, 1930, modeled by Lillian Fischer. Photograph by George Hoyningen-Huene, courtesy of the Frederick R. Koch Collection, Harvard Theatre Collection.*

and Lanvin, but she had foreseen that ready-to-wear would largely replace the couture, resulting in new and much less expensive clothes. As she wrote in 1931, "The future of fashion is very clear to me. [There will be] research into the materials used, along with the simplification of the aesthetic conception. . . . Thus fashion will democratize itself.[10]

Meanwhile, in the Soviet Union, women artists and designers, such as Liubov Popova, Varvara Stepanova (the wife of Alexander Rodchenko), and Alexandra Exter were creating abstract "proletarian dresses," rather similar in appearance to the art dresses of Delaunay.

Women artists were especially important in the Soviet Union, because of women's prominent role in the Russian intelligentsia and the radical movement. The communist regime tolerated avant-garde art for only a few years in the early 1920s, however. By 1921, artists were already being steered away from "bourgeois" easel painting toward more "utilitarian" creations — such as clothing and textile design, where women had a traditional base of strength.

Liubov Popova has been called the "strongest painter of her generation." As one comrade put it: "When she was fighting for art, she was a man; but in bed she was a woman."[11] She came from a wealthy, cultivated merchant family and had visited France and Italy, but she supported the Bolshevik Revolution of 1917.

In 1922 she called for a social "vacuum cleaner" that would "remove all this aesthetic trash from life" and bring utilitarian beauty to the masses. "No artistic success has given me such satisfaction as the sight of a peasant or worker buying a length of material designed by me," she declared.[12] In addition to textile design, she designed both theater costumes and fashion. Her fashion designs were simple and geometric and could easily be made at home from patterns. In 1924 she caught scarlet fever from her child and died at the age of thirty-five.

Like Popova, Varvara Stepanova designed textiles with "bright, simple, geometric patterns, freed from 'degenerate' bourgeois style and also small enough to save waste when cutting to match repeats."[13] Stepanova came from a peasant background and had professional training as a dressmaker; her fashions were radically simple.

In *The Dress of Today Is the Industrial Dress* (1923), Stepanova wrote:

Store windows with their dresses exhibited on wax mannequins are becoming an aesthetic leftover from the past. Today's dress must be seen in action — beyond this there is no dress, just as the machine cannot be conceived outside the work it is supposed to be doing. . . . Aesthetic aspects must be replaced by the actual process of sewing. Let me explain: don't stick ornaments onto the dress, the seams themselves — which are essential to the cut — give the dress form. Expose the ways in which the dress is sewn, its fasteners, etc., just as such things are clearly visible in a machine.[14]

ABOVE: *Varvara Stepanova, Dress designed in 1927 reconstructed by Elena Khudjakova in 1985. Photograph courtesy of Alexander Lavrentier.*

Following the Revolution a third woman, Alexandra Exter, worked for the Moscow Fashion Studio, creating utilitarian clothing for workers which could be mass produced, as well as one-of-a-kind luxuriously embroidered dresses.[15] Exter was Ukrainian (like Sonia Delaunay), and her embroidery designs were influenced by peasant art. But she had also visited Europe before the First World War, and her designs were more profoundly influenced by modern movements like Cubism and Futurism.

In 1924, the same year that Popova died, Alexandra Exter emigrated to Paris, fed up with the growing repression and artistic constraints in the Soviet Union. The Russian fashion experiment was over.

Back in France, it seems fairly likely that there were always more women fashion designers than a mere list of couture houses might indicate. In 1925, for example, the House of Drécoll was actually run by a M and Mme de Wagner, a Belgian couple. According to *Paris on Parade,* "all Drécoll gowns

are designed either by Madame de Wagner or by Mademoiselle Madeleine, who until recently was a partner in the firm Madeleine and Madeleine."[16] (Madeleine, in fact, moved about a great deal, having worked also for the houses of Paquin and Callot.)

As we have seen, the hierarchy within all dressmaking establishments was predominently female. The *premières*, or forewomen, in an atelier were sometimes more expert dressmakers than the designers, who frequently consulted with them in working out the season's line. Among the many *premières* who later opened their own establishments, Madeleine Vionnet was probably the most successful. In addition, a number of saleswomen with a personal following and designing ability were able to get financial backing to open their own establishments.

Many women designers came up through the ranks before branching out on their own. Nina Ricci, for example, was apprenticed to a dressmaker at the age of thirteen. At eighteen she was already in charge of the atelier; at twenty she was head designer. In 1932 she opened her own couture house, with the assistance of her husband, Louis, a jeweler, and her son, Robert, who later ran the business. Maggy Besançon de Wagner, daughter of Mme de Wagner, the head designer at the House of Drécoll, also became

a well-known couturière under the pseudonym Maggy Rouff. "But please note," her husband once said, "she was not in trade, she [was] an artist."[17] Rouff once described herself as a couturier, deliberately rejecting the normal female title of couturière, "for I make a great distinction between the two terms," she said. "The couturier is a general who is more or less qualified, and who has, under his command, an army of collaborators. A couturière can, indeed, be very great and important . . . but the word by itself implies a knowledge and experience of manual labor. And I scarcely know how to cut!"[18]

## POIRET'S SISTERS

The great Paul Poiret had three sisters who went into fashion and had independent careers. Poiret was closest to Jeanne Boiven, with whom he had none of the professional rivalry that spoiled his relationships with the other two. For many years a conventional wife and mother, she took over a small existing couture house only after the death of her husband in 1917.

The second sister, Germaine Bongard, began by working for her brother; she and Poiret's wife, Denise, started a department of children's clothes in 1907 (at about the same time that Lanvin did). But when she opened her own *salon de couture* in 1911, Poiret regarded it as "treason." Whereas Paul Poiret dressed the fashionable world, however, Germaine's clients tended to be among the "artistic intelligentsia," people like Mme Henri Matisse and the pianist Marcelle Meyer. Her career was short.

Poiret's third sister, Nicole Groult, was the most important. Too independent to work for her elder brother, she began cutting and sewing dresses on the dining-room table (as her daughter later recalled). Her first models were naturally influenced by her brother's style, but they were already simpler. As *Vogue* observed in April 1912, "The models of Mme Groult, although simpler and less sumptuously oriental than those of her brother, are nonetheless original and artistic, and cost only a fraction of the clothes he makes."[19]

From the beginning Poiret felt threatened by this "rivalry." By the 1920s he was on the decline, reluctant to abandon the fabulous style that had once been so successful. During the same decade, his little sister's more minimalist style became increasingly popular. *Women's Wear Daily* called her clothes "wearable" and "chic." In 1923 *Jardin des Modes* and French *Vogue* paid more attention to her clothes than to Poiret's, and her dresses were frequently featured on the cover of *L'Art et la Mode*.

Although in retrospect it is clear that Poiret was incomparably the greater of the two, Groult was more in touch with the trends of the 1920s. Like her friend, the painter Marie Laurencin, Groult was temporarily very fashionable. Indeed, in 1927 American *Vogue* described her as "the Marie Laurencin of the art of fashion." The two women shared a love of pink, pale green, and silver-gray, unlike Poiret, who had brought about a revolution when he introduced bright, "barbaric" colors. Yet as Guillaume Garnier

TOP: *Maggy Rouf, Dress and cardigan jacket, 1931, illustrated in* Art, Goût, Beauté. *Photograph courtesy of Special Collections, The Fashion Institute of Technology Library, New York.*

ABOVE: *Nina Ricci in a portrait painted circa 1932. Photograph courtesy of Nina Ricci, Inc.*

OPPOSITE: *Nicole Groult, Black evening dress with pink and green embroidered flowers, circa 1926. Groult was the sister of Paul Poiret. Courtesy of the Musée de la Mode et du Costume, Paris, and the photographer, Chantal Fribourg.*

observed, "What particularly distinguishes the dresses of Nicole Groult is *black with a discreet touch of color.*"[20]

Although Poiret's sisters are worth remembering, however, Schiaparelli was his true successor in the art of outrageous fashion. Meanwhile, Vionnet, too, had her acolytes.

## SEDUCTIVE MODERNISM

In the 1930s Vionnet's seductive modernism influenced many designers, both male and female. A fashion connoisseur like Mainbocher, for example, who found Chanel too casual and Schiaparelli too bizarre, greatly admired women like Vionnet, Augustabernard, and Louiseboulanger. Indeed, not only was the Chicago-born Main Rousseau Bocher influenced by their style, but — in imitation of Augustabernard and Louiseboulanger — he also united his first and last names.

Like Vionnet, Augustabernard was known for her use of the bias and for the sophistication of her cutting and draping. Like Vionnet, too, she was above all a skilled dressmaker, a technician, not a personality in high society. According to the fashion editor Lilian Farly, "Her appearance, down to the color in her cheeks, was that of a young woman from the country. Her curly brown hair was combed back in a knot and she invariably wore one of her tailored suits without any decoration."[21]

But for all her genuine personal simplicity, she created dresses that *The New Yorker* called "grand simple affairs." Her evening dresses were characterized by long, floating lines, which were emphasized in the photographs that Hoyningen-Huene took for *Vogue.* Her "little" afternoon dresses also only appeared to be simple but were actually cut and constructed with refinement and ingenuity.

Augustabernard began modestly, as a copyist, skillfully reproducing the models of the great couturiers. She opened her own *salon de couture* in 1924 on the rue du Faubourg Saint-Honoré, but achieved her greatest fame from 1930 to 1935. In 1932 *Vogue* chose her neoclassical evening gown as the most beautiful dress of the year. She never had many customers, only the most exclusive, such as the Marquise de Paris, who won the Concours d'Elégance in St. Moritz wearing a silver lamé dress by Augustabernard. Because she made very few dresses, her clothes are now quite rare.

Despite her renown, Augustabernard's finances were always rather fragile. Ironically, she went out of business in part because her dresses were so widely copied. She was probably also a victim of the Great Depression; like Vionnet, her clientele was heavily South American, and with the currency crisis, they were often unable to pay their bills. The financial climate was so bad that even a famous designer like Vionnet made only half the number of dresses in 1938 than she had a decade earlier.

Louiseboulanger also ran her first and last names together, presumably because Boulanger, like Bernard, was a very common name. Louise Boulanger began working as an apprentice at the age of thirteen, much like Vionnet. And later she was strongly influenced by Vionnet's use of the bias

cut. But Louiseboulanger was also influenced by the beautiful Mme Chéruit, for whom she worked before opening her own business in 1923. Like Chéruit, Louiseboulanger was a stylish woman who made stylish clothes.

"Women who dare to wear clothes that are strikingly individual and about three seasons ahead of the style naturally gravitate toward Louiseboulanger," stated one guidebook.[22] Among her select clientele were the fashionable Daisy Fellowes and the Duchesse de Gramont. Louiseboulanger did all the designing, while her husband and sister directed the business. Like Vionnet and many others, Louiseboulanger closed her couture house in 1939.

Vionnet also paved the way for a third, very important woman designer, who did *not* stop working when the golden age of the couturière came to an end. As a young girl, Germaine Barton dreamed of becoming a sculptor. But her bourgeois parents disapproved, and so she turned to making what she called "living sculptures"—dresses of extraordinary artistry. Indeed, her clothes were so beautifully constructed that Vionnet herself wore them after she closed her own house.

## ALIX GRÈS

Alix and Madame Grès are one and the same person, and both *Alix* and *Grès* are assumed names. Germaine Barton hated her real name, and in the 1930s, under the name Alix, she first became famous for her bias-draped and pleated evening gowns. After World War II she had difficulties with her business partners, so she decided to open a new house under a different name. She chose the name Grès, which was an anagram for her husband's name.

RIGHT: *Nicole Groult, 1927. Photograph courtesy of the Union Française des Arts du Costume, Paris.*

A girl from a "good" Parisian family, Alix never worked as an apprentice. Instead, she briefly studied cutting and sketching, and then family friends helped her establish herself officially as a couturière. She was so nervous that she burst into tears when she had to show her patterns to the *commissionaires* of the Chambre Syndicale de la Couture.

"In the beginning there were minor inconveniences," she recalled years later. "The dress would look *magnifique*, but I wouldn't know if the poor lady would be able to lift an arm or sit down all evening."[23] According to fashion writer Arlene Cooper, who interviewed Madame Grès in the 1980s, the couturière was, in any case, less interested in "comfort" or "women's changing life-styles" than in the ways in which fashion can "enhance the body."[24]

Because Grès saw couture as an art, and because she had training in sculpture, her initial technical ignorance of dressmaking was not entirely a liability. "Ignorance is a very important thing," insisted Grès. "It leads you to try things others wouldn't dare attempt. . . . That was one reason I took the material and worked directly on it. I used the knowledge I had, which was sculpture."

Grès "sculpted in fabric." She loved fabric, especially silk jersey and cashmere jersey. "By touching a piece of fabric," she said, ". . . it is possible to know its soul, its character. When I drape a mannequin with silk, it reacts between my hands, and I try to understand and judge its reactions. . . . I can't make [the fabric] do what it doesn't want to do. There is a complicity, like a perfect marriage."[25]

Like Vionnet, the "sculptress-designer" Alix Grès always implicitly emphasized the relationship between clothing and the female body. "Alix stands for the body rampant, for the rounded, feminine sculptural form beneath the dress," declared *Harper's Bazaar* in 1936.[26]

LEFT: *Augustabernard, Day dresses and coats; hats by Rose Valois, 1932. Photograph by George Hoyningen-Huene, courtesy of the Frederick R. Koch Collection, Harvard Theatre Collection.*

ABOVE: *Louiseboulanger, Velvet and silk tweed raglan coat (left) and Jenny, Beige tweed redingote and crepe de chine scarf, 1930, illustrated in* Art, Goût, Beauté. *Photograph courtesy of Special Collections, The Fashion Institute of Technology Library, New York.*

RIGHT: *Alix, Classical-style white silk jersey evening gown, 1937, from* Femina. *"Alix stands for the body rampant, for the rounded, feminine sculptural form beneath the dress," declared* Harper's Bazaar. *Photograph courtesy of Special Collections, The Fashion Institute of Technology Library, New York.*

OPPOSITE: *Marcelle Chaumont, Evening gown of accordion-pleated gold lamé and wrap of purple velvet, 1948. The Costume Institute, The Metropolitan Museum of Art, New York. Photograph courtesy of the photographer, Joshua Greene.*

Like Vionnet, she always gave credit to the women with whom she worked. The reason the dresses were so marvelous, she insisted, was because of their workmanship. Both Vionnet and Grès cultivated a style of austere sophistication and fluidity of silhouette.

Unlike Vionnet (and most of the other couturières of the golden age), Grès started again after World War II. There were, of course, some female designers still working in Paris after the war, but they were fewer and less influential than before.

Vionnet's former assistant, Marcelle Chaumont, designed some very elegant dresses but had to retire in 1953 because of ill health. Two other Vionnet protégées, Mad Maltezos (the designer) and Susie Carpentier (the businesswoman) collaborated from 1939 to 1957 at the couture house they named "Mad Carpentier."

Some couture houses named for women acquired male designers during this period (for example, Castillo designed for Lanvin). A few new houses opened, such as that of Carven, who is still designing today.

But Grès was special. Sometimes she seemed to repeat her neoclassical evening dresses of the 1930s. But although Grès's clothes are, in a sense, "timeless," she did adapt to changing fashions. In the 1960s she created op-art dresses and flowery gowns for "couture hippies." And in the 1970s, when thirties' nostalgia influenced fashion, she made clothes that combined the best of both decades.

In 1985 Bernard Tapie acquired 66 percent of the Maison Grès, an-

nouncing that the venerable and perfectionist couturière would now collaborate with younger colleagues to make ready-to-wear clothing. This, however, proved difficult. Nevertheless, as late as 1990, Grès was the last living and working representative of the golden age of the couturière — the last of an entire generation of great women designers.

Along with Chanel, Grès is the most important couturière of the postwar period. Anne Hollander has compared their clothes, and she concludes that Grès's clothes look timeless precisely *because* she was not concerned with women's lives, their convenience, "sexual politics [or] social signals." She was concerned purely with "fabric as a fundamental artistic substance." This commitment to basic materials allied Grès with architects like Frank Lloyd Wright and Le Corbusier. By contrast, "Chanel worked in the realm of practical use, sexual charm and social meaning." Chanel's clothes were "suggestions for new ways . . . to live." Grès's clothes "were solutions to abstract problems. . . . Beauty [was] the overriding standard."[27]

LEFT: *Mad Carpentier, Evening dress, circa 1948. Mad Maltezos and Susie Carpentier collaborated at the couture house they called "Mad Carpentier." Photograph courtesy of the Union Française des Arts du Costume, Paris.*

OPPOSITE: *Alix, Evening dress, 1937, from Femina. "There were minor inconveniences," Alix recalled years later about her early designs. "The dress would look magnifique, but I wouldn't know if the poor lady (who wore it) would be able to . . . sit down all evening." Photograph courtesy of Special Collections, The Fashion Institute of Technology Library, New York.*

ABOVE: *Carven, White embroidered dress, 1951. Photograph courtesy of Carven.*

RIGHT: *Madame Grès, Hooded coat, 1950, modeled by Natalie. Photograph by Louise Dahl-Wolfe, courtesy of The Center for Creative Photography, University of Arizona.*

# 7
# SPINACH VERSUS MINK

There were important women designers in New York, as well as in Paris in the interwar years. Two designers, in particular, seem to epitomize the independent women of 1930s' America: Elizabeth Hawes and Valentina. A third woman, Muriel King, is also included here, because her life and career seem typical of the American experience at this time.

Elizabeth Hawes is primarily remembered today as the author of *Fashion is Spinach*, which takes its title from a famous cartoon by James Thurber in *The New Yorker* that shows a child glaring at the food on his dinner plate: "Eat your broccoli, dear," pleads his mother, to which the child replies: "I say it's spinach. And I say, the hell with it." Hawes's attitude towards fashion — or, at least, the fashion industry — was similarly disenchanted.

Like many Americans, Hawes had a love-hate relationship with fashion. She loved the beauty and individuality of fashion, but she hated the fact that so many people slavishly followed whatever fashion "dictators" declared to be the latest style. Not only did she deplore the copycat tendencies and cheap production values of many American clothing manufacturers, she also attacked the conformism of individual men and women. Freedom was her goal, and she was something of a fashion maverick.

By contrast, the Russian-born designer Valentina was profoundly dictatorial. "What women want is nearly always wrong," insisted the woman known as "America's most glamorous dressmaker."[1] She bullied her customers, giving them no choice in design or even color: "Yellow is for flowers," she told one hapless woman who had indicated that her husband liked that color. Valentina was equally dictatorial with fashion editors and usually insisted on choosing the dress, styling it, and posing herself for fashion pho-

35

ABOVE: *Cartouche designed by Alexey Brodovitch for the book cover of* Fashion Is Spinach, *published by Random House in 1938.*

tographs. *"Vogue* needs Valentina drama," she told Bettina Ballard, "You photograph me like this? Horst maybe?"[2]

Muriel King was not as dramatic as Valentina or Hawes, but her designs, too, were featured in leading magazines. Launched by the department store Lord & Taylor in 1932, King then opened her own salon on East 61st Street. Her motto was "cautious daring."

Muriel King "[is] a glorious-looking young woman . . . a sort of tawny goddess," declared *Vogue* in 1933. "Today, more than any one of this exciting new group of young people who are creating an American school of design, Muriel King has kept to the real couture tradition, by designing complete wardrobes . . . for the individual. She has never designed too many things for copying."[3]

Clearly, at this time, not only was couture more prestigious than ready-to-wear, but the personality and appearance of women designers were of the utmost importance.

## FASHION IS SPINACH

Hawes approached dressmaking from the perspective of a leftist intellectual. As a student at Vassar, she claimed to have spent time "wailing around about whether or not it was really the proper thing to devote my life to the matter of clothes."[4] But she did love beautiful clothes, and after studying economics, she went to Paris.

Her first job was as a design thief for a company that copied couture fashions; then she became an apprentice at the couture house of Nicole Groult and a free-lance fashion reporter for *The New Yorker*, signing herself *Parisite.*

Although she learned a great deal in Paris, she rejected what she called "the French Legend"—that "all beautiful clothes are made in the houses of the French couturières and all women want them."[5] In 1928 she returned to the United States and opened a small dressmaking establishment in New York City.

Hawes's openings were attended by a mixed group of fashion people, socialites, artists, and intellectuals. Edmund Wilson (of all people to imagine at a fashion show!) reported in a diary entry of 1934: "Elizabeth Hawes herself had on a very pretty evening gown, not very long, white satin, just caught up over her breasts with thin white ribbons of shoulder straps, and showing off by contrast to splendid advantage her rather dark, well-muscled back . . ."[6]

At one point during the 1933 spring fashion show, the lights were turned off, to show "The Panther Woman of the Needle Trades," a fifteen-minute silent film starring Hawes herself. The film begins with the creation of the universe, runs through a time line of important historical events (the Roman Empire, the Plague, etc.), and stops at 1903: Chromosomes dance around, and Hawes appears dressed as a baby; she immediately seizes a pair of scissors and some diapers, and begins cutting out dress patterns.

Hawes's 1933 fashion collection was typical of her irreverent style:

The dresses bore names like "Five Year Plan," "The Yellow Peril," "Nazi," "Prosperity Is Just Around the Corner," "The People's Choice," and "The Revolt of the Masses"—the last named referring to a lace evening dress.

There was also the "Alimony" evening dress of 1937, the "Misadventure" cape, and others. One collection had an Alice in Wonderland theme, with the "King of Hearts" suit and the "Mad Hatter" coat, while another collection took rivers as its theme: Evening dresses bore names like "Volga," "Rubicon," "Swanee," "Ganges," and "Limpopo"; a tweed coat was called the "Amazon."

Although later in life she would attack the "rich bitches" who bought custom-made clothes, a Hawes advertisement of the mid–1930s declared that "our only ambition is to go on dressing more and more real ladies in what we and they consider to be really beautiful clothes." And she promised that her clients could wear a Hawes dress until it "falls to pieces (from one to three years)."[7]

*Vogue* regarded Hawes as "one of the inspired insane" and loved "the mad, mad quality of her concoctions." In spring of 1934 the magazine burst into "one of our periodical paeons in praise of Elizabeth Hawes, who, as usual, is up to new tricks." The way she combined pink and red made editors "swoon with sheer pleasure." They also appreciated her as the "supreme . . . purveyor of gadgets," such as gloves that "laced up the back with contrasting leather thongs ($10)," or an "unforgettable broccoli boutonniere ($2.50)."[8]

"Elizabeth Hawes has more energy than any ten women I know," declared an editor at *Harper's Bazaar*, on learning that Hawes was now designing a line of purses, "which, being by Miss Hawes, aren't like anybody else's bags you ever saw."[9]

Despite praise from the fashion press, Hawes despaired of the American tendency to copy Paris, and she was frustrated by the difficulties that American designers faced. It was much easier to work in Paris, she said. While still struggling with her own dressmaking house, Hawes received many offers from manufacturers to design for the mass market.

Sick of the "parasites" who bought couture clothes, Hawes was initially enthusiastic about the opportunity of designing for the masses. Her 1938 book, *Fashion Is Spinach*, was dedicated to "Madeleine Vionnet, the great creator of style in France, and to the future designers of mass-produced clothes the world over." As Hawes saw it, this was the issue for American designers: how to learn from the French couture, while also creating "democratic" and mass-produced clothes that answered the needs of modern American women.

BELOW: *Hawes in suspender trousers and pussy-foot shoes of her own design, circa 1940. "I've reduced dressing to a minimum: a couple of suits, trousers or shorts, pockets instead of purses," she said. Drawing courtesy of Sandra Smith-Garcéz.*

She believed that mass production could and should ensure that all American women could have beautiful clothes. But the purely businesslike approach of the American fashion industry disgusted her, and in the long run she was unwilling to make the compromises that seemed to be necessary when designing for American mass production.

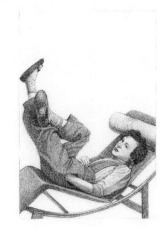

In 1932 Lord & Taylor began to promote the American designer movement. Yet Hawes, who was one of those promoted, complained that no one mentioned the designers' names: "'Our own American designs' . . . by whom? Why, by Americans. Who are they? What are their names? Never mind that, these are 'Clothes designed in America' whoopee — by perfectly nameless people, robots maybe."[10] Hawes was far from robotic. Indeed, her controversial fashion polemics garnered considerable publicity throughout her career.

After her manifesto *Fashion Is Spinach*, which argued that all women deserved to have beautiful, functional clothes, Hawes wrote *Men Can Take It* (1939), in which she advocated greater freedom, color, and comfort in men's clothing. The title referred to her belief that men's clothes were uncomfortable and physically restrictive (their collars and ties, in particular), but since "men could take it," they unquestioningly put up with standard men's apparel.

But Hawes's advice to men fell on deaf ears: "As for bright hues in clothes, men always snort at my suggestion, 'Only pansies wear colored clothes!' So I say to myself, heaven help the American male with his complex of having to be masculine."[11] She even proposed that men wear skirts.

Hawes herself tended to wear trousers during the day, even in the city. "I've reduced dressing to a minimum," she said, "a couple of suits, trousers or shorts, pockets instead of purses."[12] She designed trousers with wide suspenders and deep pockets, to be worn with soft, flat "Pussyfoot" shoes or "Foot Gloves," rather like Claire McCardell's ballet slippers. Like McCardell, too, Hawes made simple, comfortable designs for the casual American life-style.

But the two designers had rather different conceptions of the American woman, which affected the fashions they created. According to Hawes's biographer, Bettina Berch, Hawes was arty. Her clients were the "left-leaning Vasserish social set." By contrast, McCardell was "suburban," and she "was bankrolled by a sympathetic clothing manufacturer."[13] Certainly, McCardell had a much greater influence on the subsequent history of American fashion, but the fashion iconoclast Hawes is now receiving increased attention.

Hawes essentially stopped designing at the end of the thirties (except for a brief comeback in 1948). But she continued to write about fashion. Her book *Why Is A Dress?* (1942), which went to press just as the United States entered World War II, offered advice to aspiring designers. Hawes herself spent the war years working in an aviation factory.

Her experiences led her to write *Why Women Cry, or Wenches with Wrenches* (1943), in which she argued that "wenches" were oppressed by a sexist and class-stratified society. She further divided American women into several categories: "the contented cow," "les riches bitches," and "she-wolves" (like herself), who fought for the right to be full human beings. At the Federal Bureau of Investigation, J. Edgar Hoover opened a file on Hawes, who had become increasingly radical.

Nevertheless, in fashionable circles there was still a small Hawes clique. When she made a brief comeback in 1948, *The New Yorker* covered her fashion show: "She's politically Left, but this is her art," remarked one viewer.[14] The show was not a success, and this was her last attempt to produce a collection. She continued to design a little bit for friends, but mostly

LEFT: *Elizabeth Hawes, The "Alimony" evening dress and "Misadventures" cape, 1937. The Brooklyn Museum, gift of Mrs. Diana S. Field. Photograph by William Lyall.*

BELOW LEFT: *Elizabeth Hawes, White crepe evening dress, 1936. The Brooklyn Museum, gift of the estate of Elinor Gimbel.*

concentrated on writing.

Her last book, *It's Still Spinach* (1954), argued that men and women should get "naked." That is, not only should they strip off their uncomfortable clothes, they should also discard their preconceived ideas about appropriate dress. Why should men have to wear hats and ties? Why should women have to wear gloves and brassieres? Over the years, she reiterated her arguments in a host of popular articles.

"Can Ladies Wear Trousers?" she asked in one article. They already do, she concluded. Another article bore the title "Ruffles — If You Feel Like Them," and this was really Hawes's fashion ideology: You should feel free to wear whatever makes you happy.[15]

## MINK IS FOR FOOTBALL

Valentina Nicholaevna Sanina had a very different fashion philosophy. If Hawes was a fashion anarchist, Valentina was a fashion royalist. One said, "Do what you want." The other said, "Do what I say." Yet there were also striking similarities between the two women.

In 1928, the year that Hawes opened her first couture shop, so did Valentina. They shared some of the same society and theatrical clients, and (at different times) they even occupied the same town house on 67th Street. Sometimes described as Hawes's rival, Valentina also designed clothes characterized by simple, classic lines. Hawes's style developed out of a "stripped down no-nonsense" modern attitude toward dress, whereas Valentina's classicism was a "timeless but theatrical statement."[16] In personality, they could not have been more diametrically opposed, and this difference was reflected in their clothes.

Born in Kiev at the turn of the century, Valentina was studying drama when the Revolution broke out. She often recalled that she met her future husband, George Schlee, in the Sevastopol railroad station, when she was trying to escape from Russia with her family jewels. (By contrast, Hawes visited the Soviet Union in the 1930s to see how clothing for the masses was produced and to offer friendly advice.)

In Paris, Valentina and Schlee launched a theatrical revue, "Russe," which in 1923 traveled to New York, where they decided to stay. In 1928, with her husband's support, Valentina opened a dress shop. For the next three decades she designed made-to-order dresses for a hand-picked clientele, which included many theatrical personalities.

She was also known for her stage costumes: "Valentina has designed clothes that act before a line is spoken," declared drama critic Brooks Atkinson. And Valentina herself insisted that "on the stage or off, it is essential to know a woman's physical and psychological equipment . . . in order to create a dress that will . . . identify a personal style."[17]

Her clients included Katharine Hepburn, Gloria Swanson, and Lynn Fontaine. After a trip to Hollywood, she also designed for Norma Shearer, Rosalind Russell, and Paulette Goddard, as well as socially prominent Astors, Vanderbilts, and Mellons, not to mention Clare Booth Luce. Her most

famous client, however, was Greta Garbo, with whom George Schlee had a longstanding liaison. Garbo and the designer looked rather alike, although when told so, Valentina would say that she was "the Gothic version."

Valentina was an extraordinary personality: strong-willed, shrewd, funny. Occasionally she would put on a one-woman fashion show for selected guests:

"Little dress for evening to keep husband home who go out too much," she would say, as she floated around in a lovely hostess gown. Or, she would explain, "Little costume to take off weekend, so old-fashioned pack too many no good clothes — take one costume, wear many ways," and she would do an amusing striptease, starting with a handsome Valentina shirt and skirt, "For arrive by car," then off would come the blouse, underneath which was a bare top, "for take sun on terrace," then off would come the skirt to show matching shorts, "for beach with hat," and the Russian woman in the wings would throw her a pointed coolie hat. . . . Then, "for dinner in moonlight" the Russian would hand her a long skirt that she would add to the bare top. . . . She invariably ended the show in a delicious organdie dress with a little embroidered apron. . . . "Very simple for garden, darrling," and she would float out to the happy gasps of "Marvelous, sublime, you're a genius, Valentina."[18]

Valentina was described as "America's most glamorous dressmaker," and her aphorisms became famous: "Children are for suburbs," she declared. "Mink is for football." Like Diana Vreeland, Valentina was parodied on Broadway. But, like Vreeland, she also had a clear sense of style. In 1940 her striking clothes started at $250, but they were so widely copied that journalists often referred to a copy as "a poor woman's Valentina."

"She made many wonderful clothes, but nobody looked as well in them as she did," said designer Bill Blass, who made some linen dresses for Valentina in 1970.[19]

Her clothes were always deceptively simple and fashioned according to the female anatomy. *Vogue* explained that "the Valentina idea" was to work "from the figure first."[20] Like the clothes of Vionnet and Alix Grès, Valentina's dresses were intended to be timeless. "Simplicity survives the changes of fashion," she declared, "Fit the century, forget the year."[21] Whether she made a stark black velvet evening gown or a rough linen shirt-waist, she insisted that the *line* of her clothes was crucial. Jewelry obviated the need for trimmings.

"A dress that does not give a woman freedom gives her nothing," declared Valentina. The "swift-moving rhythms of America" require clothing that permits "freedom of movement and freedom of mood," she continued. "A dress must be all one swoop," without distracting details or encumbering embroidery, if a woman is to "develop her own mood." In the wrong clothes, "she is marooned, falsified."[22]

Valentina closed her couture house in 1957, but she deserves to be remembered for her workmanship and sense of theater. She epitomizes the heights attained in the field of American couture.

Hawes and Valentina were exceptional figures, but many other women played a vital role in American fashion during the 1930s. To understand their contributions to the history of American fashion, we need to look at the structure of the fashion industry. Many women worked in the exclusive tradition of made-to-order styles, just as they did in Paris. Indeed, women were especially prominent in the area of custom dressmaking. In America, however, there was also another body of women, who worked for the ready-to-wear industry, designing affordable and comfortable clothes for ordinary American women. Some women designers, such as Hawes and King, worked in both areas. At Lord & Taylor, King's originals were priced at about $125, her copies at $30 to $50.

ABOVE: *Muriel King, Sketch for an evening dress, circa 1935. Photograph courtesy of Special Collections, The Fashion Institute of Technology Library, New York.*

After World War II, ready-to-wear would become far more important in America than indigenous couture, resulting in a gradual loss of influence for women designers. Moreover, as the public relations industry increasingly created a veritable cult of personality around designers, only a few women — like Claire McCardell — caught the popular imagination. But in the smaller fashion world of the 1930s, a modest but genuine talent like King's could flourish.

"Miss Muriel King is a Seattle girl [who is] . . . prouder of her amateur watercolors than of her severely elegant clothes," declared *Fortune* in 1933.[23] In fact, King had studied art at the University of Washington before she went into fashion design, and she spent ten years doing free-lance fashion drawing for *Women's Wear Daily, Vogue,* and *Femina* before she actually began designing clothes.

As she herself put it, she always began designing "backwards": Only after she had a complete color sketch did she choose the fabric and begin work on the dress itself. According to one account, "Contemporaries agree that if she knew more about cutting and sewing, she might be restrained by technical difficulties from trying for certain effects."[24] Yet her dresses turned out well, and her sketches are exceptionally beautiful.

Among her couture clients was the famous photographer Margaret Bourke-White (whose diary attests to the fact that she adored clothes). Beginning in 1935 King also designed costumes for Hollywood films, such as *Sylvia Scarlet* and *Stage Door.* "At fittings," said King, "Ginger whirled, Hepburn strode like a lithe young goddess, Gail Patrick practiced walking, sitting and standing to be sure that these costumes moved with fluidity and grace."[25]

In December 1936 *Harper's Bazaar* illustrated a piece by the sculptor Isamu Noguchi inspired by a dress by Muriel King: "a dress that is the calla-lily come to life," enthused the magazine. "And only, emphasizes Miss King, for the young lady who is not afraid of Destiny."[26]

Back in New York in 1937, she moved to a large salon on East 51st Street, only to close three years later at the height of her success. "I stopped because my work suddenly seemed anachronistic," she told an interviewer in 1940. "I don't think people really want to spend that much time and money on clothes. And for my part, I did not want to be so individualistic in my whole activity. It just seemed too bad not to make a highly specialized talent more useful to more people." In 1943 she came out of retirement to design the "Flying Fortress Fashions," an all-blue safety wardrobe for women workers in the aircraft industry.[27]

Although a forthcoming chapter will focus on fashion editors and photographers ("Think Pink!"), there is one woman whose sophistication and independence set her apart from the typical fashion journalist and ally her with the "independent women" of American fashion and in particular with Elizabeth Hawes. Her name is Lois Long, and she wrote *The New Yorker's* fashion column, "On and Off the Avenue," from 1927 until 1970.

Brendan Gill described Long as "an exceptionally intelligent, good-looking, and high-spirited girl . . . the embodiment of the glamorous insider."[28] After graduating from Vassar, she plunged into New York's party life. Not only were she and her roommate, actress Kay Francis, known for their own parties, but Long also began to review nightclubs, restaurants, and cabarets for *The New Yorker*, writing under the sobriquet *Lipstick*. She was one of the few women to break into *The New Yorker's* golden circle, and this prior to her brief marriage to *New Yorker* cartoonist Peter Arno.

Her real forte, however, proved to be fashion reportage. She had an original, ironic, and slightly disillusioned view of fashion. She was never afraid to criticize even fashion's greatest icons — not from malice but in defense of the ordinary woman shopper. Thus, both in style and content, Long's fashion journalism was a far cry from what Gill called "the sedulous puffing of certain favored shops and designers." In his memoir *Here at the New Yorker*, Gill wrote: "Long cared not a straw for anyone but her readers." She sought "to instruct and entertain them by the extraordinary device of taking clothes seriously and writing about them honestly."[29] In one typically memorable column of 1936, for example, Long fearlessly analyzed the latest designs of fashion's three greatest designers:

Chanel's little daytime dresses look ordinary and well bred, instead of smart, unless worn by a woman with enormous chic. . . . I am at a loss to understand why the big houses all fell for Schiaparelli's wool suit with the slightly flaring hip-length jacket which has a one-button closing so high-waisted that all look of slimth through the waistline is gone. And I stand or fall by my contention that Vionnet's things are overrated. When she sticks to those sculptured, simple lines she has done for years, her clothes are lovely enough; when she goes haywire with lots of fabric, they are sloppy and clumsy beyond words. I am still enraged by a chiffon evening thing at Saks Fifth Avenue which, so far, stands unchallenged as the horror of the season: huge harem trousers, very full front and back so that you can't avoid looking dumpy, and those unspeakable full Vionnet folds, crossing high at the front and back to wrap around the neck. I could howl.[30]

There was nothing catty in all this, since in the very same column Long generously praised two other dresses by Vionnet as "divine" and "a honey." A week later she also described "an infinitely flattering . . . perfect Vionnet" at Bloomingdale's "that costs but $19.95."[31]

But Long absolutely detested the way "fashion writers sat in their offices and told their awestruck public that Vionnet was Vionnet and that any model she turned out, no matter what it did to your charm, was automatically veddy smawt."[32] Grecian drapery might be lovely, she added, but the Greeks didn't wear girdles.

Rather than simply following (and promoting) the latest fashion trends, Long *analyzed* phenomena like the New Look. In 1947, for example, she described how American buyers were suffering "their usual schoolgirl crushes on talented newcomers," such as "the new darling," Christian Dior.[33] She also studied the phenomenon of "buyers' resistance," noting that it was "possibly related to buyers' contemplation of present-day price tags."[34]

Fashion is "a schizophrenic girl," wrote Long, with "a kleptomaniac attitude toward other women's pocketbooks." But, she admitted, if you didn't follow her slavishly, she was often a lot of fun. Long signed off one column on swimsuits with the words: "Nice, isn't it, to dream of all these things during our dreary hibernation in our long woolen underwear?"[35] Fashion historians have tended to focus on men, such as New York's Norell, Hollywood's Adrian, and the Paris-based Mainbocher, but the periodicals of the day also featured women designers such as Jessie Franklin Turner, Nettie Rosenstein, Claire Potter, and many others who worked in a variety of styles. If we single out Hattie Carnegie, it is because she, more than any of her contemporaries, succeeded in the *business* of fashion.

Hattie Carnegie is widely regarded as the "mother" of American high fashion. The "father" was Norman Norell, who worked as Carnegie's most famous designer. In contrast to the usual pattern in France, where the female designer tended to work in association with a male business partner (often her husband or son), in this case the woman was in charge.

A tough, ambitious immigrant who could neither cut nor sew, Carnegie was a savvy entrepreneur who became the head of a multi-million dollar business with her own factories, wholesale operation, and retail stores, and more than a thousand employees. One of Carnegie's stable of designers was Emmett Joyce, who was mentioned in the late 1930s in an article in the *World Telegram*, entitled "Men Are Designing, Too" — as though this were an unusual occurence.[36]

Meanwhile, to the extent that fashion was associated with Frenchmen (even in the 1930s), the real role of American women may have been underappreciated. One American woman, Pearl Alexander Lipman, for example, gave her "sketch house" a French masculine name — *André* — to capitalize on the desire that Americans felt for fashions designed in Paris. (The name *André* may also refer obliquely to the Hollywood designer Adrian.) When Lipman opened her house in 1931, most French designers were women, but the prestige of the male couturier (established by Worth and Poiret) continued to exist — and would grow much stronger in the 1950s.

# 8
# ALL-AMERICAN

W hen World War II broke out and Schiaparelli went into exile in America, she argued that New York could never replace Paris as the capital of fashion, because of the commercialism and lack of creative freedom on Seventh Avenue. She also believed that American women lacked interest in fashion and elegance. What she failed to recognize was that American women were in the process of developing a different type of fashion, a casual and functional style that could be mass-produced.

Claire McCardell is probably the most important American ready-to-wear designer of the twentieth century. It is her name, in particular, that is associated with the phenomenon known as "The American Look." Paris had Chanel, America had McCardell. But there was more than one woman designer in America.

Just as women dominated Parisian couture in the 1920s and 1930s, so also did women play a very important role in the American ready-to-wear industry, especially in the 1940s. Among the women working at this time were Louella Ballerino, Hattie Carnegie, Bonnie Cashin, Ceil Chapman, Jo Copeland, Sophie Gimbel of Saks, Tina Leser, Vera Maxwell, Mollie Parnis, Claire Potter, Nettie Rosenstein, Carolyn Schnurer, Pauline Trigère, and Valentina. They worked in a variety of styles, of course, but we shall concentrate here on several pioneering women who helped make this period the golden age of American sportswear.

"Women Designers Set New Fashions," declared *Life* in 1946. Cited as "outstanding . . . designers of U.S. warm-weather wear" were Claire McCardell, Tina Leser, Frances Sider, and Carolyn Schnurer. "The ideal of all four is the long-legged tennis-playing, swimming girl."[1]

ABOVE: *Claire McCardell, Sketch for blue denim bare-back dress, 1943. "I've always wondered why women's clothes had to be delicate," said McCardell. "Why couldn't they be practical and sturdy as well as feminine?" Photograph courtesy of The Brooklyn Museum.*

OPPOSITE: *Claire McCardell, Tweed suit, 1945. France had Chanel, America had McCardell. Photograph by Louise Dahl-Wolfe, courtesy of The Center for Creative Photography, University of Arizona.*

McCardell "looks exactly like . . . The Typical American Girl," declared *Vogue* in 1941, "just as real as real, only prettier. She's glowing with health . . . Her figure is long and lithe . . . and she's young, fresh, . . . full of slang and laughs."[2]

McCardell made clothes that were "right, ready and revolutionary for every girl in America," agreed *Harper's Bazaar* in 1944. There was "something of the pioneer woman in the frugal but beautiful cut of the suit, the black cotton stockings . . . something of our workmen in the stout welt-seaming . . . something of Flash Gordon in the adventurous hood."[3]

McCardell was born in 1905 in Maryland, the daughter of a banker and a southern belle. She studied fashion at the Parsons School of Design, and spent her sophomore year — 1926 — in Paris. Back in New York, she began working for Townley Frocks, a Seventh Avenue wholesale manufacturer that specialized in sportswear.

In the 1930s American fashion was still in an embryonic stage of development. McCardell herself admitted, "I did what everybody else did — copied Paris."[4] Her sketchbooks (now at Parsons) indicate, for example, that she copied Molyneux, Maggy Rouff, and Alix. But whereas most designers simply copied, McCardell also analyzed and dissected dresses by Alix and Vionnet. "I was learning the way clothes worked, the way they felt," recalled McCardell.[5]

Like Vionnet, McCardell was attentive to the nature of her materials and sensitive to the three-dimensionality of a woman's body. Like Vionnet, McCardell may have represented a female design sensibility. Her intentions and her market (college coeds, career girls and housewives) were different than Vionnet's, however, and she simplified Vionnet's cut, because she was creating ready-to-wear, not couture.

"Don't forget, Claire invented all those marvelous things strictly within the limits of mass production," said Norman Norell. "I worked more in the couture tradition — expensive fabrics, hand stitching, exclusivity, all that — but Claire could take five dollars worth of common cotton calico and turn out a dress a smart woman could wear anywhere."[6]

Her sketchbooks are filled with notes indicating, for example, "4 yards of tweed $5.70 . . . 1 belt $2.50 . . . 16 buttons $1 a dozen . . . 1 yard lining taffeta $2.75 . . . 7 hooks and eyes $1.25 a dozen." She lists fabrics like plaid cotton, linen, onionskin taffeta, chambray, and checked gingham.

"Clothes ought to be useful and comfortable," said McCardell. "I've always wondered why women's clothes had to be delicate — why they couldn't be practical and sturdy as well as feminine."[7] She made denim suits, skirts with big pockets, dresses, and jumpsuits that a woman could really move in. Her inspiration, she claimed, came from solving problems. Thus, for the woman traveler, she created a six-piece interchangeable wardrobe, consisting of a skirt, jacket, blouse, slacks, shorts, and halter or brassiere-top, either in denim or black butcher cloth.

McCardell's first famous design was the "Monastic" — a waistless, dartless, bias-cut tent dress. According to McCardell's biographer Sally Kirkland, the dress caused a sensation: "Drop everything!" an agitated dress manufacturer shouted to his designer. "There's a girl up the street

making a dress with no back, no front, no waistline, and my God, no bust darts!"[8] Extremely radical for 1938, the "Monastic" nevertheless proved tremendously popular. Unfortunately, it was also extremely easy to copy, and Townley Frocks went (temporarily) bankrupt.

Hattie Carnegie recognized McCardell's talent and hired her to create a line called "Workshop Originals." But Carnegie's customers wanted something fancier for their money, so in 1940 McCardell returned to Townley Frocks to design under her own name.

Most American designers were anonymous at this time, and it says something about McCardell's strength of character that she was credited for her designs. Even the publicity for the "American Designer movement" tended to emphasize the name of the store rather than the designer. It is

ABOVE: *Claire McCardell,
"Baby-doll" dress in black
wool jersey, 1946. Photograph
by Louise Dahl-Wolfe,
courtesy of The Center for
Creative Photography,
University of Arizona.*

important to note, though, that McCardell was not the only designer creating casual "American" styles; other recognizably similar American designers of the period include both women like Tina Leser and men like Tom Brigance.

"Before and during the war there was a terrific vogue for what were called 'the American Designers,' who were being discovered and promoted by Dorothy Shaver at Lord & Taylor's," recalled fashion editor Bettina Ballard. "During the war they received an inordinate amount of publicity, what with Paris dead to the press, and also because they represented a good national fashion story." Although Ballard disliked "the glorified covered-wagon quality" of the genre, she recognized that they had put Seventh Avenue on the map.[9]

World War II undoubtedly helped McCardell's career: Cut off from French fashion by the Nazi occupation of Paris, American manufacturers and department stores were desperate for homegrown design talent. They

especially wanted designers who could work within wartime restrictions, creating simple, inexpensive clothes. McCardell had always been drawn to simple, unpretentious clothes, and she regarded wartime restrictions as a welcome challenge.

One of McCardell's most famous dresses was a 1942 design, which Lord & Taylor christened the "Popover." It was an unstructured, waistless, wraparound dress, made of unpretentious materials such as denim and calico. The "Popover" was "made at *Harper's Bazaar*'s request to fit the requirements of wartime ladies whose servants had gone off to the defense plant." It was featured in the magazine with the caption "I'm doing my work" — together with accessories such as a potholder. It was given the name "Popover" because "you just pop it over something nicer underneath."[10]

Priced initially at $6.95, the "Popover" continued to be produced for years; it sold for $23 in 1955, when it was featured in *Vogue*. According to McCardell, "the 'Popover' started out as a wartime Victory Garden cover-up—moved into the house when servantless living arrived. . . . By the summer of 1951, it played its role as dress, coat, beach wrap or hostess dress. The victory of the basic dress is this type of versatility."[11]

Many of McCardell's dresses had little or no "hanger appeal" and depended for their effect on being worn. Often only a belt gave the dress its shape (and McCardell liked "important" belts). She disliked shoulder pads, and her dresses were almost the exact opposite of the typical structured forties' fashions.

The decade of the 1940s was McCardell's most productive period. Among her classics were the "Kitchen Dinner Dress" (1940) in which a woman could both cook and serve her guests; the "Diaper Bathing Suit" (1942); a silk gingham plaid playsuit with bloomers (1942); a one-piece jumpsuit (1943); and the black wool empire-style "Baby-doll Dress" (1946). As this partial list indicates, McCardell emphasized "playclothes" and sports clothes more than formal wear. Even her evening dresses tended to be comfortable "hostess gowns" for entertaining at home.

In retrospect, McCardell's jersey bathing suits look particularly modern. Without the heavy structural underpinnings that date other bathing suits of the period, and equally free of surface decoration, they rely on clean, bold lines and unexpected shapes, such as a halter top or a wrapped "diaper" bottom. In contrast to the shiny, colorful Lastex bathing suits coming out of California, McCardell used plain black or beige wool jersey. Her bathing suits bore a recognizable similarity, in fact, to her jersey dresses, skimpy jersey jumpers, and halter tops.

McCardell was also one of the first to incorporate the leotard look into everyday fashion. From 1943 on, she used leotards (which *Life* called "funny tights"), thus anticipating the beatnik or modern-dancer styles of the 1950s, to say nothing of the aerobic styles of the 1970s and Donna Karan's wildly successful bodysuits and leotards of the present day. She also used ballet slippers and other flat shoes, which gave the McCardell woman a youthful stride.

In January 1950, *Vogue* looked back on the previous decade and concluded that the American woman of the 1940s had "a frugal, space-silhouetted American primitive look that Martha Graham helps her to visualize, and Claire McCardell and Capezio help her to achieve: her dress a jersey tube . . . (or a skimpy jersey jumper over a skimpy leotard); her Phelps belt and bag bold . . . ; her feet flat on the ground."[12]

Although McCardell liked long, full skirts and gently fitted bodices, her clothes were also quite different from Dior's New Look dresses with their intricate interiors. Hers were easygoing clothes—easy to make and easy to wear. A customer at Manhattan's Lord & Taylor was quoted in *Time* as saying, "Just what I want. Smart, you know, but casual."[13]

McCardell's jersey dresses appealed especially to young, sophisticated women (often other designers or fashion editors), precisely because they recognized how *new* her unstructured, undecorated, comfortable, casual clothes really were. "She put women into brief jersey bathing suits and amusingly mad play clothes. She made the jersey sheath an American uniform," wrote Bettina Ballard (who was, however, the rare fashion editor who did *not* become a "Claire McCardell fan"). In her memoirs, Ballard slightingly remarked that "Claire McCardell had a natural instinct for publicity that spread her name rapidly across the country."[14]

Shortly after the war, a *Harper's Bazaar* copywriter, Alice Morris, had to write a caption for a photograph of a McCardell dress. "Tell me, what's so great about this dress?" she begged editor Diana Vreeland. "But, Alice, it's wonderful. It's so pathetic," said Vreeland. "I knew immediately what she meant," recalled Morris. "I couldn't use the word 'pathetic,' but she was so right. It was a new frugal silhouette with that tight top so close through the shoulders." *Pathetic* became *frugal*.[15]

Whether the copy limped along or soared in Whitmanesque enthusiasm, the photographs of McCardell's clothes were usually exemplary. Louise Dahl-Wolfe, in particular, took dozens of outstanding photographs of McCardell's clothes for *Harper's Bazaar*. The ongoing collaboration between Dahl-Wolfe and McCardell throughout the 1940s was one of the magazine's greatest achievements. (Indeed, it is possible that some of Bettina Ballard's hostility comes from the fact that *Harper's* featured McCardell so much more effectively than did *Vogue*.) Certainly, Dahl-Wolfe thought that it was virtually impossible to take a poor photograph of a McCardell dress.

The golden age of American sportswear was more than McCardell, however. "During World War II," writes Caroline Milbank, "[the designer] Mildred Orrick submitted an idea for leotard-based dressing to Diana Vreeland, then at *Harper's Bazaar*, who liked it so much that she arranged for Claire McCardell to oversee its production, which resulted in McCardell getting the credit."[16]

Subsequently, Orrick was able to design innovative sportswear under her own name, although later she reverted to designing anonymously, first for Anne Fogarty and later at Townley, where, according to Milbank, she supervised the collections while Claire McCardell's was ill and after her death.

Many people have seen Tina Leser's playclothes in photographs by Dahl-Wolfe . . . and mistaken them for designs by Claire McCardell. An innovative designer in her own right, Leser deserves to be better known.

She did hand-painted prints before Pucci and toreador pants before Saint Laurent, and is even credited with having designed the first cashmere dress. In 1945 Leser was given a Coty Award for her "complete freedom and originality in the design of playclothes, and for establishing the bare brown look, as well as the wrapped skirt silhouette."[17]

Born Christine Shillard-Smith in 1910, she was the daughter of a stockbroker and a painter. While still a child, Tina traveled throughout Asia, Africa, and Europe; at the age of twelve she spent six months living with the family of the Indian poet, Rabindranath Tagore. After living in California and studying art in Paris, she came back to Philadelphia, where she had been brought up, to be presented to society. In 1931 she married the ichthyologist Curtin Leser and moved to Honolulu, where she opened a dress shop stocked with clothes by Nettie Rosenstein — and with her own

designs made from colorful hand-blocked textiles.

In 1940, on a buying trip to New York, she showed one of her ethnic-inspired playsuits to *Vogue* and *Harper's Bazaar*. Saks Fifth Avenue ordered 500 of them. She had problems finding fabric printers willing to produce her large and unusual designs, then she had union troubles and had to borrow money from her mother, but eventually her career was launched. For ten years she designed for the firm of Edwin Foreman; after he retired in 1953, she started her own business.

Leser once described her designs as "half Asiatic and half just pretty and feminine."[18] Her designs were often Asian in inspiration — "Hindu waterboy outfits," "coolie coats," and "Persian hostess pyjamas," which were "Americanized and glorified." She used lush color combinations, such as green and gold satin, which gave her leisure clothes "an Arabian-nights look." Her gilt-studded Turkish slacks were particularly popular, and she put sequins even on leather. In 1945 *Women's Wear Daily* announced: "Fabulous eastern influences make for exciting loungewear."[19]

"Wandering down Main Street or riding in a bus, these fashions would look absurd and ridiculous, comfortable as they might be," warned journalist Catherine Roberts. But, she continued, worn "at the beach or . . . in your own backyard or . . . for dancing at the club . . . these clothes will lend glamor."[20]

When Leser married for the second time in 1949, to former Pan Am pilot James Howley, her honeymoon inspired additional "global fashions," influenced by the indigenous costumes of Japan, Siam, India, and the Middle East.[21]

LEFT: *Claire McCardell,
Linen suit with shorts, 1950.
Photograph by Louise
Dahl-Wolfe, courtesy of the
Edward C. Blum Design
Laboratory, The Fashion
Institute of Technology,
New York.*

Her two-piece bathing suits were "the most daring attire to appear on American beaches to date," declared the photography magazine *Click,* approvingly, in 1944: "Scanty swim suits . . . are designed to give the girls a maximum of vitamin D—and the boys an eyeful."[22] In addition to these bathing suits that were "bare practically everywhere," Leser was also known for rayon jersey bathing suits that were "twisted and draped in mermaid manner." She also created strapless (and even boned) bathing suits.

One of the first to franchise her bathing-suit designs, Leser often complemented them with "futuristic . . . sun fashions," such as beach dresses, terry-cloth "dry-off suits" and wrapped "sarong" skirts to be worn "over the shortest-yet shorts."[23]

Obviously, Leser was not the only designer doing sexy swimsuits. A *Cosmopolitan* article on "male-tested fashions" noted that men like Bob Hope and Desi Arnaz also appreciated Claire Potter's "strapless black sharkskin number which fits like a grape peeling." And Claire McCardell's bathing suits were strictly "for the young and brave," since it took either "a perfect figure or perfect nerve" to wear them.[24]

Carolyn Schnurer also designed creative sportswear for the mass market. And like Leser's designs, Schnurer's collections for Peck & Peck were often inspired by her travels. Her Africa collection, for example, included an embroidered square-cut jacket inspired by the clothing of Hausa men. Her Japan collection was also influenced by traditional garments—not only the kimono and obi but also men's hakama trousers. Schnurer's

"Hakama" dress used pleats to give the look of a divided skirt. She also designed a pearl-haltered swimsuit.

Caroline Milbank notes that "at her peak [in the 1950s] annual volume was $7 million a year, the average price for a dress around $30." Her sun dresses and bathing suits were particularly popular, but she also "moon-lighted, anonymously, as an evening-dress designer for one of the best New York custom houses." According to Milbank, "When she divorced her husband (and business partner), she quit fashion design."[25]

Meanwhile, as the forties gave way to the fifties, McCardell continued to develop her major themes. In May 1955, she was featured on the cover of *Time* — the first American designer to be so honored. The author of the cover article, Osborne Elliot, observed that "from America's lively leisure has evolved a new homegrown fashion, as different from Paris fashion as apple pie from crepes suzette."[26]

McCardell was one of the first to design for the new suburban "life-style." As Elliot put it, the French might still dress for "Veblenesque lei-sure," but Americans enjoyed active leisure in the form of social events like backyard barbecue parties.

Recently, Elizabeth Hawes's biographer, Bettina Berch, has suggested that "McCardell was suburban," in contrast to Hawes, who was "arty."[27] There is some truth in Berch's characterization, but it relies too heavily on McCardell's image in the 1950s and not enough on an analysis of the clothes themselves, which in the forties were often extremely radical. She was an American Primitive, considered as radical as modern dancer Martha Gra-ham.

McCardell's own book, *What Shall I Wear?*, is a fascinating mixture of typically fifties' opinions and beliefs that many Americans still hold today. The woman who popularized Capezio ballet slippers later insisted that she had never meant them to be worn outside the home. In a section on shoes, she sounds like designer Anne Fogarty, author of the infamous *Wife-Dressing*, which was based on the principle that a married woman dressed to please her husband and to help him get ahead in his career.

"When you buy shoes," writes McCardell, "you are *not* just buying for your own feet. You are buying for your husband's taste. . . . Would he rather help poor delicate little you into a taxi?. . . . If there is an outdoor man in your life, don't annoy him by getting a blister when you follow him in a golf tournament. If you have a taxi-lover in your home, be sure you have plenty of spindly heels . . ."[28]

Even her more modern-seeming pronouncements have that fifties' tone: "Fashion should be fun"; "Disguise the less-than-perfect dimension"; "Are you impeccably groomed?" McCardell, of course, strongly empha-sized her Americanism: "We [designers] specialize in what we know best. For me it's America — it looks and feels like America. It's freedom, it's de-mocracy, it's casualness, it's good health. Clothes can say all that."[29]

A Lord & Taylor advertisement of the 1950s echoed McCardell: "You'd Know That Was An American Dress Anywhere." Such statements combine valid insights about differences in national styles of life with an unquestioning ideological assumption that a particular style really does represent freedom and democracy. And, of course, there is a long tradition in Anglo-Saxon countries of using Paris as the symbol of sartorial slavery. "When [McCardell] is in Paris on vacation, she visits no collections lest she be influenced by what she sees," *Time* reported.[30]

ABOVE: *Window display of Carolyn Schnurer dresses, circa 1954. Photograph courtesy of Special Collections, The Fashion Institute of Technology Library, New York.*

Another source of her popular appeal lay in seeming outside of fashion altogether, and it is true that many of her designs seem unusually "timeless." Indeed, several designs were reintroduced commercially in the 1970s and 1980s, although they were not always exactly like the originals. A McCardell retrospective at the Fashion Institute of Technology in 1972 led journalists to declare, "These are styles that can be worn today." And: "By any yardstick it was the smash fashion collection of the season."[31]

Even today, McCardell is often referred to as "the designer's designer." As designer Lee Evans said in 1972, "When I was a student, she was my inspiration. There were other designers who were important, like Adrian, but I always thought they made clothes for my mother — she made clothes for me."[32]

One reason McCardell's clothes still look fresh is that she often designed for younger women. "Claire McCardell dresses will be going back to college soon," announced a newspaper article of 1944. The journalist went on to describe McCardell as "the most youthful of the designers, and the one who creates almost exclusively for school girl figures and fancies."[33] For example, McCardell's "pet hate" was man-tailored slacks, so she designed ballet breeches.

Did the fact that McCardell was a woman influence the clothes she designed? McCardell's partner, Adolphe Klein, was quoted in *Time* as saying, "With these dames, you don't know where they get their inspiration. It may be from a crack in the wall."[34] According to her own testimony, she was inspired by the realities of women's lives.

"First of all, I am a woman," insisted McCardell. "Quite secondarily, I am a designer. . . . Most of my ideas come from trying to solve my own problems — problems just like yours. I like to be able to zip my own zippers. . . . I need a dress that can cook a dinner and then come out and meet the guests."

McCardell identified with her customers and their lives: She was not only a fashion designer, she wrote: "Sometimes I am a hostess. Sometimes I am a guest. I have a job to go to. I have a market list to plan. I *love* clothes."[35] She assumed, though, that her readers needed help:

Are you constantly tormented with the thought: "What shall I wear?" or . . . "I have nothing to wear"? Your clothes closets are full but somehow have holes in them. No dress that is exactly right for lunch with a sophisticated mother-in-law. Nothing — but *nothing* — to wear to your husband's company picnic. This simply means that the clothes you have chosen — beautiful and becoming as they are — don't match your life. . . . Your job is not so much tracking down the clothes as tracking down yourself.[36]

Which, come to think of it, is still good advice.

# 9
# WIFE-DRESSING FOR SUCCESS

ABOVE: *Louise Dahl-Wolfe portrait of Anne Fogarty, used on the dust jacket of* Wife-Dressing: The Fine Art of Being A Well Dressed Wife, *published by Julian Messner in 1959.*

OPPOSITE: *Jacques Fath with model Bettina, 1950. Photograph by Louise Dahl-Wolfe, courtesy of The Center for Creative Photography, University of Arizona.*

In 1954 the French couturier Jacques Fath told the United Press: "Women are bad fashion designers. The only role a woman should have in fashion is wearing clothes." And he predicted that "some day all great designers will be men." His remarks caused considerable controversy, especially among what the press called his "feminine rivals."[1]

"Men are the great designers? No! The great designers are women," declared Sophie of Saks Fifth Avenue, citing Vionnet and Chanel as examples of truly creative figures. Chanel herself laconically replied, "Mr. Fath's statement needs no answer. Facts will answer him." A few months later, she reopened her couture house — and began lambasting male designers for putting women in uncomfortable, impractical clothes.

Women, Fath insisted, can only see fashion in personal terms. "But a man sees fashion as hundreds of women like it." Women designers disagreed. "I never design for myself," replied the American sportswear designer Tina Leser. "I'm a big girl. All my designs are for little people."

Carolyn Schnurer admitted that "it would certainly be foolish . . . to confine your designs to yourself," since "there aren't many people in the world like you." But she argued that most women designers avoided that trap: "It's silly to say sex makes a difference in designing," she insisted. "Creative people are creative people, irrespective of sex."

Others believed that there *was* a difference between male and female designers — but that it worked to the women's advantage. Ready-to-wear designer Ceil Chapman argued that a man draws pictures and assumes that "he can take his sketch and drape it around a figure and any woman can wear it," whereas a good woman designer works directly with the cloth to

114

make a dress: "She isn't thinking of a drawing. She is thinking of a live person wearing it." (In fact, of course, some male designers did drape, just as some women designers sketched.)

The most famous American sportswear designer, Claire McCardell, insisted that men "never understand the way clothes feel." She argued that male designers "must go to a woman for final judgment. She may be a model or wife. But there's always a woman behind the throne." And she cited Fath's wife, Genevieve, as his ideal model.

In a reversal of Fath's prediction, McCardell concluded that "someday all designers will be women. Men, I hope, will be busy with masculine things." This type of sex-role stereotyping is, of course, the mirror image of Fath's, and as such, it does not necessarily work to women's advantage. But it was very typical of the 1950s' mindset.

Moreover, behind Fath's provocative rhetoric lurked an undeniable fact: In the 1950s, for the first time since the age of Worth, men dominated the world of high fashion. Although there were still many women fashion designers in America and a few important ones in France (Alix Grès continued designing, and Chanel reopened her couture house in 1954), the fashion industry was increasingly dominated by men such as Christian Dior, Cristóbal Balenciaga, and Fath himself.

A few designers, such as Mainbocher, recognized this historic change. "In the past there have been more great women designers," he said, but "the opposite would seem to be true today." And he added: "Whether history will again repeat itself remains to be seen."

*Why did men dominate high fashion after 1945?* According to Fath, the answer was obvious: male superiority. Others have proposed a different explanation: male conspiracy.

According to the fashion photographer Louise Dahl-Wolfe, when the textile millionaire Marcel Boussac decided to start a new couture house, he had to choose between Dior and Madame Mizza Bricard, a beautiful, stylish Frenchwoman, who was "Miss Fashion herself." Said Dahl-Wolfe: "He picked Dior, I think, because he was a man."[2]

Despite its plausibility, Dahl-Wolfe's conspiracy theory is, ultimately, no more convincing than Fath's theory of male superiority. Certainly, Dior was surrounded by women. Bricard was officially in charge of Dior's millinery. Then there was Mme Marguerite, Dior's technical director, who turned his sketches into clothes. Even more important was Mme Raymonde, who had been Dior's colleague at Lelong and whom he described as "my second self."

Dahl-Wolfe, in fact, may have conflated Mmes Raymonde and Bricard, since she mistakenly identified Bricard, rather than Raymonde, as Dior's "right hand" at Lelong, when, in fact, Bricard had been at Molyneux. No doubt, Bricard was a very stylish woman: Dahl-Wolfe insisted that she even taught Diana Vreeland "an awful lot about fashion."[3]

But according to other accounts, Bricard functioned primarily as Dior's muse. According to Raymonde, "Dior always had a need for beautiful things around him, and he loved to look at Madame Bricard." Dior himself said, "Madame Bricard is one of those people, increasingly rare, who makes elegance their sole *raison d'être*. I knew that her presence in my house would inspire me towards creation."[4]

Back in the 1930s, a few women of great personal style exerted a tremendous influence on fashion. Clients at the top of the social pyramid were at least as important as designers. "Women of fashion were at their most powerful — dictators, in a sense, of a luxurious and capricious way of life." As fashion editor Bettina Ballard recalled, this "small egocentric group of women" dominated high fashion "by making fashionable what they chose for themselves."[5] Women like Mrs. Reginald "Daisy" Fellowes and Princess Jean Louis "Baba" de Faucigny-Lucinge were known as *Les Dames de Vogue*. Someone like Bricard might then have become a fashion leader.

In the 1950s, however, fashion was geared toward a less sophisticated mass audience. In this context, dressing to please men became more of an issue, and many women may have preferred to follow a male designer. *Life*, for example, referred to "that friend of your wife's named Dior."[6]

The leading role seemed to shift toward the male couturier-genius. Many people in the general public were predisposed to believe in the distinction between male creators and female technicians, just as they romanticized the relationship between the male designer and his female clients and muses.

There is no question that Christian Dior was a brilliant designer. But talent alone does not necessarily result in success. Money is necessary, too. Dahl-Wolfe may have been partially correct in sensing that businessmen felt more confident backing male designers. But it was not that businessmen were necessarily more "sexist" in the 1950s than they had been earlier. Rather, the changing structure of the industry gave financial backers both more power and less incentive to take risks.

When big money was at stake, the chosen designer had to be marketable as a superstar. According to this new definition, the male designer *might* have had an edge. Certainly, the press that Dior received — and he was covered as thoroughly as a war — made much of his role as the *king* of fashion. This fit the popular stereotype of the male fashion genius — but it would not be the first time that stereotypes actually influenced the real world.

Certainly, the number and significance of women in Paris fashion declined as the structure of the couture moved from the *atelier* to the global corporate conglomerate. As noted earlier, Jeanne Lanvin opened her own business in 1880 with only 40 francs saved and a loan of 300 francs! Even in the 1930s many well-known couturières had relatively small businesses, or at least they needed only a small initial capital investment. One wealthy client was often all a woman required to go into business for herself.

After 1945 women lost the leading role in fashion, in part because they now needed (and failed to obtain) much greater financial backing. As fashion became "big business," women's participation was adversely affected. Chanel was able to reopen in the fifties because she already had a recognized name and a profitable perfume business, but hers was an exceptional situation.

Additional widely held cultural assumptions also militated against women's success. Society has historically accepted women's endeavors only when the work itself was defined as suitably "feminine."

"Fashion is art," insisted Jacques Fath. "Art is creative and men are the creators."[7] A century earlier, Charles Worth, the father of haute couture, had also presented himself not as a skilled dressmaker but as a great artist. When fashion was interpreted as high Art (with a capital A), then men might more easily fit the stereotype of the great artist. But to the extent that dressmaking was defined merely as an *artistic* endeavor, an expression of "feminine taste" and "love of beauty," it was regarded as good for women.

Similarly, when fashion was a small-scale enterprise, society accepted it as appropriate women's work. But when fashion was seen as a *business* (like the automotive industry), businessmen increasingly took over, leaving only the crumbs for would-be "career girls."[8]

Nevertheless, there were many more crumbs for women in a traditionally feminine industry such as fashion than in a "masculine" business like the automotive industry. Indeed, throughout the fifties, fashion continued to be a stronghold of careers for women. But cultural assumptions about femininity influenced their work.

## FASHION AND THE FEMININE MYSTIQUE

Women's fashions of the 1950s tended to be ultrafeminine, with long skirts and wasp waists, petticoats, and stiletto heels. Many people have wondered whether male designers were responsible for the unliberated fashions of the 1950s. Chanel, as we have seen, insisted that "men were not meant to design for women. Men make clothes in which one cannot move."[9]

French feminist Simone de Beauvoir wrote movingly about the bondage of fashion in her book, *The Second Sex*. She argued that maintaining an elegant appearance was like housework: It requires constant effort. Even worse, it tends to make women regard themselves as objects. A few years later, Betty Friedan made a similar point in *The Feminine Mystique*, a book whose title expressed an era.

One of the best studies of 1950s' fashion, by Barbara Schreier, concludes that women's dress really was, in many ways, "a metaphor of the mystique," expressing a veritable cult of femininity.[10] Women's fashions in the 1950s were highly artificial, with exaggerated forms that amounted almost to a burlesque of feminine curves — a parody of a male-defined "femininity."

But were men primarily responsible for the exaggerated femininity of 1950s' fashions? Automobiles designed in the 1950s were also highly stylized, exaggerated, and glamorous. If women's fashions changed more rapidly and dramatically than ever before, so also did automotive fashions. Yet we interpret 1950s' automobiles as "populuxe" artifacts, the products of postwar affluence and Cold War conformity, whereas the clothing fashions of the 1950s are almost always too narrowly interpreted in terms of female oppression.

Certainly, there was a decided reaction against restricted wartime styles. "We were emerging from a period of war," wrote Dior, "of uniforms, of women soldiers built like boxers. I drew women-flowers, soft shoulders, flowering busts, fine waists like lianas and wide skirts like corollas."[11] The female-dominated fashion press responded with great enthusiasm to the New Look, as did millions of female consumers who cannot all be dismissed as deluded slaves of fashion.

Moreover, the romantic style in women's dress was already emerging *before* World War II. It was not born in the fifties, and can clearly be seen in many of Chanel's neo-Victorian evening dresses of the late 1930s. The war years simply put the style on hold until Dior's New Look was triumphantly launched in 1947. In the context of the period, then, it is not surprising that a number of women designers also created extravagantly feminine clothes and were unconcerned with mundane questions of comfort or practicality.

In fact, what one might call the *ideology* of ultrafeminine fashion was defined in the public consciousness by a woman.

In her 1959 book, *Wife-Dressing*, the American fashion designer Anne Fogarty advocated wearing a girdle "with everything" — a practice that she happily compared with Chinese foot-binding. Fogarty boasted about her "eighteen-inch waist" and favored cocktail dresses so tight that she had to stand up. She felt "very strongly" that clothes should fit snugly, especially after 5:00 p.m. "You're not meant to suffer," she reassured her readers, but the feeling "should be one of *constraint* rather than comfort."[12]

As a young woman, Fogarty had wanted to be an actress, but in retrospect she believed that "what I really wanted . . . was simply to dress up."[13] After a brief stint as a fitting model, she began designing clothes for teenagers and junior sizes. She specialized in dresses with fitted bodices and full petticoats — a youthful, inexpensive take on the New Look, which (as Fath pointed out) was perfect for her own figure. In 1951 Fogarty won a Coty Award for her "paper doll" silhouette.

But although she had a successful career, Fogarty always insisted that she thought of herself "first and foremost as a wife." And wife-dressing involved more than corsetry.

"The first principle of wife-dressing is Complete Femininity," argued Fogarty. Whereas the independent "bachelor-girl" might dress to please herself, a wife should always remember that "it's your husband for whom you're dressing." She warned: "Never underestimate the power of a man . . . for he who pays the bills deserves consideration in the way you look as wife, mother . . . or working home-maker."[14]

Wife-dressing not only pleased a husband, it even helped *his* career. During the 1950s, more and more men worked for large corporations, where they were under considerable pressure to conform. Hence, of course, the stereotype of the Man in the Gray Flannel Suit. But the wife's appearance was also an issue, "especially when promotions to high-echelon jobs are in the offing."[15]

"In any social situation, remember that you are an appendage of your husband," warned Fogarty. An "ultra-glamorous negligee" was nice, but appropriate and glamorous attire for entertaining was at least as important. In return, men were to bear in mind that "if you adore her, you must adorn her. There lies the essence of a happy marriage."[16]

Dungarees had no place in wife-dressing, Fogarty counseled, even when cleaning the house: "Don't look like a steam-fitter or a garage mechanic when what you are is, purely and simply, a wife." Vulgarized Freudianism was a pillar of the feminine mystique, and Fogarty cited one child psychologist who interviewed a little girl about what she thought of her mother: "a dust mop," said the child. Fogarty concluded from this that even when the husband was not at home, comfort was of much less importance than an attractive appearance.[17]

To understand both Fath and Fogarty, it is necessary to realize that during the 1950s, the ideology of the "feminine mystique" influenced many women to leave the work force and return to the home, where they were encouraged to cultivate the roles of wife and mother.

Even women who continued working (as many did) were expected to conform to a narrow image of appropriate womanly behavior and appearance. "Working wives must cultivate two separate fashion philosophies," advised Hollywood fashion designer Edith Head in 1959. "No man wants a brisk, executive-looking woman at the dinner table, and no man wants a too-alluring creature gliding around his office."[18]

## FASHION AS A CAREER

If fashion design in the 1950s was dominated by men, what happened to all the women who had risen to such prominence in the industry before? Paradoxically, they were still there and in some ways were already setting the stage for a new era of women designers.

The 1950s and 60s saw the publication of numerous books with titles like *Fashion As a Career* and *Your Future in Fashion Design* (the latter "by 15 famous members of the Fashion Group," an international organization of women executives in all branches of the fashion industry). In a typical passage, Sophie Gimbel wrote: "As a designer and as a woman, I feel that Fashion is a sixth sense, [the] desire to look feminine and gracious."[19] Fashion seemed so glamorous that Anne Klein felt that she had to warn young people, "This is *not* the easy life!" As she wrote, if your image is "that female designers (in ubiquitous hats or horn-rimmed glasses) and male designers (in cravats and tails) function and create in sumptuous, crystal-chandeliered salons . . . [and] lunch daily on champagne and caviar—you are laboring under a delusion!" You might well begin, she warned, by "being a man or girl 'Friday' to the designer" for coolie wages.[20]

To the extent that making and wearing clothes were regarded as "feminine," careers in the fashion industry were seen as appropriate for women. And, indeed, these books were primarily addressed to young women.

In her book *Fashion As a Career* (1962), Janey Ironside, a well-known English professor of fashion design, described life "in the garment jungle" and identified the jobs available "for him (or her)." Significantly, she wrote:

I am sorry about all this "him" or "her" business, but while it was fairly easy to establish the "him" when we were dealing with haute couture, as we get to mass production, it is more likely, though of course not invariably, to be "her." Why? Yet another question which one can only answer by guesses and half-baked psychology. Possibly women prefer a more routine job, are more adaptable, amenable, less resentful of chores, do the work for the money while thinking about husbands or boyfriends and children, like to be practical, see themselves wearing these good cheap garments and appreciate them.[21]

Psychology (whether half-baked or not) probably explains as little as "superiority" or conspiracy, however. More important are the social, cultural, and economic reasons why women were directed toward one rather than another branch of the profession.

Historically, it seems fairly likely that there were always more women fashion designers than a mere list of fashion businesses might indicate, since many women worked anonymously in businesses that carried men's names. Indeed, well into the twentieth century, most American designers, *both male and female*, were kept "in the back room." As Bill Blass has observed, until recently many manufacturers "didn't want it known that they even *had* designers."[22]

Most manufacturers, of course, have traditionally been men, but even a great female entrepreneur like Hattie Carnegie was not supportive of female designers. "Miss Carnegie used to say that she could not understand a woman designer," recalled Pauline Trigère, who worked at Hattie Carnegie as Travis Banton's assistant in 1937. "She never believed in them. She liked male designers. There were no female designers with Hattie Carnegie." (Or none who lasted long, anyway, since Claire McCardell had a brief tenure there, as did Pauline Potter.) "Maybe there is something that frightens women to start their own business," mused Trigère, who, like Carnegie, was an exception to the rule.[23]

Trigère opened *her* own business in 1942 and — half a century later — continues to design luxurious, sophisticated clothes. Perfection in cut is a passion of hers, and draping — not sketching — is her method. "In France, where I come from, the couturier never sketched," she told *Vogue* in 1989. "Mme Lanvin, Mlle Chanel — *non.* Molyneux, Patou, no one ever sketched. . . . Today, the young designers will sketch a garment, but how do they know how it will turn out? They hand the sketches to an assistant designer, who makes the garment for them. I never worked like that."[24]

In America in the 1950s, male designers only slightly outnumbered their female counterparts, but Americans of either sex were overshadowed by the men in Paris. Ultimately, however, the rise of the big-name (male) designer worked to the long-term advantage of both men and women in fashion design. So when a ready-to-wear designer broke out and became known by name, his or her image was extremely important.

If "name" designers tended disproportionately to be men, women designers had the task of creating a new, strong image. And this is precisely what they did.

LEFT: *Pauline Trigère, Navy silk cocktail dress, 1950. Photograph by Emma Gluehom, courtesy of Pauline Trigère.*

# 10
# THINK PINK!

ABOVE: *Actress Kay Thompson portrayed Maggie Prescott, a Diana Vreeland-like fashion editor who declared, in a famous sequence of the 1956 film* Funny Face, *"Think Pink!" Photograph courtesy of The Kobal Collection, New York.*

OPPOSITE: *Louise Dahl-Wolfe photographs model Bijou Barrington while Diana Vreeland and an unknown assistant look on, 1942. Photographer unknown. Photograph courtesy of The Center for Creative Photography, University of Arizona.*

The flamboyant fashion editor in the film *Funny Face* who tells her subordinates to "think pink!" was based on Diana Vreeland. Obviously, it is a fictional portrait, a caricature — but Mrs. Vreeland did once send out a memo, urging her staff: "Today let's think *pig white!* Wouldn't it be wonderful to have stockings that were *pig white!* The color of baby pigs, not quite white and not quite pink!"[1]

An extraordinary woman in many ways, Vreeland was typical in one respect: The majority of fashion editors and journalists have been women. Except for the publishers themselves, who were men, "white-glove" fashion publishing in the twentieth century has been essentially a "matriarchy." The central personnel office at Condé Nast, for example, was run for many years by Mary Campbell, who was often compared to the dean at a women's college, assigning young women to work at *Vogue, Mademoiselle,* and *Glamour.* Fashion magazines functioned as something of a finishing school for debutantes and graduates from Seven Sisters colleges. Most of these women worked a few years, married, and then disappeared, but some of them became highly influential.

By contrast, there have been relatively few women who achieved fame as fashion photographers. Just as there exists the stereotype of the male fashion designer, there is also a stereotype of the male fashion photographer. Films like *Funny Face* and *Blow-Up* emphasized his romantic and/or sexual relationships with the female fashion model. Even today, many people think that a male photographer brings out the best in a female fashion model, just as a male designer supposedly knows best how to make a woman beautiful.

124

The technical aspects of photography may have militated against women in the early years, when a knowledge of practical chemistry was necessary. Moreover, as Horst recalls, in the prewar period, "the 8 x 10-inch studio cameras were so heavy and unwieldy that it was assumed that no woman could ever be a *Vogue* photographer."[2] And yet, there have always been a certain number of women fashion photographers, among the best known being Louise Dahl-Wolfe. No history of women in fashion can omit the roles of the fashion editor and photographer, and the personal histories of influential image-makers may tell us how and why women achieve success in one or another branch of the fashion industry.

## MRS. CHASE VERSUS MRS. SNOW

Edna Woolman Chase was editor in chief of *Vogue* from 1929 until 1951, during which time she was probably the single most powerful person in the international fashion press. The greatest challenge to her authority came in 1932, when her subordinate, Carmel Snow, left *Vogue* for *Harper's Bazaar*. In *Magic Names of Fashion*, Ernestine Carter gives a vivid description of this event:

ABOVE: *The stereotype of the male fashion photographer as sexual conquistador was captured in the 1966 film* Blow-up. *Actor David Hemmings played a character based on real-life London photographer David Bailey, who once compared the camera to a phallus. Photograph courtesy of The Kobal Collection, New York.*

The atmosphere . . . was reminiscent of a prize fight. At either end of the ring were the promoters: *Vogue's* publisher, Condé Nast, and *Harper's Bazaar's* publisher, William Randolph Hearst. The protagonists were the editors: for *Vogue*, Quaker Edna Woolman Chase; for *Harper's Bazaar*, Irish Carmel Snow — powerful and resourceful fighters behind their fragile, feminine exteriors, with sharp brains under their delicately blue-rinsed white hair.[3]

In her memoirs, *Always in Vogue*, Edna Chase recalled how she was "always looking for the right young women" to work in *Vogue's* editorial offices. In 1921 she found Carmel White, the daughter of an Irishwoman who ran a dressmaking business in New York. White was delighted to work for *Vogue*, even though the magazine was a bit too "la-di-da" for her taste.[5] In her memoirs, she recalled that while the work was fascinating, Chase "seemed to criticize everything I did." She also found it mortifying to hear people joke that Edna was Condé's wife and Carmel was his mistress.[6]

In 1926 Carmel White married Palen Snow — and (as Chase put it) "our vicissitudes began" since the couple's parties and vacations "became Carmel's primary interest and she sought to rearrange her *Vogue* schedule accordingly." Chase admitted that "when Carmel got to her desk in the morning she was as alert and capable as ever," despite the parties. But "then there were the children, whom she had in remarkably swift succession. This also disrupted the office schedule, but she had so won our hearts that we treated her as a favored daughter."[7] Snow denied this account vehemently, claiming that even her honeymoon was divided between business and pleasure.

In 1929 Snow became the editor of American *Vogue*, but Chase remained editor in chief. According to Snow Condé Nast had assured her that she would eventually succeed Chase, but she did not believe it. "I happened to know that *she* had promised the succession to several other people, and besides, I didn't believe she had the least intention of retiring." Moreover: "Under her I would always be a subordinate, and I was beginning to find that position as intolerable as I found it under my mother." Nast became worried when Snow's brother Tom went to work for his competitor, Hearst, and he tried to get Snow to sign a contract with *Vogue*. "She was indignant," Nast told Chase. "She said nothing would induce her to work for Hearst." [10]

In October 1932, Snow was in the hospital, having just given birth to her daughter. She asked Chase to come to the hospital, where she told her that she was leaving *Vogue*. According to Snow, "a storm broke over my head." Chase berated her furiously: "*Vogue* trained you, *Vogue* made you, now you propose to make out of *Vogue*'s rival a copy of the magazine that trusted you!" [11]

"I was stunned," wrote Chase. "I sat beside her for a long time unable

LEFT: *Louise Dahl-Wolfe, photograph of plaid cotton evening dress by Mildred Orrick, 1947. Photograph courtesy of the Edward C. Blum Design Laboratory, The Fashion Institute of Technology, New York.*

to speak. . . . I tried every argument I could think of to dissuade her, but it was useless."[12]

"Before I knew what was happening the entire staff of *Vogue* was grouped around my hospital bed," wrote Snow, "arguing, pleading, threatening. 'This is Treason!'" Even twenty years later, one *Vogue* editor told a reporter: "To discuss fashion in relation to Mrs. Snow is like writing a history of the United States from the viewpoint of Benedict Arnold."[13]

Chase and Snow competed to attract talented collaborators. Without *Vogue*'s international network behind her, Snow had a more difficult time, but since she was temperamentally more adventurous than Chase, she seized talents that *Vogue* neglected: Munkacsi's daring action photographs, for example, appeared in *Harper's*. According to Louise Dahl-Wolfe, Munkacsi was "a newspaper man [who] had never done fashion." But when Snow saw his picture of a girl holding an umbrella and jumping, she immediately saw the potential for fashion photography. She rounded up socialite Lucille Brokaw, put her in an evening dress and had Munkacsi photograph her, running and jumping in the countryside. Chase dismissed the pictures as "farm girls jumping over fences."[14]

Ernestine Carter claims that *Vogue* made Edna Chase a power in the world of fashion, but it was Carmel Snow who made *Harper's Bazaar* a major fashion power. Dahl-Wolfe also credits Snow with transforming *Harper's Bazaar* from a "terrible" magazine that "you never read" into a very exciting magazine, at a time when *Vogue* was staidly "ladylike."[15]

She was "hard as nails," recalled Dahl-Wolfe, but she was a brilliant editor, who recognized talented people and let them work.


### IN LIVING COLOR

As a young woman, Louise Dahl-Wolfe studied painting, but, inspired by Anne Brigman's photographs of nudes, she turned to photography. Throughout her life, she was always far more interested in art than in "looking at dresses done by third-rate designers."[16] But fashion photography offered both artistic and financial rewards.

She approached *Vogue* first with her photographs, but that day she had the flu, so she was not looking her best. When *Vogue*'s art director, Dr. Agha, returned her portfolio, his memo to Condé Nast was still accidently attached. It read: "This work has definite possibilities, but it's by a middle-aged woman who probably won't develop much farther."[17]

"I just wanted to go through the floor," remembered Dahl-Wolfe. "His criticism was so merciless. He thought I was too old. I think I was thirty-nine. I knew I could never work there."[18] She then brought her portfolio to *Harper's Bazaar*, where art director Alexey Brodovitch hired her. Snow recalled: "I knew that the *Bazaar* was at last going to look the way I had instinctively wanted my magazine to look."[19]

Dahl-Wolfe began working at *Harper's Bazaar* in 1936, ultimately publishing more than 600 photographs in the magazine, as well as 86 covers. A number of pioneering women photographers were working at the time, such as Bernice Abbott and Margaret Bourke-White, but not many worked in fashion. There was Toni Frissell at *Vogue*, and Genevieve Naylor, and the principle photographer at *Harper's* before Dahl-Wolfe, the Baroness Toni von Horn. "She was so Germanic," recalled Dahl-Wolfe, "you know, that heavy, heavy look. . . . And that's what Carmel was trying to get rid of."[20]

Most of the best fashion photographers of the day, though, were men like Horst and Hoyningen-Huene, who created images of ideal elegance. Dahl-Wolfe was revolutionary in that she portrayed active, approachable women — and she did it in color. She was one of the first to photograph "healthy outdoor women" — on the beach, in the country, and on location in places like Brazil and Florida. She was known for her technical skill in dealing with the new color films.

"A fashion photographer is not a free agent," she observed. "You must try to express in the photograph what the designer is saying without being literal, corny, or unnatural."[21] There were "not many talents like Claire McCardell or Vionnet," recalled Dahl-Wolfe. Many clothes ("pearls of little price") had to be photographed, because the manufacturers advertised in the magazine. Perhaps "there would be nothing about the garment that had even a touch of inspiration; you'd be disgusted — and then you'd appeal to Diana [Vreeland] to help brighten up the dress." And if the clothes were really horrible, "Carmel would say, 'Just hide as much of it as you can.'"[22]

## D. V.

Diana Vreeland was another of Carmel Snow's discoveries. A fashionable young representative of the international set, she eventually became the most famous fashion editor of the twentieth century.

Vreeland first came to public attention in 1936 with her notorious column for *Harper's Bazaar*, "Why Don't You . . . ?" which included suggestions such as "Why don't you turn your old ermine coat into a bathrobe?" and "Why don't you rinse your blond child's hair in dead champagne to keep it gold, as they do in France?"[23] Naturally, these tongue-in-cheek suggestions were much parodied, but Vreeland wasn't really joking. Rather, she spoke in a kind of code. She treated fashion "not commercially but romantically," said one colleague. Vreeland herself explained the "Why Don't You . . . ?" column by saying that "one could have the fantasy, even if one did not have the rest."[24]

A visual person, she had an eye for color and an insistence on the importance of details. She was often inspired by romantic or glamorous images from the past: "Why don't you wear olive-green corduroy breeches, a loose chemise shirt, knitted white cotton stockings, and strong shoes of black leather with silver buckles like a boy of the eighteenth century?" And she was never afraid to seem absurd: "Why don't you put all your dogs in bright yellow collars and leads like all the dogs in Paris?" (It was the way she said "*all* your dogs" that was so typically Vreeland.) Occasionally, she struck the wrong note. In the November 1936 issue, for example, she asked, "Why don't you wear bare knees and long white knitted socks, as Unity

ABOVE: Vogue *cover, August 1, 1965.* Vogue *editor Diana Vreeland coined the term Youthquakers which appears as a cover line on this issue of the magazine. Cover photograph by Bert Stern, courtesy of* Vogue, *copyright © 1965 by The Condé Nast Publications Inc.*

TOP: *Sheila Metzner,* Joko
Passion, *1985. Photograph
© Sheila Metzner.*

ABOVE: *Photographer
Roxanne Lowit. Photograph
by Jesse Frohman, © 1991,
courtesy of Roxanne Lowit.*

Mitford does when she takes tea with Hitler at the Carlton in Munich?"

Vreeland refused to revive the column after the war, but she continued its spirit in memos to her staff. "There was a brisk trade in Vreeland stories — apocryphal and otherwise," recalled her successor at *Vogue*, Grace Mirabella.[25] Her aphorisms became notorious throughout the fashion world: "Pink is the navy blue of India." "The bikini is the most important thing since the atom bomb."

Vreeland once advised a junior editor, "Never fear being vulgar, just boring, middle-class or dull."[26] *She* certainly never was. "We musn't be afraid of snobbism and absurdity," she declared. "And we mustn't be afraid of luxury."[27] Luxury, yes, glamour, allure, elegance. And sex: Vreeland described a sexy dress as "something for the chaps."[28] But not boring good taste. She once said to a journalist, "Why do you worry about good taste? . . . . Lots of people have terrible taste, you know, and make a damn good living off it."[29]

Vreeland was fashion editor at *Harper's Bazaar* from 1937 to 1962 and editor in chief at *Vogue* from 1962 to 1971. But this tells only half the story. "She was and remains the only genius fashion editor," says Richard Avedon.[30] "She didn't *report* on fashion. The designers . . . [and] the fashionable world had to *follow* her." Before her it was "society ladies putting hats on other society ladies," and after her, only "promotion ladies."[31]

"I hate the past," Vreeland said once. "I can never remember last week. I can only remember three months from now."[32] A fashion Sibyl, she insisted, "I know what they're going to wear before they wear it! I know where they're going before it's even *there*!" Her motto at *Vogue* was: "Give them what they never knew they wanted."[33]

In 1962 Vreeland left her job as fashion editor at *Harper's* to become editor of *Vogue* — which caused a tremendous uproar, in light of the deadly rivalry between the magazines. Many years later she was asked why she changed sides. "Money," she said. "Why, does anyone work for anything else?"

"At *Vogue*, I was what you might call an *enfant terrible*," Vreeland recalled. Fashion photography was not art, she insisted, as she created composite pictures — one model's legs, another person's torso, and everything retouched ("I never took out fewer than two ribs"). Fashion is "all *trompe l'oeil*," she said — "artifice [and] perfection. . . . For the same reasons, I *approve* of plastic surgery." But she noted that "half the things I did" couldn't be published, notably a series of photographs of an eye-lift operation. One member of her staff "left immediately to throw up, others were gagging and carrying on . . . these were *professional* women working on a *woman's* magazine, you understand — not a gaggle of housewives. It was unbelievable!"[34]

Her enthusiastic and idiosyncratic coverage of sixties' fashions made for an extraordinary magazine. She invented or popularized terms like *Youthquake* and *Beautiful People*. She rejected the narrow WASP standard of beauty, bringing in black models like Naomi Sims, unconventional stars like Barbra Streisand and other unusual models like Twiggy.

But in 1971 Vreeland was fired. Some say that her dismissal "had something to do with the mini-midi debacle," others that "there was controversy at *Vogue* over hot pants," or that "Vreeland started to get 'pressure from upstairs' (particularly from *Vogue's* editorial director, Alexander Liberman) and began to behave 'erratically.'"[35] It is clear, though, that the fashion industry was in trouble in 1971, and Vreeland's publishers probably felt that her individualistic and aggressively frivolous aesthetic was increasingly problematical. *Harper's Bazaar* was also radically revised at this time to become more "practical." The era of the all-powerful fashion editor was coming to a close.

ABOVE: *Photograph by Deborah Turbeville of British designer Jean Muir and models in suede dresses from Muir's Spring 1975 collection. Photograph courtesy of Jean Muir.*

### A Tough Profession For A Woman

At the same time, the number of women working in fashion photography crept upwards. Today they include Roxanne Lowit, Dominique Issermann, Sheila Metzner, Sarah Moon, Bettine Reims, and Ellen von Unworth, to name only a few. Perhaps the best-known is Deborah Turbeville.

"I *adore* Turbeville's girls," Vreeland once said. "These worn-out girls at a thousand dollars a day — they *kill* me! We don't know who they are, or *where* they are, or *why* they are where they are, or why they *are* . . . but the lines are so beautiful. We don't think about it. The girls keep looking in the mirror . . . which is alright by *me*. I loathe narcissism, but I approve of vanity."[36]

Turbeville began her career as a model (as did von Unworth). She later became a fashion editor at *Harper's Bazaar* and then at *Mademoiselle*, where she worked closely with the photographers.[37] "This is a tough profession for a woman," says Turbeville. "It requires a lot of physical strength and endurance besides sensitivity. I don't know if I'd ever have become a photographer if I hadn't worked for a fashion magazine. I'd never hire a woman assistant. I'm a woman myself, and there are some things I couldn't demand from a woman." (Another photographer, Elizabeth Novick, agrees: "I would never have a woman assistant. There are so many women on a fashion shooting that you need some men around.")[38]

Turbeville's images have always been controversial. Her photographs are often slightly out of focus, while the figures seem isolated, with a "disturbing . . . sense of mystery."[39]

Whether or not women photographers have a uniquely female perspective, it is usually not a feminist one. "I'm not a feminist in the least," says Turbeville. "As a woman, I'm very dependent on men, which shows in my photographs: The women are always depending on the environment or something else. Where the woman is isolated, there's a certain fear in that isolation."[40]

# 11
# FASHION LIBERATION

The sixties marked a very important stage in twentieth-century fashion for two reasons: because young people created their own styles; and because the idea soon spread that people should be free to wear what they liked.

In her book *Looking Good: The Liberation of Fashion* (1976) journalist Clara Pierre argued that

Women designers came back on the scene in the sixties. . . . At their helm was Betsey Johnson . . . [followed by] Liz Claiborne, Jeanne Campbell, Luba, Mary McFadden, Britta Bauer, Carol Horn, Maxime de la Falaise, Hanae Mori, Diane von Fürstenberg, Holly Harp, Cathy Hardwick, and Donna Karan. . . . In the United States the current preeminence of female designers is due partly to the fact that they originate ideas for their own use. . . . The other reason is that in these days of female emancipation, the ladies have shown that they can make it in business.[1]

From the perspective of the 1990s, however, the role of women in sixties' fashion is more difficult to assess, both because the most influential fashion designers tended to be men (such as André Courrèges, Pierre Cardin, and Yves Saint Laurent), and because the ideal woman of the sixties was the adolescent "dolly bird" or "chick." Nevertheless, it is indisputably true that one of the most famous fashion designers of the sixties was Mary Quant, whose life and career epitomized the rise of Swinging London. And it is also true that there were a number of other women in England, France, and America who helped create the new look.

ABOVE: *Barbara Hulanicki, Minidress for Biba, 1966. Her London shop was known as the "mother house of the dolly birds." Photograph courtesy of Barbara Hulanicki.*

OPPOSITE: *Barbara Hulanicki, Velvet jacket, trousers, and helmet, circa 1968. "Battle dress for the female sex." The child in the photograph wears a velvet maxi coat and helmet. Photograph courtesy of Barbara Hulanicki.*

"To me, adult appearance was very unattractive, alarming and terrifying, stilted, confined, and ugly," said Mary Quant. "It was something I knew I didn't want to grow into." "Squares," she claimed (even those on the best-dressed list), did not know how to look exciting.[2] Barbara Hulanicki (creator of the fashion emporium, Biba) agreed: "Fashion in the late 1950s was designed for 30-year-olds and over," the shops were full of "matronly" clothes, and the standard look was "three rows of pearls and a black dress." But soon "the first signs of fashion that came from the street" emerged.[3]

When Quant opened her first shop in 1955 on King's Road, it was already a fashion promenade for London's mods and rockers. But Quant was one of the first to capitalize on the emerging popular culture: "I had always wanted the young to have a fashion of their own. . . . I wanted to make clothes . . . that would be fun to wear."[4]

When she could not find enough "exciting" clothes for the store, Quant began to try to make them herself, "going to a few frantic evening classes in cutting." She had no idea you could buy fabric wholesale, so she bought her material over the counter at Harrod's. She worked in her bed-sitting-room, where her Siamese cats ate the paper patterns.

Despite these difficulties, customers routinely stripped her store, even before she could finish putting up her eye-catching window displays. Soon her clothes were featured in fashion magazines throughout the world.

There is some controversy about whether it was Quant or the French designer Courrèges who "invented" the miniskirt. Courrèges insists, "I was the man who invented the mini. Mary Quant only commercialized the idea." But Quant dismisses his claim: "That's how the French are. . . . I don't mind, but it's just not as I remembered it. . . . Maybe Courrèges did do miniskirts first, but if he did no-one wore them." This is obviously an exaggeration, however, and Quant was closer to the mark when she added, "It wasn't me or Courrèges who invented the miniskirt anyway — it was the girls in the street who did it."[5]

In retrospect, some feminists have questioned whether the sixties' feminine ideal was genuinely liberating for adult women. Minis were undoubtedly an important element in sixties' youth culture, but didn't they turn women into nymphet sex objects? This attitude was alien to the sixties' mentality, however.

In her memoirs, Hulanicki enthusiastically describes how "the postwar babies . . . grew into beautiful skinny people. A designer's dream." And she insists that "in the 1960s, the girls were prepared to suffer to look good. Our long skinny sleeves were so tight that they hindered the circulation."[6] These clothes were designed by and for the young. In her autobiography, Quant proudly quoted an American journalist who declared that she was spreading "the subversive word that being a girl is a much more rewarding occupation than being a Lady Senator or even a Lady President."[7]

Meanwhile, there were other young women designers working in London. The partnership of Sally Tuffin and Marion Foale was especially productive. Like Quant and Hulanicki, they disliked the fashions of the 1950s.

"There weren't clothes for young people at all," recalled Tuffin. "One just looked like one's mother."[8]

Tuffin's mother, in fact, had been a dressmaker, and Foale's father worked for a menswear manufacturer. But the two really discovered fashion while studying at the Royal College of Art. A guest lecture by Quant and her husband encouraged them to set up their own business, rather than going to work for a conventional clothing manufacturer. Lack of start-up capital was no problem: Their rent was six pounds a week. "We were dressing ourselves and our friends," recalled Tuffin, "and it just happened to be the sort of things that people wanted."[9]

Tuffin and Foale became especially famous for their pantsuits, which were quite a new idea. In a recent book, Betsey Johnson was quoted as saying, "The cut was incredible. . . . I'm sure Saint Laurent was influenced by them."[10] Soon Tuffin and Foale designs were featured in *Vogue, Harper's*

*Bazaar,* and *Woman's Wear Daily,* worn by models such as Twiggy and Jean Shrimpton.

In 1965 the film *Kaleidoscope* appeared, starring Susannah York, who wore Tuffin and Foale designs in her role as the owner of a London clothing boutique. Cathy McGowan, the "Queen of the Mods," wore clothes by Tuffin and Foale, Hulanicki, and other young designers in her role as hostess for the music television show, "Ready Steady Go."

Many, if not most, of the young women entering the field of fashion design in Great Britain in the 1960s came from working-class backgrounds. They had no experience of the world pictured in glossy fashion magazines; when they encountered the couture as design students, they rejected it and all that it stood for. Instead they created their own styles, which then spread throughout the world, although not without some initial resistance from older people.

Chanel thought that miniskirts were disgusting. And pantsuits worried conservatives, who fretted that women were becoming masculinized at the very same time that long-haired men were obviously falling into degenerate effeminacy. A little later there were also maxidresses and caftans and thrift-store clothes — and thus, gradually, the mods turned into hippies.

Laura Ashley was no hippie, but her floral printed dresses and other gently romantic styles fit perfectly with the new spirit. "When we started

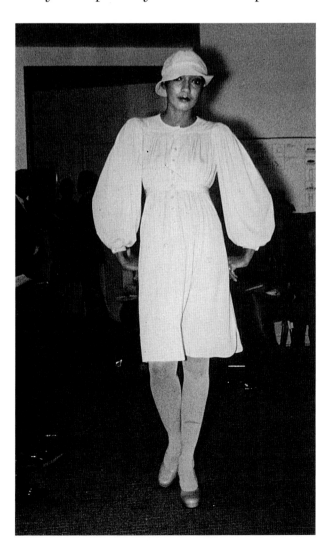

OPPOSITE: *Barbara Hulanicki, Velvet mother and daughter dresses for Biba, 1969. Photograph courtesy of Barbara Hulanicki.*

LEFT: *Jean Muir, White matte jersey dress, 1967, shown in Paris, where Muir was acclaimed as "La Reine de la Robe." Photograph courtesy of Jean Muir.*

RIGHT: *Sally Tuffin and Marion Foale, Mod suit, 1966, worn by actress Susannah York in the film* Kaleidoscope. *York was cast as the owner of a London fashion boutique who is wooed by a fortune hunter, played by Warren Beatty. Photograph courtesy of Warner Brothers Pictures.*

doing clothes in the sixties there were all these dolly-bird minis about — we were sort of against all that," she recalled in 1983 in an interview in *Harper's and Queen*. "It seemed so wrong, so unnecessary. I'm not the least interested in clothes. I like to forget what I'm wearing. Ideally I'd like to have four sets all the same."[11] Ashley herself died in an accident several years ago, but her clothes, sold in boutiques bearing her name, continue to be popular with many women around the world.

## Yé Yé Fashion

Just as women like Quant emerged in London, so also in Paris designers created their own versions of Youthquake fashions, although they tacitly acknowledged the influence of London when they spoke of "*yé yé*" fashion and "*le style anglais.*" Most of the big names in Paris, however, were men: Courrèges, Cardin, Paco Rabanne, and Saint Laurent.

"In the 1960s, there were few women in fashion," recalls Jacqueline Jacobson, the designer behind Dorothée bis. But women like Sonia Rykiel, Emmanuelle Khahn, Michèle Rosier, and Christiane Bailly did emerge to design youthful clothes, with what Jacobson calls "that 'sexy-modern' aspect that is now inherent in fashion."[12] Most of these *créatrices* worked in the ready-to-wear industry.

"Haute couture is dead," declared Emmanuelle Khanh in 1964. "I want to design for the street." A Parisian orphan, Khanh says that she became a model by calling the first name listed under "Couture" in the telephone book — "it was Balenciaga." But where others then and now worshiped Balenciaga, Khanh reacted against the ultrasophistication of 1950s' couture. The couture made "Rolls Royces," she explained: chic but rigid. Recalling her days as a teenage model, she said, "Balenciaga treated us like chairs, and I think the fact that he couldn't care less about us — women — reflects on the way he creates dresses."[13]

Khanh became known for her youthful tailored suits and culottes. Wearing her trademark big glasses, she frequently modeled her own clothes for the pages of French fashion magazines.

Michèle Rosier "has done for ready-to-wear what Courrèges has done for the couture" — created "a style without nostalgia," declared the *International Herald Tribune*.[14] Even before the first moonshot, Rosier (the daughter of a French fashion editor) gave a space-age twist to active sportswear. Nicknamed "the Vinyl Girl," she created rain ensembles in silver PVC that looked like something from Andy Warhol's Factory, while those she did in black were deliberately androgynous and menacing.

Jacqueline Jacobson helped popularize pantsuits and shorts. Her company, Dorothée bis, employed a variety of talented young creators. One such was Christiane Bailly, another pioneer of *stylisme* and also an ex-

LEFT: *Laura Ashley, Neo-Victorian floral-print dress, circa 1969. "I'm not the least interested in clothes," said Ashley. Photograph courtesy of Laura Ashley, Inc.*

Balenciaga model, who popularized trench coats and aviator jackets and explored the possibilities of simple shapes and "rough" materials.

According to Jacobson,

A woman creates clothes that correspond to her. . . . There is an *identification* — whereas men who create clothes *sublimate* the women that they dress. It is, perhaps, for that reason that the clothes made by women are less spectacular, because we know the needs of other women, the defects that one wants to conceal and the advantages that one wants to show. Today women designers are the equal of men designers, although they do not create clothes in the same way — sublimation for the men, identification for the women.

Sonia Rykiel, "the queen of knits," was the most important of the women designers who emerged in France during the 1960s. The clothes that she designed for her husband's boutique, Laura, were worn even by the trendiest British mods.

RIGHT: *Emmanuelle Khanh, Halter-top dress, 1965 (right), and Top decorated with plastic squares, 1965, shown with flared trousers by Dorothée bis. Photography by Traeger/Photo Trends.*

### "Wow! Explode! The Sixties!"

In America, the young look also had its adherents. What Mary Quant did for England and Emmanuelle Khanh did for France, Betsey Johnson did for the United States. Dressing "should be as uninhibited as possible," Johnson said in 1966. "My clothes are for young people who are saying, 'Look at me — I'm alive.'"[15]

"Wow! Explode! The Sixties," recalled Johnson. "It came to life in a pure, exaggerated, crazed-out, wham, wham, wow way. The Beatles, Hendrix, Joplin, the Velvet Underground exploding so wonderfully."[16] Johnson's work has always been associated with the music scene in all its changing forms, from rock and roll in the sixties — when she was (briefly) married to John Cale, bassist for The Velvet Underground — to disco and punk in the seventies and MTV in the eighties.

Johnson designed clothes for the legendary New York boutique Paraphernalia, making teeny-tiny skirts and skinny T-shirts. Another Paraphernalia designer, Elisa Stone, became famous for paper dresses. And electrical engineer Diana Dew designed Paraphernalia's famous light-up dress, powered by a miniature battery pack. But Johnson was especially close to the world of pop art, designing dresses of clear plastic, colored paper, and metal. Warhol "superstar" Edie Sedgwick was her most famous fitting model, and Johnson designed her wardrobe for the film *Ciao Manhattan*.

In 1971 Johnson became the youngest designer to win a Coty Award. *The New Yorker's* Kennedy Fraser reported, "Betsey Johnson belongs unmistakably to the new fashion generation."[17] But as the seventies wore on, and fashion increasingly focused on the working woman's wardrobe, Johnson encountered difficulties: "I'd be doing petticoats and the market would be thinking three-piece suits; it was basically menswear done for women," she recalls, ruefully.[18]

Meanwhile, in California, as the 1960s moved into its hippie phase, several local designers emerged. In San Francisco, Linda Gravenites designed one-of-a-kind costumes for rock stars like Janis Joplin. In Los Angeles, Holly Harp also designed within the counterculture, working in nostalgic crepe and exotic tie-dye.

## BONNIE CASHIN

Not all the sixties' designers were young, however. Bonnie Cashin pioneered liberated fashion even before the sixties. A true independent, she created a type of advanced sportswear that still looks modern today.

Cashin was born in California in 1915 and spent the 1940s working as a costume designer in Hollywood, before coming to New York where, in 1950, she won the first of five Coty Awards. In 1956 she was featured in Beryl Williams's book, *Young Faces in Fashion*, and in 1962 she was the subject of a major retrospective exhibition at the Brooklyn Museum. But it was only as the sixties got under way, when Futurism merged with ethnic hippie styles, that she was widely recognized as a true original.

Cashin had always been drawn to the pure forms of ethnic clothing and the possibilities inherent in "natural" materials such as leather and suede. In 1945, for example, she designed a short midriff-baring top inspired by an Indian *choli* (the blouse worn under a sari). When it was featured in her 1962 retrospective, noted fashion journalist Bill Cunningham wrote in *Women's Wear Daily*, "Her 1945 cut-out midriffs were very exciting and looked 1963 to me. These clothes . . . made me feel as if I were shot into the 21st century."

"What she has done for leather!" Cunningham added. "That sinister Marlon Brando mood is gone, replaced by a sleek, caressable, modern material. . . . This is the comfortable future!" The effect, he said, was simultaneously "splendidly effortless" and "too sexy for words."

"Miss Cashin is as American as the bald eagle," declared Cunningham.

"The French should see Bonnie's clothes—they would really rejuvenate Chanel." Unfortunately, Cunningham complained, most Americans did not yet appreciate such avant-garde fashion.[19] This, however, would soon change.

As *The New York Times* put it in 1968: "Fashion catches up to Cashin."[20] Her fringed leather garments (which she created as early as 1953) were as hip as anything worn by a sixties' rock star, and she did layering before the term was even coined. Always "anti-gimmick," her work had an integrity that others' often lacked. Cashin's mother had been a dressmaker and had taught her how to work in leather and suede years before these materials came into fashion.

ABOVE: *Bonnie Cashin, Hooded coat, circa 1967. Photograph courtesy of Bonnie Cashin.*

An avid traveler, she not only drew inspiration from ethnic costume, she also conceived practical travel wardrobes for the busy, adventurous woman. Thus, her use of layering grew naturally out of her research into both ancient Chinese costume and the modern American style of life. *Sports Illustrated* gave her an award in 1963 for her role as "the master equipper of all travelers" and noted that "a fully organized Cashin traveler looks as efficiently engineered as a jet plane."[21]

Cashin's clothes were functional: She pioneered the use of hardware fastenings and made pockets big enough to carry a paperback book, "security" purses to deter purse-snatchers, and hooded sweatshirts to keep warm. In 1977 she even designed freewheeling, high-visibility bicycle fashions, featuring shorts, tights, hoods, and backpacks—anticipating by more than a decade the late–1980s' craze for "bike messenger" styles.

Although she began as a costume designer for Twentieth Century Fox and ultimately collected more than sixty screen credits, her clothes were never theatrical. "I wasn't designing for fashion," she wrote, "but for characteristics—which is the way I still like to design clothes for daily wear. I like to design clothes for a woman who plays a particular role in life, not simply to design clothes that follow a certain trend."[22] Thus, in *Laura*, Gene Tierney played the title role wearing Cashin's typical casual, uncluttered style.

*Anna and the King of Siam*, on the other hand, brought out Cashin's love of traditional ethnic costume; throughout the filming, Cashin herself frequently wore a wrapped sarong-type skirt. When she was awarded The Fashion Critics' Hall of Fame Award in 1972, she was described as "closer kin to the first desert wanderer to draw on a djellaba, or the first Indian to cut hide into clothing, than she is to what's generally called a fashion designer."[23]

Cashin has criticized the commercialism, lack of creativity, and the sheer abrasiveness and ugliness of Seventh Avenue. Yet she finds clothing itself "fascinating" and has always looked for what she called the "simple, elegant solution."

Bonnie Cashin believes that there are few significant differences between the work of male and female designers. She will admit only that "perhaps" women design "more wearable" clothes, because as a woman one is "emotionally closer to the work." As she says, "You wear the clothes, you feel them. You are your own guinea pig!"[24]

TOP: *Bonnie Cashin, Fringed suede minidress, circa 1968. Cashin had explored the possibilities of fringed suede and leather as early as 1953. Photograph courtesy of Bonnie Cashin.*

ABOVE: *Bonnie Cashin, Parabola skirt, hooded sweater, and tights, circa 1968. Photograph courtesy of Bonnie Cashin.*

The Youthquake fashions of the 1960s were wonderful, but they were not necessarily right for all women, especially those in the work force. By the 1970s many working women were tired of youthful fashion fads and began demanding classic clothes that *didn't* change every season or constantly bare a new erogenous zone. The "baby-doll" look was over, but what would replace it? Throughout the 1950s and 1960s Anne Klein had designed reasonably priced mix-and-match blouses, skirts, and slacks that appealed both to suburban housewives and career women. Now, in part due to the influence of feminism, more designers moved into that area.

Fashion inspiration had to be "ideologically compatible with the feminism of the seventies," writes stylist Alain Sorel. Feminism initially contributed to the rise of unisex sportswear, which, although practical, was unsophisticated. How could designers reintroduce sophistication without falling into sexist stereotypes? In France, Sonia Rykiel's thirties'-inspired style allowed women "to be sophisticated again without feeling submissive." It was both "elegant and emancipated."[25]

In America during the 1970s, Diane von Fürstenberg had a similar success with her little "bourgeois" jersey wrap dresses, which could be worn to work but were also sexy enough for evening.

Liz Claiborne also aimed at providing relaxed separates for a wide range of "ordinary" working women — a strategy that has resulted in the creation of one of the largest and most successful women's apparel firms in the world, with a $1 billion-plus sales volume. When she and her husband first founded the company in 1976, Liz did all the designing. (After all, she had previously worked for Tina Leser and designed dresses for Jonathan Logan's Youthguild division.) But as the company grew ever larger, she increasingly delegated responsibilities to her design team, which has always included both men and women.

Looking back on the 1970s, fashion historian Jane Mulvagh concluded that "some of the most outstanding designers of working clothes were women." She named, as examples, Jean Muir, Sonia Rykiel, Laura Biagiotti, and the Fendi sisters. "What distinguished their collections was a profound evolution of style rather than random changes," Mulvagh wrote. "Perhaps an intelligent, intuitive woman will always have an edge over her male counterpart when producing clothes that women really feel comfortable in."[26]

Back in the 1960s, Norma Kamali flew to London almost every weekend, bringing back the new mod fashions to sell in the Manhattan boutique that she and her husband ran on East 53rd Street; by 1967 she began to design herself.

The spirit of the sixties proved stimulating to Kamali: "Maybe it was all a little too fantasy," she told *Women's Wear Daily* years later, "but dreams are important. People . . . weren't afraid to try anything. Some wonderful changes happened to all of us as a result. It was the most creative time I've

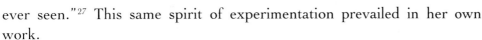

ever seen."[27] This same spirit of experimentation prevailed in her own work.

Kamali was one of the first to bring the new trend for physical exercise into fashion, and frequently emphasized that the contemporary woman was in much better shape and much stronger than her predecessors. She is perhaps best known for her fashions made of sweatshirt material, which were enormously influential in the late seventies and early eighties. After her divorce, in 1978, she conceived the idea of down coats while resting in a sleeping bag.

Kamali also emphasized glamour, and many of her styles featured shoulder pads and other historicizing elements. At one point Kamali had a lot of trouble with the unions and virtually disappeared — except for her bathing suits, which continued to be very popular, and which many women regard as among the sexiest and most flattering around. She has begun to reemerge, however, and is still widely regarded as one of the most genuinely creative talents in contemporary American fashion.

In 1985 Kamali was quoted in *The New York Times* as saying: "In every kind of career — medicine, politics, law — more and more women are growing in numbers in their chosen field. I see it happening in our industry, which has always been male-dominated. The timing is right for women designers."[28]

# 12

# LONDON: FEMININE NOT FEMINIST

"The role of women in British fashion continues to grow," reported *The New York Times* in 1984. "Women have always been the backbone of the fashion industry and have always been more visible than female fashion designers in other countries, but now they are wielding even more influence. . . ."[1]

## THE OLD GUARD: ZANDRA RHODES

"For a long time my hair was green," says Zandra Rhodes, "but the pink is easier to keep."[2] The offbeat practicality of this remark is typical of the London designer. In the late sixties, when she had a shop on Fulham Road, her partner used to say, "Don't come in! You'll frighten the customers."[3] Even seen-it-all New York City cab drivers still stop and stare in astonishment when she walks down the street.

Like many who came of age during the "swinging sixties," Rhodes admires individuality and freedom of dress and abhors straight fashion "uniforms." Yet Rhodes's designs are not really extreme, just a bit exotic and quite wearable in a romantically feminine way. She is known in England as the "Queen of the Party Dress."[4]

Rhodes says:

I'm not a women's lib lady. I think it's rather wonderful to have a man think you look nice in something. But most male designers do not really know about what attracts another man. They see the dress as a design *object*. The

ABOVE: *Zandra Rhodes, Lace Mountain textile design, 1975. Photograph courtesy of Zandra Rhodes.*

OPPOSITE: *Zandra Rhodes. Photograph by Robyn Beeche. Hair by Nick at Trevor Sorbie. Make-up by Phyllis Cohen. Photograph courtesy of Zandra Rhodes.*

short, puffy dress with a lot of workmanship that's very expensive is a male-dominated image, but would real men like their wives in it?

I think women, because they're wearing the clothes, have more awareness of comfort. I give myself feedback, and that's what I think the men can't do. Sometimes in my workroom I've got boys working and I say, "I think that bodice is too low. Would you want to go around with your balls hanging out of your trousers?" And they look at me, quite appalled. But a woman can tell, because she knows how she feels and how people are going to react to her.

Zandra—with a *Z*—is an unusual name, and it is not surprising to learn that her mother had an original sense of style. "She sprayed her hair silver and wore lilies behind her ears," recalls Rhodes, who used to plead with her mother, "Please don't wear that hat. . . . People will *look* at you."[5]

Her mother had been chief fitter at the House of Worth in Paris and later taught fashion at the Medway College of Art, so "at home there was always someone draping fabric." But Rhodes did not learn dressmaking from her mother, never having been inspired by "all these Parisian lines."

Instead, she became a textile designer. But she was dissatisfied with the way other designers used her fabrics, so in 1968 she began to make clothes that would allow her textiles to speak for themselves. Her breakthrough came when she discovered the traditional patterns and shapes of ethnic costume, which were not only "extraordinary and timeless" but also extremely flattering and comfortable.

In 1970 Rhodes created her felt "Dinosaur" coat with the seams pinked and turned inside out; in 1971 she designed her first "ripped" dress. She experimented with "tattered" hems and pinned-on sleeves. In 1978 her "Conceptual Chic" collection created a sensation, with its glamorized version of the Punk look, complete with jeweled safety pins. Rhodes once commented that she didn't see why there should be anything intrinsically frightening about holes in clothing; after all, she observed, lace has holes in it too.

Rhodes sees herself as an artist working in the medium of clothes. Coming from most designers this would sound pretentious, but in her case it is clear that each dress really is the product of a complex artistic process.

First she creates the design, based on her own sketches. For example, after she drove across the United States, she created a series of textile designs derived from cactus and cowboy motifs; her lily designs were inspired by a visit to Japan, as well as by the study of old Parisian lace. The design is then hand-stenciled on the fabric, in such a way that the shape of the clothing enhances, rather than interferes, with the integrity of the textile design. "I don't want to put all that energy into something that's just a throwaway item," says Rhodes, who has described her fantasy dresses as "the Rolls Royces of evening clothes."

This sense of clothing as art makes her feel close to designers of the past who also viewed their creations as animated works of art:

I think Schiaparelli was a true original, because she brought together . . . art and fashion. I'd like to think that's something I've contributed, too, in

my own way, mainly by letting the textile influence the clothing.

In fact, when you think about it, some of the most extraordinary designers were women like Schiaparelli, Chanel, and Mme Vionnet, possibly because they had some great individuality. I suppose I'm trying to create things that people haven't seen before, a new pattern or a different look at color, that will appeal to their imagination.

Despite her great personal success in a field that is still dominated by men, Rhodes claims that she is "not convinced that women have actually achieved equality with men. I would like to think that I'd make it whether I was a man or a woman. The only difference is, it's easier for a man to have a family. I know Sonia Rykiel has a daughter, but I feel I haven't been able to have children, because I've had to put so much into my art."

## AND JEAN MUIR

"I design *feminine* not feminist clothes,"[6] says Jean Muir, or *Miss* Muir, as she is always addressed. "I like my clothes to be womanly, with rounded, soft lines, feminine in the true and natural sense, not fussy . . . not sex symbol." She adds: "I don't like that fussy kind of femininity any more than I like the feminist kind."[7]

Since 1967, when Muir was acclaimed in Paris as "La Reine de la robe," she has been recognized as a world-class designer. She has been called "the world's best dressmaker."[8] Her version of simple chic reflects an elegant and somewhat austere persona. She wears only navy blue clothes, for example, and her home is decorated entirely in white. She is known above all for her technical genius, the sheer *craft* of her work, which is based

ABOVE: *Zandra Rhodes,
Conceptual Chic dresses,
Autumn/Winter 1977–1978
collection. Photograph by Clive
Arrowsmith, courtesy of
Zandra Rhodes.*

ABOVE: *Jean Muir, Intarsia cashmere sweater, Autumn 1990 collection. Cashmere is treated like an artist's canvas in this sweater, which Muir thinks is probably the best designed and crafted garment her house has ever made. Photograph courtesy of Jean Muir.*

TOP LEFT: *Jean Muir, Black matte jersey dress with asymmetric chiffon frill across the body, Spring 1990 collection. Photograph by Clive Arrowsmith, courtesy of Jean Muir.*

LEFT: *Jean Muir, Pale yellow wool crepe swing jacket with black matte jersey leggings and a stitched wool beret, Spring 1990 collection. Photograph by Clive Arrowsmith, courtesy of Jean Muir.*

ABOVE: *Vivienne Westwood in a ripped Destroy T-shirt, circa 1975. Photograph by Norma Moriceau, from* Punk, *1978, courtesy of Dike Blair.*

primarily on cut and on meticulous detailing. The creative side "never seemed to be difficult," she says, "one does it so naturally." She prefers to think of herself as a maker of clothes, rather than a designer, and she believes that fashion is "an exacting trade" requiring work and intelligence. "I love the fittings, getting the shape right, the mathematics of it."[9]

She favors soft, flexible fabrics, especially matte jersey, which she *tailors* rather than drapes, and she never uses darts, only tucks. "I like structure, but I like it to be fluid. So that, therefore, I make structured shapes in jersey. They have a fluidity but they've still got a structure — which is rather like classical ballet."[10] She also works with liquid-soft suede and leather, emphasizing a purity of line.

"Because I'm small, I never liked extra weight," says Muir, "and that contributed to the rather spare clothes that one makes." But there is also a practical logic behind her style. "When I started my own business in 1967, I wanted to make clothes that looked like couture, that had that kind of cut, but were ready-to-wear." But in translating the couture look to ready-to-wear, she remarks, "you had to eliminate a lot." By contrast, "when you made jersey, you *didn't* have to line it or interface it. So that, in fact, you really *could* do a lovely couture shape that could be made for ready-to-wear and machined."

Women are very prominent in British fashion, "but I don't know *why,*" says Muir. "It just happened that way. I don't think there's any particular significance in it." She does believe, though, that a woman "understands the female anatomy." She adds:

If you're making clothes for women, the fact that you're a woman who knows what it feels like to wear clothes has to have an effect. Also I've always loved dancing — the classical ballet has always been a passion of mine — and so, therefore, one understands the anatomy and how it moves.

And you emphasize comfort. Women designers all make comfortable clothes. I think men rather superimpose shapes on women. In today's rather complex world, I think a woman has got infinitely more *common sense* and is infinitely more practical.

The modern woman is "loose-limbed, open-minded, and not afraid of her body," Muir says. "One must realize what the body does. It MOVES."[11]

If Muir and Rhodes represent London's old guard, then Vivienne Westwood and Katharine Hamnett epitomize the next generation.

## THE NEW GUARD: VIVIENNE WESTWOOD

Vivienne Westwood, the revolutionary creator of Punk fashion (ripped T-shirts, bondage clothes, fetishist accoutrements), feels an affinity with Coco Chanel. "Chanel probably designed for the same reasons that I do really: irritation with orthodox ways of thinking and a certain perversity. She was a street-fashion designer."[12] Westwood once wondered what it would be like if she were to design an entire collection inspired by Chanel. Admittedly, this idea would probably make Mademoiselle roll over in her grave. But although Westwood's clothes have frequently been described as decadent, degenerate, and unwearable, they have also exerted a powerful influence on international fashion.

"I'm very antibourgeois," says Westwood. "I think it was Bertrand Russell who said, 'What is orthodox is unintelligent,' and I hate anything which is unthinking. *Orthodox* is a much better word to use than *Establishment*."[13] Chanel was unorthodox, too, according to Westwood, "especially when she first started — the way she dressed in men's tweeds and trousers, made comfortable clothes, and raised hemlines."

Westwood has great admiration for Chanel and regards her as a true innovator who "contributed a lot towards the climate of liberation" in her day.[14] Consequently, Westwood is "irritated" by the way the Chanel Look has frozen "in a mold" and become "very trendy." She believes that Chanel herself "would not be doing anything of the kind if she were alive today."

She considers Chanel a street-fashion designer, not so much because Chanel thought fashion should go down into the streets, but rather because Chanel's clothes have all kinds of "social and cultural associations." By contrast, Westwood sees many other designers "making shapes," doing things "just for the sake of doing something that nobody's ever done, in this sort of grand manner of What a Designer Ought to Do."

Westwood became a fashion designer in the mid–1970s, when the emergence of Punk put London back on the fashion map for the first time since 1965. Just as the Mods, Rockers, and Hippies of the 1960s had embraced particular styles of dress and music, so also did the Punks create their own subculture. The Punk "style in revolt" was a deliberately "revolting style" that incorporated into fashion various offensive or threatening objects like tampons, razor blades, and lavatory chains.

As Dick Hebdige writes in *Subculture: The Meaning of Style*:

Safety pins were . . . worn as gruesome ornaments through the cheek, ear, or lip. "Cheap" trashy fabrics (plastic, lurex, etc.) in vulgar designs (e.g., mock leopard skin) and "nasty" colors, long discarded by the quality end of the fashion industry as obsolete kitsch, were salvaged by the punks and turned into garments . . . which offered self-conscious commentaries on the notions of modernity and taste. . . . In particular, the illicit iconography of sexual fetishism was . . . exhumed from the boudoir, closet, and the pornographic film and placed on the street.[15]

Westwood's "confrontation dressing" captured the essence of the Punk style. Westwood herself was a primary-school teacher until she met Malcolm McClaren, who achieved notoriety as manager of The Sex Pistols, a Punk music group starring Sid Vicious and Johnny Rotten. "We're into chaos, not music," said Johnny Rotten, summing up the Punk musical aesthetic, which was deliberately crude, amateurish, and anarchistic.

In the beginning McClaren came up with the ideas and Westwood translated the ideas into clothes. "It did take me a long time to think of

ABOVE: *Vivienne Westwood, Lycra fashions, Spring/ Summer 1989 collection. Photograph courtesy of Vivienne Westwood.*

FAR LEFT, TOP: *Vivienne Westwood, Suit inspired by eighteenth-century menswear, from the Pirates collection, Autumn/Winter 1981–1982.*

FAR LEFT: *Vivienne Westwood, Dress with "tribal" design, from the Savages collection, Spring/Summer 1982. Photographs courtesy of Vivienne Westwood.*

LEFT: *Vivienne Westwood, Shirts, vests, trousers, and hats, from the Pirates collection, Autumn/Winter 1981–1982. Photograph by Robyn Beeche.*

BELOW: *Vivienne Westwood, Bra worn over layered clothing, from the Buffalo Girls collection, Autumn/ Winter 1982–1983. Photograph by Robyn Beeche.*

OPPOSITE: *Vivienne Westwood, Glamour and gloves, Spring/Summer 1989 collection. Photograph courtesy of Vivienne Westwood.*

ABOVE: *Vivienne Westwood, Tailored suit. Autumn/Winter 1989–1990 collection. Westwood has redefined classic British tailoring: "Shades of Miss Marple on acid," Tatler commented. Photograph courtesy of Vivienne Westwood.*

myself as an independent designer," she says.[16]

But after they broke up in 1983, Westwood kept designing successfully, and her interpretation of their past collaboration took on a slightly different tone: She dismissed McClaren as "the perfect orthodox rebel . . . intelligent, very glossy, and action-packed." Even worse, "Malcolm wasn't a craftsman. At one time he used to refer to me as 'the seamstress.' He didn't like the idea that anything could be done without him—which was true at the beginning. I needed Malcolm's ideas."[17]

In 1971, with establishment fashion divided between mass-market late-hippie looks and incipient neoconservatism, McClaren and Westwood opened a fifties' revival shop in King's Road, London, named Let It Rock. By 1974 it was transformed into the notorious S&M, bondage, and fetish store, Sex, which pop star Adam Ant called "one of the all-time greatest shops in history." As Punk became more overtly political, the shop was given the appropriately anarchistic name Seditionaries (1977).

Then in March 1981, Westwood and McClaren produced the "Pirates" collection, which heralded the beginning of the New Romantics movement and finally established Westwood as an internationally significant designer. Westwood says, "When we finished punk rock we started looking at other cultures—up till then we'd only been concerned with emotionally charged rebellious English youth movements. . . . We looked at all the cults that we felt had this power—comic-book Apache Indians, pirates, even Louis XIV, who had the same sort of style. . . ."[18]

Historical revivalism was the new trend in London street style: Adam Ant's music video, "Stand and Deliver" (1981) made a hero of the eighteenth-century highwayman. Similarly, Westwood's "Pirates" collection continued her recent theme of "Clothes for Heroes"—it apotheosized those much-romanticized and *very English* seagoing robbers. The "Pirates" collection featured eighteenth-century dandified frills, along with sumptuous colors and fabrics and a looser silhouette. One of Westwood's pirate outfits (complete with the traditional pirate hat) is now a centerpiece of the costume collection of the Victoria & Albert Museum.

Subsequent collections in the early to mid–1980s were "Savages," "Buffalo Girls," "Hobos," and "Witches." As McClaren and Westwood gravitated toward a "tribal" look, their store was renamed World's End. They also opened a second shop, Nostalgia of Mud (1982), a corruption of *nostalgie de la boue* (the bourgeois attraction to low-life) that also expressed their search for "something primeval in old dirt."

The "Savage" collection reflected their research into "primitive" tribal societies. The name seems to have been deliberately offensive and shocking. It also recalled the Punks' ambivalent identification with West Indian culture and reggae music. The clothes in the "Savage" collection tended to be oversized and made of rough fabrics, with exposed seams and bold geometric prints. Valerie Mendes of the Victoria & Albert Museum's fashion department declared that "the Savage Collection . . . was simply wonderful. . . . [Westood] is in the forefront of ideas, her impact on the cut of clothes has been considerable and, while her ideas can be extreme, her clothes are wearable."[19]

Soon avant-garde French designers, such as Jean-Paul Gaultier, began to "borrow" from Westwood. "I don't care about people copying me," insists Westwood. "Their clothes never look as grand or important as mine . . . there's no feeling in them. I didn't mind Zandra [Rhodes] copying the punk rock thing because she did it in her own way."[20]

ABOVE: *Vivienne Westwood in elegant attire, 1989. Photograph courtesy of Vivienne Westwood.*

Every modern subversive movement from Dada to Punk has stolen, juxtaposed, and transformed objects and symbols from the dominant culture. Westwood continued this form of anarchic collage, mixing styles from past and present and ripping them out of their traditional contexts. The "Buffalo" collection, for example, fractured images from American folk culture and featured urban cowgirls and cowboys in layers of sheepskin and mud-colored cloth, rags tied in their hair, falling-down socks, and bras worn *over* dresses.

Just as her inspiration for ripped clothing came partly from old movie stills with "film stars looking really sexy in ripped clothes," so also was the "underwear-as-outerwear" theme deliberately sexy.[21] Westwood's bras worn over dresses were much copied by more orthodox fashion designers, stylists, and photographers. According to Westwood: "The giant thing about my clothes — the way they make you feel grand and strong — is to do with the sexy way they emphasize your body and make you aware of it."[22]

The "Witches" collection took its name from a book about voodoo in the tropics. The clothes were intended to fall off the body slightly and were related to the then-current style of "robotic dancing."

After an absence of several seasons, Westwood returned in autumn 1985 with a new garment, a bell-shaped skirt supported by collapsible hoops: the mini-crini. You "take something from the past which has a sort of vitality that has never been exploited — like the crinoline — and . . . you get so involved with it, that in the end, you do something original," explains Westwood. "People loved it yet didn't understand it, they thought the crinoline was just fantasy and not for commercial reproduction."[23] Spurned as unwearable, the mini-crini turned out to be the forerunner of Christian Lacroix's much-copied pouf skirts of the late 1980s. Even feminist periodicals like *Ms.* carried articles debating the pouf skirt.

"I can never say that I'm a feminist, I wouldn't ever say that," Westwood said recently. "Why not? Well, women are the most conservative section of society, they will not risk anything. Margaret Thatcher really exploited that. I'd much rather promote or defend homosexuals than women, because they've contributed . . . much more to our society."[24]

Have homosexuals also contributed more to fashion than women? "I don't think so," says Westwood. "I was just defending unorthodoxy, and homosexuals have been forced to consider that there may be at least two viewpoints, whereas most people are programmed into the orthodox received view." Orthodox fashion, for Westwood, means "being trendy, following fashion trends, being a fashion victim." Unorthodox fashion means "having your own sort of chic, being an innovator."

"There probably is a distinction between men designers and women designers," she adds, "just as there are distinctions between men and women." But what Westwood notices most is that, "[the] men who work around me, homosexual or not, often say they wish they were women, because they'd have so much more scope in choosing what to wear. Sometimes they see some really nice things that men really wouldn't be allowed to wear. Women have so much more scope, because they can go from the most extreme masculine style to the most extreme feminine style, which men can't do."

Westwood's ideas and forms have evolved considerably since her Punk period. In 1982 Westwood told *Women's Wear Daily*: "I try to relate fashion to the really important things in life, like politics and young people on the streets. Clothes are the only way most people can express themselves. Fashion is an emotion and people want to wear what they want to feel."[25]

Today Westwood has "completely reversed" some of her earlier expressed opinions:

I don't have any great faith in youth or politics, the way I did when I was doing Punk. The jungle beat was supposed to rock the establishment and threaten the Puritan ethic and all that sort of thing, but I realized that it didn't.

*Elegance* is my favorite word at the moment, because it has to do with culture, and the only thing I really do believe in is culture, civilization. If someone looks elegant, that suggests that that person is interested in cultural things.

Not that her clothes or persona have gotten any more bourgeois: In April 1989, Westwood appeared on the cover of *Tatler*, under the headline "This Woman Was Once a Punk." Wearing a wig, pearls, a conservative Aquascutum suit, and an anxious expression, she was cleverly disguised to look eerily like Margaret Thatcher. Says Westwood: "I imagined myself standing over a child in a hospital bed—*caring*. I then thought of the TV camera as being just over *there* and achieved her 'anxious' look by wondering if I looked caring enough."

*Tatler* described her 1989 styles as "anarchic reworkings of Little Old Ladies' Clothes (shades of Miss Marple on Acid)."[26] Certainly, since 1986 and 1987 Westwood has radically redefined classic British tailoring. "I've utilized the conventional to make something unorthodox," explains Westwood. "Fashion design is almost like mathematics. You have a vocabulary of ideas which you have to add and subtract from each other in order to come up with an equation that's right for the times." No longer Punks, in 1987 Westwood's street creatures dressed in Harris tweeds and twinsets, John Bull hats, and black velvet breeches.

They even played with "the vocabulary of royalty," wearing crowns and fake ermine. "Dressed like this . . . you look like you've got power and culture," claims Westwood. "It's a move away from middle-class bourgeois dressing, but it's also a move away from the underground. . . . There's no status in it. . . . You have a much better life if you wear impressive clothes."[27]

Another recent collection was "Britain Goes Pagan," which focused on the idea that "Britain must go back to the ideas of Greece and Rome. Their morality was more sane, it wasn't about sin. And it's a question of the skeptical point of view, they knew you have to keep an open mind." Westwood continues:

It's very difficult to come up with something shocking and original. In my last collection I surprised myself by making a garment that shocked me. I realized that the statues of Adonis in Greece have a tiny bit of drapery that enhances the sensuality of the nude. Suddenly, it clicked, I thought of those men they called *Incroyables* during the Napoleonic era, when the whole emphasis of men's clothes was on the genitals, with very, very light-colored tight leather trousers. And I realized that those men were trying to look like those Adonis figures. I wanted the look for women, so I did tights worn with the shirt hanging out loose, so it looked like a guy just about to rape you, but it was worn on a woman. When I tried the tights on, I just shrieked: It looked pornographic. It was terribly sexy, just because it was the reverse of what was fashionably sexy.

Westwood claims that "sexuality is always really an interplay between the polarities of masculine and feminine." Hence her criticism of the padded shoulder. As she once said, "I've never thought it powerful to be like a second-rate man. Feminine is stronger, and I don't know why people keep plugging this boring asexual body."[28] In her view, "the big shoulder was just too obvious, it became very bourgeois in the end." That's the problem: "Things become sort of stale and bourgeois, not alive."

Westwood said once that she was "really inspired by the Queen," so she chose as her logo the orb and satellite, the orb being what the Queen of England holds in her hand as a symbol of her power, and the satellite signifying the future.[29] Westwood's admirers might say: "Long Live the Queen!"

ABOVE: *Katharine Hamnett in a "Stop Acid Rain" T-shirt, from her Spring/Summer 1985 collection. "Integrity is sexy," says the designer. Photograph by Roxanne Lowit.*

### AND KATHARINE HAMNETT

An ordinary fashion designer would not say, as Katharine Hamnett has, "Yuk, fashion . . . blah, blah clothes. I find it difficult to talk about trends when we need an awakening worldwide."[30]

Sometimes called a "loony leftist," Hamnett has said that "America is bad" and has described both the Queen and Mrs. Thatcher as "garbage." Yet she insists, "I am not left-wing, or right-wing. I am a mother. I am doing this for my two kids, so we can have a life."[31]

"Katharine Hamnett is a *provocateuse*," declared British *Vogue*. "She has made her reputation with a combination of startling public gestures and a design imagery that speaks of sex, rock, and rebellion. . . ." Says Hamnett: "I don't feel I have to be a man, look like a man, to succeed. Being a woman is wonderful. We can get away with murder."[32]

In 1985, during a time when there was a public outcry about the proposed stationing of American missiles in England, British Prime Minister Margaret Thatcher hosted a cocktail party to honor British fashion design-

ABOVE: *Katharine Hamnett, Minidresses, 1989. Photograph by Roxanne Lowit.*

OPPOSITE: *Katharine Hamnett, Denim bustiers with velvet miniskirt and hot pants, Spring/Summer 1989 collection. Photograph by Roxanne Lowit.*

ers. Hamnett staged a publicity coup by wearing a T-shirt proclaiming: "58% DON'T WANT PERSHING." Mrs. Thatcher later complained, "We don't have Pershing, we have Cruise." But Hamnett had made her point.

She is most famous for mixing fashion and politics, especially via T-shirts emblazoned with messages like "Stop Killing Whales," "Heroin-Free Zone," "Choose Life," "Preserve the Rain Forests," and "Worldwide Nuclear Ban Now." The profits from the sale of these shirts go to a charity that fights child abuse.

"Integrity is very sexy," says Hamnett. "I find people who care about the world tremendously attractive — people who stay true to their beliefs and aren't afraid to show through their clothes and actions what they think."[33]

Indeed, all fashion is ideological, she argues: "People who think alike tend to dress the same." But she does not take a simple leftist or feminist stance; although many of her clothes are derived from street fashion, it is not proletarian chic. Nor does she have much patience with the usual feminist critique of "sexist" fashion: "I really hated that old-fashioned idea which said looking sexy was bad and that you shouldn't try to attract men!"[34]

"Men and women both, to an extent, get dressed to get laid," says Hamnett. "Most of the male designers are gay, and that can't help but affect how they design. I'm very interested in the sexual power of dressing, but it's ostensibly a heterosexual interest. . . . I love to create clothes that make people look like heroes and heroines. The knack, though, is to do that without the clothes themselves taking over. They have to be wearable and, at the same time, invisible."[35]

"There is a new feminine force emerging" in fashion, she says. "Some people call it androgyny, but it's not really that at all. It's that both sexes are borrowing from each other to make themselves look more attractive."[36]

Recently, for example, she noticed that "men look very sexy in suits, whereas they looked very sexy before in jeans." So she designed a sexy "Power Dressing" collection, inspired by young bankers. "The establishment is where the power is. You have to beat them at their own game, be chicer than Chanel."

Hamnett once bought herself a Chanel suit on sale. She says, "It's very interesting fighting a Chanel suit, which basically turns you into a fascist unless you watch out. It really does. It gives you such a rise. You can completely obliterate anyone seeing you in a Chanel suit."[37]

# 13
# PARIS: LA VRAIE FEMME

**W**omen no longer dominate Paris fashion the way they did in the 1930s, but there are signs that the decades-long period of male dominance may be winding down. "Women designers are emerging here [in Paris], too," observes British *Vogue*, although most of them have not yet made much "impact in the international market."[1]

### SONIA RYKIEL

ABOVE: *Sonia Rykiel, Black knit dresses, Spring/Summer 1989 collection. Photograph courtesy of Sonia Rykiel.*

OPPOSITE: *Martine Sitbon, Black-and-white tailored suits, Autumn 1990 collection. Photograph by Roxanne Lowit.*

"The woman I am interested in is *la vraie Femme*. Put that with a capital *F*," says Sonia Rykiel. Rykiel is probably the most successful woman designer in France today, so her belief in the eternal feminine may be culturally significant. Not all women are Women, she insists: "You have to be a woman in your mind."[2]

"I am a woman," says Rykiel. "Consequently, I think as a woman, I design as a woman, I invent as a woman with my woman's passions and desires. Obviously, everything finds itself in my essentially womanly creation."[3] Her first book, *Et je la voudrai nue . . . (And I Would Like Her Naked . . .)*, consisted of a series of poetic meditations on fashion, life, and love. In it, Rykiel described a woman of pleasure, work, power, desire — a mother, wife, mistress, creator . . . *une vraie Femme*.

"Naturally," says Rykiel, the clothes created by male designers are different than those created by women, "because the men won't be wearing the clothes." She continues, "a man's eye is often more graphic, more decorative. They are not so close to it. One could say, therefore, that a man is

ABOVE: *Sonia Rykiel,
Sweaters with a message,
Spring/Summer 1989
collection. Photograph courtesy
of Sonia Rykiel.*

sometimes more creative than a woman, because he will not wear the clothes himself."

She elaborated on the differences in another interview. For male designers, she said, "practical considerations are secondary, and they can create magnificent designs. Women designers define things with a more practical eye because of the limitations of their body. A collar that looks attractive on the drafting board might be difficult to pull over the head. And pants that appear elegant can be constricting."[4]

Clearly, Rykiel does not accept the popular idea that women designers have an advantage over their male counterparts because they actually wear the clothes. Indeed, she sees female practicality as something of a liability. But this is not to say that she prefers the creations of male designers.

In the past, claims Rykiel, men dominated fashion design "because women didn't work, they didn't have a *métier*, a profession; they took care of their homes and children." Now that women have assumed responsible roles in the working world, says Rykiel, they play two roles — one masculine, the other feminine. Women designers have attained equality with men — "absolutely."

But the source of their strength, she implies, lies in their innate femininity: "As a creator I live with a woman, as a woman I live with a creator," Rykiel told fashion editor André Leon Talley. "And when I work, I make more of a study of woman, rather than a craft of fashion design."[5]

Rykiel's success rests on the emergence of a modern generation of working women, who identify with her liberated and sophisticated style. Yet in her work there is also a very strong emphasis on what she calls "the primitive instinct to be a mother and a lover."[6]

Untrained, Rykiel began to design in 1962, almost "by accident," because she was pregnant and wanted to make a beautiful maternity dress. Pregnancy for Rykiel was "ecstasy." Other women may be embarrassed by their huge bellies, but Rykiel felt herself to be "superb" and "beautiful": "Indifferent to the rest of the world, I promenaded my belly and my swollen breasts the way a standard-bearer carries the flag. . . . Huge, full, striking, I surrounded myself with enormous dresses, flowing, flowered, baby-dresses filled up with all the newborns of the world that I spread out around myself like a circle, round like the earth. . . . Equivocal dresses made to hide and to display. Pregnant, I made my first dress."[7]

This body-consciousness remains a characteristic of Rykiel's clothes. Her first fashion breakthrough came in 1964 when one of her body-hugging "poor boy" sweaters was featured on the cover of *Elle*. When she had first tried to market her sweaters, the buyers sneered: "Who is supposed to wear that little sweater — a twelve-year-old?" But by 1964, journalists in the United States were calling her the "Queen of Knitwear," and in 1967 Marylou Luther of the *Los Angeles Times* announced, "Couture is not enough — you need a Rykiel."[8]

Rykiel's second breakthrough came in the early 1970s, a time when ready-to-wear was dominated by unisex sportswear that was practical but unsophisticated. By contrast, Rykiel proposed soft knit separates in colors like black and cream, in a style that seemed both liberated and sophisticated. They were sensuous without looking like a caricature of femininity.

Rykiel was also becoming famous as a personality. In 1970 a poll of Frenchwomen voted her one of the fifteen most sensuous women in the world. She insists, however, that "no form of fashion makes a woman sexy. The woman must provoke, she must shock the look or attention of others. . . . What is a thousand times more important than clothes are gestures, the way a woman moves, the way she uses her eyes."[9] She says that she makes clothes to dress women — and to inspire men to want to undress them.

What woman does she think of when she designs? "First of all, myself!" she told a journalist from *Liberation*. "The woman who interests me is the bisexual woman." She paused. "I want to say: the *garçon manqué*."[10] A former "tomboy" herself, Rykiel often describes herself in interviews as "androgynous." She thinks that very feminine women are both masculine and feminine — forceful, aggressive, yet also sensuous and mysterious.

Rykiel recalls: "When I was little, I hated clothes. I only liked them when they were old and worn. I always wanted to wear the same skirt and the same pullover. It was a war between my mother and me." One day, in desperation, her mother got rid of Sonia's old clothes. "Very well, mamma," Sonia said, "I'm going out naked." She opened the door and went out. Her mother caught up with her in the garden.[11] The little girl who always liked to wear the same old sweater grew up to design fluid knits whose form changed only gradually. The girl who went out naked created clothes that were as comfortable and sensual as a second skin.

TOP: *Chantal Thomass, Lingerie dress, 1989. "I was the first to rehabilitate sexy lingerie," says Thomass. Photograph by Roxanne Lowit.*

ABOVE: *Chantal Thomass, Print dress and kerchief, 1989. Photograph by Roxanne Lowit.*

## FROU-FROU-FROU

Not all French clothes are *frou frou*, by any means, but in comparison with the relative classicism of the Italians and Americans or the avant-garde styles of the English and Japanese, French fashion remains dedicated to the eternal feminine.

Chantal Thomass is known for sexy clothes, especially for her lingerie looks. Her press releases are filled with words like "coquettish," "seductive," "mysterious," and "*un succès frou-frou-frou*," and we are told that Chantal herself is "*une femme. Une vraie.*" The magazine *Libération* calls her a "post-feminist" designer.[12]

"Women's big defect is their hips," says Thomass, bluntly. On the other hand, she notes, "all women have something interesting to show. There are some women who like to show their breasts, others their legs, others their buttocks. . . . I always try to show some part of a woman's body."[13] The "big difference" between male and female designers, according to Thomass, is that "the men create an image of women and it is always the same image. Often this limits them. At the outset, I think of myself, . . . then of women near my age who have a life like mine. . . . There are always a dozen women, my friends, whom I think of when I make something. I don't have a feminine ideal. . . . I don't think: 'This would be good for Marilyn Monroe.'"[14]

ABOVE: *Myrène de Prémonville, Fringed jacket and trousers, Spring/Summer 1989 collection. Photograph courtesy of Maria Chandoha Valentino.*

BELOW: *Agnès de Fleurieu, the designer behind Agnès B. Photograph courtesy of Agnès B.*

BOTTOM: *Agnès de Fleurieu, Sketch for cardigan sweater. Photograph courtesy of Agnès B.*

Not only does Thomass often incorporate elements of lingerie into her clothes — lace, underwear shapes, bustier tops, petticoats — she also has a line of lingerie and stockings. "I was the first to rehabilitate sexy lingerie," says Thomass. Although she is not well known in America, her pretty, feminine clothes are quite popular among young Frenchwomen.[15]

"Naughtily sexy, athletically Parisian, with peek-a-boo slits [and] garter-belt clips," said *Vogue* of Corinne Cobson's contribution to the Parisian fashion-scape. Her clothes are "based on the principle of the striptease." And *Vogue* quotes another young designer with the evocative name of Lolita Lempika as saying, "I like the spirit of the naughty *naïf.*"[16]

Myrène de Prémonville is another young French designer who creates fresh-looking, sexy clothes and colorful suits. "I don't try and think about women at large." she says, "Otherwise I'd end up not pleasing anyone."[17] Instead, she says, "I take influences from books, from paintings, from what I see around me. But I don't make any particular statement about women."[18]

Not all French designers are wild and sexy, of course. Kim Hastreiter of *Paper* magazine once divided the world into Plain Janes (pure, basic) and Mad Mollies (wild, eccentric): Nantucket versus Tijuana, cotton versus fun fur, khaki versus Day-Glo pink, Agnès B. versus Vivienne Westwood. . . .[19]

Agnès de Fleurieu is the designer behind Agnès B., where Plain Janes find great generic fashion with a Left Bank sensibility. Before she began designing, she worked at *Elle*, choosing the clothes to be photographed, but she seldom found the simple clothes she wanted. "I think real fashion interests maybe two thousand people in Paris. People like to look at fashion magazines, but in the end they like to be themselves."[20] The neutrality of r designs is the secret of their appeal, according to the designer.

"I like the fashions I see now on the street," she says. "They are often much more poetic than the clothes that designers create. Actually I think designers have very *little* influence on the clothes that people wear. There is a very strong popular way of clothing oneself. You saw it with the miniskirt, with shorts and blue jeans, which change very little from year to year."

De Fleurieu designs for men as well as women. "I think, 'If I were a man, what would I like to wear?' You get inside people's skin. Some men, like Saint Laurent, know women, and his clothes work very well for women." She claims that the fact that she is a woman influences the clothes she designs for women — and those she designs for men. She tries to make men look less conformist and to liberate them from fashion rules and codes.

Her view of fashion history recognizes the traditional importance of the female designer. "In the past, men were ashamed to make women's clothes; it was not really a respectable profession for men. It was really *women's* work. But now there are both men and women." She doesn't think that male designers outnumber female designers in France, but adds, "perhaps it is different in America and there are more men there?" The question of numbers is complicated by the fact that many women designers are known primarily in their own country.

Anne Marie Beretta's ideal woman is Katharine Hepburn, who

dressed in men's trousers and shirts—and made them look chic. Although her accessible, serious style might appeal to buyers across the Atlantic, her clothes are not widely sold there. In France Beretta is respected as an "architect of fashion," whose clothes are characterized by strong lines, well-structured shapes, and innovative cutting.

"What interests me is not to glorify a woman's body, but to lead her into feeling exalted," says Beretta. Like many other women designers, she notes that she wants her dresses "to be comfortable and wearable." And she insists, "I cannot make clothes that I would not wear." However, she adds, "I dress not only the body, but also the spirit, the mind." Her clothes are intended to express women's "mystery, dignity, and elegance." [21]

ABOVE: *Anne Marie Beretta, Tailored suit, Winter 1989–1990 collection. Photograph courtesy of Anne Marie Beretta.*

## SITBON PRETTY

Martine Sitbon has been called "France's best-kept fashion secret." [22] Although not yet well known in America, she is one of the hottest young designers working in Paris today and the only woman mentioned in the same breath as Jean-Paul Gaultier.

The daughter of a French businessman, Sitbon grew up in Casablanca and moved to Paris when she was an adolescent, but she frequently traveled to England, where she came into contact with the London music scene. On her first trip to New York, she became equally enamored of The New York Dolls and *les Velvets* (The Velvet Underground).

Sitbon admits that she "would have loved to have been in the music industry," and her clothes often rework the pop styles of the 1960s and 1970s. [23] But music is only one of many influences on her work. She also loves the designs of Balenciaga, Dior, and Schiaparelli.

In 1974 she graduated from the Studio Berçot, an avant-garde fashion school in Paris. After a decade spent free-lancing and traveling, she began designing her own line. Her 1986 "Cinderella" collection was followed by others, whose influences ranged from Alice in Wonderland to L.A. Hell's Angels. (Kenneth Anger's cult biker film, *Scorpio Rising*, was another influence.) She produced other collections based on Carnaby Street, Twiggy, psychedelic styles, and dandyism—often basing her clothes on masculine attire, even classic Savile Row tailoring.

"This is good French taste with a Barry White Beat," declared *i-D* magazine, praising her "hip-hugging Trashy seventies'" look. Because music is her first inspiration, the background music for her shows is especially revealing—whether it is the rock of the seventies, from the Kinks to The Velvet Underground, or soul—everything except heavy metal. What she likes about fashion, she says, is the energy.

In 1988 Sitbon was chosen as the new designer of ready-to-wear at Chloé (the company where Karl Lagerfeld first made his mark and that had been in the doldrums since he left in 1983). Sitbon's work for Chloé is relatively classic: dandyish evening suits rather than skin-tight panne velvet jeans. Her cutaway jackets, billowing bell-bottoms, doublets, and tights have caught the attention of the fashion world.

RIGHT: *Martine Sitbon,
Blouse with elaborate collar
and cuffs, Autumn 1990
collection. Photograph by
Roxanne Lowit.*

Sitbon's own collections are produced by Roberto Albini's Reflection, an Italian company that finances her use of rich fabrics like velvet and luxurious decoration, embroidery, and sequins. Her art director, boyfriend, and right hand is Marc Ascoli, who started the catalogue craze among avant-garde designers. Sitbon credits Ascoli with pushing her to do her own collections. In the fashion business "there is always the tendency to repress creativity in order to enter a kind of system," says Sitbon. "He encouraged me to be different and protected me from the pressure to assimilate."[24]

If there are relatively more women designers in London than in Paris, this

LEFT: *Martine Sitbon, Jacket and hat, Autumn 1990 collection. Photograph by Roxanne Lowit.*

reflects national differences in the fashion industry. In Great Britain there is a lively youth culture and several innovative design schools, which encourage the emergence of individual talents. On the other hand, there is little institutional support for these young designers, so many of them go out of business or (like Katharine Hamnett) move their base of operations to Europe. In France, there is tremendous institutional support, but it tends to be focused on the couture (which is still heavily male-dominated) and on the stars of ready-to-wear, most of whom are also men. Ironically, the great prestige of fashion in France has tended to work against women's participation at the highest levels.

# 14

# MILAN: ANGELS HAVE NO SEX

I n 1981 the Italian fashion designer Laura Biagiotti told journalist Daniela Petroff that she felt that "a woman designer faces the same odds as a woman trying to get a job as a 747 pilot." In fact, Petroff noted, the statistics indicated that "about 25 percent of today's Italian designing force is made up of women."[1] Today, Biagiotti thinks that female designers are on par with male counterparts.[2] Nevertheless, it is certainly true that most people think of Italian design in terms of male superstars like Giorgio Armani and Gianni Versace. Where do women fit in the picture?

### THE ROMAN SPRING OF FASHION

If we look at the history of Italian fashion, we find many outstanding women designers. Today, in addition to Biagiotti, there are the Fendi sisters, Mariuccia Mandelli of Krizia, Rosita Missoni, Mila Schön, and others. In the past the many distinguished female names included Albertina, Maria Antonelli, the Fontana sisters, and Simonetta.

There probably were relatively more women involved in Italian fashion a generation or two ago than there are today. The Italian fashion industry as a whole has evolved from its roots in couture (based in Rome) to deluxe ready-to-wear (based in Milan). The first generation of great Roman couturiers that emerged after World War II included many women. Both working-class and aristocratic women worked in fashion.

Maria Antonelli, for example, began her career as *la piccina*, the little girl who picks up pins and runs errands in a couture house. Born in Tus-

ABOVE: *Fontana sisters, Sketch for an evening dress, circa 1945–1950. Drawing by Antonio Pascali. Photograph courtesy of the Centro Studi e Archivo della Communicazione, Università di Parma.*

OPPOSITE: *Laura Biagiotti, Day dress, Spring/Summer 1983 collection, modeled by Paulina Porizkova. Photograph courtesy of Laura Biagiotti.*

ABOVE: *Fontana sisters,*
*Black lace and taffeta dress,*
*1957, worn by Ava Gardner.*
*Photograph courtesy of the*
*Neal Peters Collection.*

RIGHT: *Actress Ava Gardner*
*trying on a dress for her role*
*in* The Barefoot Contessa
*at the Fontana sisters' atelier,*
*1953. Photograph courtesy of*
*the Centro Studi e Archivo*
*della Communicazione,*
*Università di Parma*

cany in 1903, Antonelli opened her own dressmaking shop in Rome during
World War II. Over the years she dressed many famous actresses, from
Anna Magnani to Elizabeth Taylor.

The Fontana sisters — Zoe, Micol, and Giovanna, born respectively in
1911, 1913, and 1915 — served their apprenticeships in their mother's dressmaking shop in the 1930s, as well as sewing in the private atelier of an
aristocratic Roman lady. They then worked individually for several designers before opening their own establishment in Rome in 1943.

From the beginning they had many noble clients who were especially
eager to buy their exquisite evening dresses. Beginning in 1951, they also
showed their models in the United States. Perhaps most importantly, the
Fontana sisters dressed many film stars both on and off the screen. Ava
Gardner, for example, was dressed by the Fontana atelier for her role in the
1953 film, *The Barefoot Contessa.*

Within the Roman couture, women like the Fontana sisters shared the
spotlight with male couturiers like Emilio Schuberth. "The women who
were the star designers of the Italian fashion world of the past were very
talented, and they dressed even more distinguished personalities than the
ones that come to our boutiques nowadays," says Mariuccia Mandelli.
"They were very discreet about their work: It was considered more elegant
not to talk about it." But, she adds, they were still subject to the dominance
of French fashion. "Perhaps the male stylist such as Schuberth, who was
less discreet (a little like Lacroix nowadays) was more famous."[3]

Because the aristocracy had an intimate personal understanding of
couture fashion, it is perhaps not surprising that when poverty threatened,

members of the Italian nobility entered the world of fashion. "Dressmaking is a suitable employment opportunity," declared one Italian fashion magazine in 1949. "In Rome, four princesses, three countesses, and two marchionesses deal in fashion."[4]

Elsa Schiaparelli, of course, had established her couture house in Paris in the 1920s, as had Vera Borea, another upper-class Italian-born woman designer of the period. When Elvira Leonardi met Vera Borea at the Agnelli home in the early 1930s, Leonardi, too, was inspired to become a designer. The poet Gabriele D'Annunzio called her "Domina," but when she opened her Milan boutique she chose instead the name "Biki." Among those who have worn the Biki label were opera star Maria Callas and actress Sophia Loren.

Simonetta (Duchessa Simonetta Colonna di Cesaro), born in 1922 of Italian-Russian heritage, became a leading Roman designer in the 1940s, signing her first collections *Simonetta Visconti*, using the name of her first husband. In 1952 she married the designer Alberto Fabiani. They continued to maintain separate fashion establishments until 1962, when they moved to Paris and formed Simonetta et Fabiani. The transplant failed, Fabiani moved back to Rome, and within a few years Simonetta ceased designing and went on a pilgrimage to India, where she established a leper colony. In her heyday during the 1950s, however, Simonetta was recognized internationally, especially for her chic cocktail dresses.

The Princess Irene Galitzine, born in Russia in 1918, was another aristocrat who entered the world of fashion. After working briefly with the Fontana sisters, in 1946 she opened her own business, which relied creatively, however, on a changing roster of young designers. She was especially well known for her 1960 "Palazzo Pyjamas" — so named by Diana Vreeland.

## Italian Women Today

The Italian fashion world of today also boasts a number of women designers who are internationally famous. Among this second generation is Laura Biagiotti, whose mother owned a dressmaking establishment.

As a girl, Biagiotti accompanied her mother on trips to Paris to see the couture collections and later went to New York to get a sense of American tastes in fashion. This type of American connection was typical of the experience of many postwar Italian designers. After a stint producing ready-to-wear collections for several Roman couturiers, Biagiotti began to design under her own name in 1972.

A shrewd businesswoman, in 1981 Biagiotti told Daniela Petroff that she resented the fact that "there is always an air of diffidence when a woman assumes a role of responsibility."[5] As of 1991, however, Biagiotti felt that women encounter "more or less the same [situation] men have to face."

She believes that there are, moreover, certain advantages to being a woman. A woman designer knows "what kind of clothes a working woman needs," Biagiotti told Petroff. "I need them myself." The fact that she is a

TOP: *Maria Antonelli, Sketch for a pink and white evening dress, circa 1950–1955. Drawing by Antonio Pascali. Photograph courtesy of the Centro Studi e Archivo della Communicazione, Università di Parma.*

ABOVE: *Simonetta, Sketch for a pink cocktail dress, Autumn 1960 collection. Drawing executed for Bergdorf Goodman, New York. Photograph courtesy of Special Collections, The Fashion Institute of Technology Library, New York.*

BELOW: *Laura Biagiotti. Photograph by Dick Ballarian, courtesy of Laura Biagiotti.*

TOP: *Designer Laura Biagiotti and models in China, 1988. Photograph courtesy of Laura Biagiotti.*

ABOVE: *Laura Biagiotti, Jacket, skirt, top, and hat, Spring/Summer 1991 collection. Photograph by Marco Glaviano, courtesy of Laura Biagiotti.*

woman certainly does affect her designs, she added a decade later: "My fashion reflects my way of being a woman, and I project and filter my vision of the contemporary world through my designs. I try to build my fashion through short stories that speak of myself, that transmit my passion to others as well."

Biagiotti is known as the Queen of Cashmere. She speaks of "my love story with cashmere and linen, my favorite materials." She is also noted for what she calls her "passion for white, the color of purity, of tradition, and of femininity, by which I have always been inspired."

"Elegance, taste, and creativity have belonged to the Italian tradition and character for centuries," says Biagiotti, "and I share this privilege with all other Italian designers." This historical and cultural link is symbolically expressed by her headquarters in the Roman castle of Marco Simone, where she has also exhibited opera costumes.

The five Fendi sisters—Paola, Anna, Franca, Carla, and Alda—have been described as a "solid matriarchy" and as the "empresses of Roman fashion." They inherited a leather business begun by their mother, Adele Fendi, in 1925. After she married, Adele and her husband, Edoardo Fendi, worked together; and, after Adele was widowed, her daughters, then students, joined the business and expanded into furs.

"Mamma had to fall back on us, and she was sorry to do that," Carla says. "We were still girls, and were studying, and anyway she liked to think of us as just being housewives. For us, on the other hand, it was natural to start working with Mamma, but once we found ourselves there in the firm, we felt we wanted to do something of our own. It wasn't easy, you can imagine: We were young, and women, and the fur industry has always been dominated by men."[6]

Today all of the sisters are married, and with the exception of Anna's husband, who is a doctor, all of their husbands and seven of their children work with them. "Without love, the kind of love you find in a family, you can't succeed," says Carla Fendi. They also had the foresight to hire Karl Lagerfeld as their principal designer. Yet, as Carla adds, all of their designs, from handbags to furs, are consciously created to suit "women like us, people who work."[7]

## KRIZIA

Perhaps the most striking figure in Italian fashion is Mariuccia Mandelli, the founder of Krizia. Her career began in 1950, when she was a primary-school teacher who was interested in dressmaking. Together with a friend, Flora Dolci, she began designing clothes, mostly skirts at first, and selling them to shops.

Mandelli named her fashion company Krizia, after Plato's dialogue on women's vanity. But she wants to make it clear that she believes that "men are as vain as women." When she founded the company in 1954, she explains, "it wasn't common to name your collection after your first and last name." Instead, many Italians used "references to French fashion," but that

LEFT: *The Fendi sisters (from left): Anna, Franca, Paola, Carla, and Alda. Photograph courtesy of Fendi.*

was something she wanted to avoid. She recalls that "I remembered from my school days the name of a man, a Greek man, who had gone broke because of women. By naming my company after him, I hoped to find many others like him."

This witty, irreverent approach epitomizes Mandelli's approach to clothes. In 1957, when she first presented a collection to the public, the clothes were made of fabric printed with large fruits. As fashion historian Colin McDowell wrote about her designs, "Their humor frequently makes one smile with pleasure, a rare and welcome thing with fashion."[8]

Mandelli herself says that "women's clothes are more witty and amusing simply because there is more freedom and an increased willingness to accept changes just for the fun of it. A man usually does not like to provoke fun." But she quickly emphasizes that "a sense of wit is not an exclusively feminine characteristic." And although she admires the madcap Schiaparelli, Mandelli says that she has been more influenced by Balenciaga and the Art Deco artist Erté. "If I have to name a woman," she says, "I admire more Chanel for her clean look [and] the easiness of her clothes."

When she first began designing, the Italian fashion industry was in a period of transition, as the first ready-to-wear shows were being staged at the Pitti Palace in Florence. It was the Indian summer of the Roman couture, and the giant Milanese fashion conglomerates had not yet been born.

"Little dressmakers were disappearing," Mandelli has recalled, "and the demand for something ready-made began to be felt." Within a few years, however, Florence began to seem stifling — with its "inferiority complex with regard to France," and with American buyers snapping up clothes and putting their own labels inside — so Mandelli shifted to Milan, and per-

TOP: *Fendi, Wool crepe suit with satin piping, Autumn/Winter 1990–1991. Photograph courtesy of Fendi.*

ABOVE: *Mariuccia Mandelli for Krizia, Animal sweaters, Spring/Summer 1989 collection. Photograph courtesy of Krizia.*

suaded others, such as the Missonis, to go, too. Once in Milan, she mediated between designers and industrialists.[9]

Inspired, she says, by a "love of freedom" and a "sense of irony," Mandelli stresses a "practical, balanced, and rational" style of dressing. "Being a woman helped me in the sense that I have a deeper and more direct knowledge of a woman's life-style, all her roles and problems," she says. But she insists that "Armani, Ferré, and Versace are equally sensitive to feminine styles, in their own ways."

Among other women designers working today, she especially admires Cinzia Ruggeri, whom she describes as "a true artist," and Laura Biagiotti, "a creative woman who is also a good manager with a feeling for precious fabrics," as well as Enrica Massei, Muriel Grateaux, and the Sanlorenzo sisters, "who should be more well known." But she adds, "I still maintain that nowadays we should not make these distinctions" [between male and female designers].

Mandelli insists that "creative people are like angels: They do not have a sexual identification. Or perhaps they have it in their privacy, but this is beside the point." A good designer may be a man or a woman, she says, just as "there are both men and women in all professions, from architecture to law, and even as head of state."

Mandelli is head of design at Krizia. Among her team, her first assistant is Anna Domenici, whom Mandelli calls her "right-hand," and who has been with her for more than twenty years. Rosella Mauri is another assistant. Mandelli's husband, Aldo Pinto, is her business manager. "Of course, from a business point of view, I owe it all to my husband," she says, while also admitting that she is a "perfectionist . . . who wants to know everything about her company — even about the administration."

"To be successful in the fashion world," she concludes, "you must have talent and an innate passion — and in my case, an incredible stubbornness — and the capacity to love one's work to the point of transforming it into a game for adults. How can you avoid playing with the toy you love the most?"

Mandelli tends to socialize with people from the film and publishing industries, rather than with aristocrats. And many of her designs are explicitly experimental and artistic, rather than simply pretty evening dresses. Back in 1981, for example, she created an extraordinary pleated jumpsuit, which was subsequently included in an exhibition on "Intimate Architecture" at the Massachusetts Institute of Technology — not the usual venue for fashion.

"This is an example of how geometric expression, the architecture of an outfit, can be combined with the feeling of freedom," explains Mandelli. When the wearer moves, the clothing moves also in wavelike forms. "There is often a sense of architecture in my clothing; in fact, one of my collections was inspired by the Chrysler Building." But this sartorial architecture "should never be rigid," says Mandelli. "It must allow the maximum freedom of movement."

If fashion connoisseurs are attracted by avant-garde design experiments, the general public loves best Krizia's famous animal sweaters, which

feature a new animal every year. "Many years ago, Agnona, the famous producers of precious woolen fabrics, called me for a photo session to design a few pieces," recalls Mandelli. The result was a sweater decorated with a sheep, to promote the use of wool. It was so popular that Mandelli followed it with a cat, "then the ferocious wild beasts, the felines which I have always loved, and so forth. Year after year it was like a game that continued because of the clients' requests. The irony is that I am afraid of a simple fly, and I now find myself surrounded by an entire zoo."

In her book *The Italian Look Reflected*, Silvia Giacomoni observed that Mandelli is sometimes known in Italian press as "Crazy Krizia" because she sometimes presents herself as a neurotic, moody person, who is "never content with what she's done." But as Giacomoni puts it, "being neurotic means she's on the same wavelength as the public." And besides, when it comes down to the facts, "of the Italian fashion designers it is she who has met with international success for longest, she who has done most to reinforce the Italy image."[10]

"I would be ashamed to dictate to women that they should dress in this or that style under the pretext that this is fashionable," Mandelli once told a French journalist. "Each should dress in her own way, so that whatever she chooses becomes like a second skin."[11]

ABOVE LEFT: *Mariuccia Mandelli for Krizia, Two evening dresses, Autumn/ Winter 1990–1991 collection. Photograph courtesy of Maria Chandoha Valentino.*

ABOVE: *Mariuccia Mandelli for Krizia, Evening dress with ornamental bodice, Autumn/ Winter 1990–1991 collection. Photograph courtesy of Maria Chandoha Valentino.*

# 15
# MADRID: WILD CHILD

ABOVE: *Spanish fashion designer Sybilla. Photograph by Juan Carlos Retama, courtesy of Sybilla.*

OPPOSITE: *Sybilla, Raincoat dress and umbrella, Autumn/Winter 1988–1989 collection. Photograph by Javier Vallhonrat, courtesy of Sybilla.*

Until the 1980s Spain was nearly invisible on the fashion scene. There were no Spanish designers, male or female, with international reputations, nor had there been since Balenciaga. Most well-dressed Spaniards bought their clothes abroad. Elsewhere, a Spanish label in clothes was more likely to be seen as a sign of cheap workmanship than of interesting design. On the other hand, says the designer Sybilla, the very lack of a fashion system, combined with a new spirit among young Spaniards, meant that "everything was much freer."[1]

## SYBILLA

"I didn't speak when I was young, so I used to dress up," says Sybilla. "I had a terrible problem communicating, but I always felt I would be able to find my friends and my boyfriends with my clothes, which would be like a flag, with which I could call out my ideas and feelings."

A shy, beautiful girl from a wealthy bohemian family, Sybilla is the hottest fashion news to come out of Spain since Balenciaga. She creates what she herself calls "weird and outrageous designs" — whimsical dresses that are draped and knotted, sculpted dresses with wired hems.

"Fashion's child prodigy"[2] was born in 1963 in New York City, the child of an Argentine diplomat and an aristocratic Polish mother who worked as a fashion designer under the name "Countess Sybilla of Saks Fifth Avenue." When she was seven years old her family moved to Madrid, where she lives and works today. Although she frequently visits New York,

Sybilla considers herself thoroughly Spanish, and it annoys her when journalists describe her as an American designer. Even her clothes, she says, are very Spanish, not the stereotype of Spain, "not *olé, olé*," but in the refined and classical sense of Spain.

When she was seventeen she apprenticed as a cutter and seamstress at Saint Laurent's couture atelier. But Paris taught her "what [she] didn't want to do." "In France," she says, "fashion is snobbish, cold and professional. Paris scares me. 'Fashion' is too serious. In Spain, you can still play."[3]

"I was very lucky that I started working in Spain," she notes. "In any other country, a young person would never have had the chance to do what I've done. If I had been French, I would still be waiting. But in Spain, people are not so logical, they are more emotional, so people believed in me — even though it wasn't logical that they should believe in me and help me."

Spain was in the midst of a cultural renaissance when Sybilla began designing, and she felt that "every day away from Madrid I was missing something important. We were the first generation after Franco died," says Sybilla, "and we tried to be different and personal and creative."

At first Sybilla created made-to-measure shirts and dresses, unique pieces for herself and her friends. "It was utopian," she admits — an extension of the years when she "looked through the flea markets of the world to find the pieces with which I could express what I felt."

"I always hated sewing," she confides, suddenly. "I was kicked out of my sewing classes at school, because I was kind of boyish, I was only interested in politics. I only really learned to sew when I went to Paris. Now I'm doing a lot of things that I learned in Paris that I didn't want to do."

Specifically, she went into mass production. In 1987 the Italian fashion company Gibo offered to provide financial backing if Sybilla produced and showed her collections in Milan. She continues to work in her studio in Madrid, making the prototypes that are later mass produced in Florence.[5] Initially, she found the commercial set-up "asphyxiating, but little by little I started to enjoy the notion that people unknown to me could wear the clothes." Now she is trying to make "the Industrial Revolution in reverse," to turn a factory "into a massive couture workshop." Sybilla says, "Even the seamstresses in the factory appreciate this. Although it's harder work, it's more personal, because they've got the responsibility for what they're doing. It's not assembly line, like cars." She does not create for a particular type of woman; on the contrary, she wants her clothes to be malleable and multiple expressions of the women who wear them. "I'm like the furniture dealer," she told American *Vogue*. "I sell the pieces, but the women do the interior design."[4]

"Being a woman," notes Sybilla, "I'm very aware of small details, the way clothes feel. I'm more into sensuality than sexuality. I try on all of the clothes I do. I'm very aware of the body. Clothes always make the body more beautiful." She wants her clothes to be about "seduction, comfort, laughs." She adds:

TOP: *Sybilla, Travelling clothes, Autumn/Winter 1988–1989 collection. Photograph by Javier Vallhonrat, courtesy of Sybilla.*

ABOVE: *Sybilla, Coats and rucksack, Autumn/Winter 1990–1991 collection. Photograph courtesy of Maria Chandoha Valentino.*

I work very hard on colors, which may have something to do with being a woman. I think very much about how color affects the way you feel. I look at women, and I wonder: Why do we have this tendency to dress in black? It's too easy, discreet, you're always okay. I work with colors to try to get the same easy wearing as black, but also with the feeling you get when you wear red or yellow. And the calm that a blue dress gives you, like bluejeans. I try to make happy or sensual colors, creating, for example, a red dress that has the same easy wearing as a black dress that you can put on at eight in the morning when you feel terrible, but it has the same warmth and sensuality of a red dress that you wear when you're ready to eat the whole world!

# 16
# TOKYO: LIKE THE BOYS

Japan "is still a male-centered society," Rei Kawakubo told *Women's Wear Daily* in 1983. "Women say it's hard if you're a woman. But if you know what you really want to do . . . then it is not difficult."[1]

ABOVE: *Rei Kawakubo for Comme des Garçons, Geometric wool coat, from the Wrapped collection, Autumn/Winter 1983–1984. Photograph by Hans Feurer for Comme des Garçons Co., Ltd.*

OPPOSITE: *Rei Kawakubo, "Lace" sweater and cotton jersey padded skirt, Autumn/Winter 1982–1983 collection. The designer's "ripped" clothes were especially controversial. Photograph by Peter Lindbergh for Comme des Garçons Co., Ltd.*

### REI KAWAKUBO

Rei Kawakubo, the creator of Comme des Garçons, is widely regarded as one of the most important avant-garde fashion designers working today. In an article entitled "Feminist versus Sexist," the London *Times* correspondent Suzy Menkes described the sensational effect of Kawakubo's Spring 1983 Comme des Garçons collection: "Down the catwalk, marching to a rhythmic beat like a race of warrior women, came models wearing ink-black coat dresses, cut big, square, away from the body with no line, form, or recognizable silhouette." While admitting that she was "intellectually with the Japanese in their search for clothing that owes nothing to outworn concepts of femininity," Menkes nevertheless felt that the French "can have my body to dress."[2]

When *Vogue* featured Kawakubo's clothes in 1983, an outraged reader demanded to know why anyone would want to pay $230 for "a torn . . . shroud."[3] Women wearing avant-garde Japanese clothes looked completely different than those in European or American fashions, and most observers initially recoiled in horror from a style that so thoroughly rejected the traditional ideal of sexy and pretty femininity. Hostile or bewildered journalists described the look in funereal or atomic terms, as resembling "a bedrag-

TOP: *Rei Kawakubo, Washed cotton elastic dress, Spring/Summer 1983 collection. Photograph by Peter Lindbergh for Comme des Garçons Co., Ltd.*

ABOVE: *Rei Kawakubo, Bonded cotton stretch jersey dress, Autumn/Winter 1986–1987 collection. Photograph by Steven Meisel for Comme des Garçons Co., Ltd.*

RIGHT: *Rei Kawakubo, Patchwork wool knit sweater dress, Autumn/Winter 1984–1985 collection. Photograph by Peter Lindbergh for Comme des Garçons Co., Ltd.*

gled shroud" or a "nuclear bag lady." As one writer put it: "The dread and hopelessness that pervade so many of the recent clothes by Japanese designers, notably Rei Kawakubo, are nowhere to be found in Saint Laurent's collections. . . . The woman who wears Comme des Garçons (Kawakubo's label) is . . . unwilling to dress herself up so that other people have something pleasing to look at . . ."[4]

Even the trivial fact that Kawakubo herself wore no makeup seemed strange to many fashion journalists. The English fashion editor Geraldine Ranson recalls that she "had been told in Tokyo that Rei Kawakubo was a tough feminist." But Kawakubo dismissed her critics, saying, "Most men don't like women who are capable of working hard. They do not like strong, independent women. So why should they like clothing that is not cute or soft, that doesn't fit a man's image of a woman?"[5]

Kawakubo has said that she believes that "the goal for [every woman] should be to make her own living and to support herself, to be self-sufficient." This, she says, is the "philosophy" of her clothes: "They are working for modern women. Women who do not need to assure their happiness by looking sexy to men, by emphasizing their figures, but who attract them with their minds." This "dream of anonymous self-sufficiency" has been Kawakubo's ideal since childhood.[6]

Kawakubo was born in 1942, the daughter of a professor at Tokyo's prestigious Keio University. In 1964 she graduated from Keio with a degree

ABOVE: *Rei Kawakubo, Menswear for Comme des Garçons Homme Plus, Autumn/Winter 1985–1986 collection. Photograph by Arthur Elgort for Comme des Garçons Co., Ltd.*

LEFT: *Rei Kawakubo, Silk organdy blouse and multi-layered silk organdy and silk georgette pants, Spring/ Summer 1989 collection. Photograph by Peter Lindbergh for* Six 3, 1989, *published by Comme des Garçons Co., Ltd.*

ABOVE: *Rei Kawakubo, Wool gabardine wrap jacket, asymmetrical wool flannel plaid skirt, and straight wool skirt, Autumn/Winter 1986–1987 collection. Photograph by Peter Lindbergh for Comme des Garçons Co., Ltd.*

in Aesthetics. Without any clear sense of direction, she began working in the advertising department of a manufacturer of acrylic fibers. "I was at the bottom of the ladder," she recalled, "but the boss was a man who, unusually, believed in allowing women to make a full contribution."[7]

Kawakubo thus came into contact with many people in the fashion world, including a woman named Atsuko Kozasu, who is now a fashion journalist and editor. When Kawakubo got "a new boss with less enlightened ideas," Kozasu encouraged her to try to work free-lance as a stylist. When she could not find the clothes she wanted, Kawakubo moved into fashion design, founding her own company in 1973.

*Comme des Garçons* is the name that Rei Kawakubo chose for her fashion company. Foreign words are popular in Japan, and Kawakubo has said that she simply liked the sound of the French phrase. But the term also implicitly signifies that henceforth women would be more "like the boys," in clothes whose muted colors and abstract forms recalled the sobriety of menswear.

The fact that the new Japanese clothes tended to be big and loose rather than body-hugging led some observers (such as France's Sonia Rykiel) to argue that the Japanese must be "afraid of the body."[8] But puritanism is not a part of Japanese culture. "I do not find clothes that reveal the body attractive," Kawakubo told *Vogue*, thus challenging the entire idea of "sexiness" in women's clothes.[9]

Although people have often found her work shocking, it has never been Kawakubo's intention deliberately to shock. Indeed, her infamous ripped sweater, for example, which she calls a "lace" sweater, is now in the clothing collection of the Victoria & Albert Museum and is justifiably recognized as an important development in twentieth-century style.

What, then, did it mean when Kawakubo designed a sweater so pockmarked with holes that it looked as though moths had all but devoured it? The seemingly random pattern of holes were the result of careful thought and technology. According to Kawakubo, "The machines that make fabric are more and more making uniform, flawless textures. I like it when something is *off*—not perfect. Handweaving is the best way to achieve this. Since this isn't always possible, we loosen a screw of the machines here and there so they can't do exactly what they're supposed to do."[10]

Irregularity, imperfection, and asymmetry are important elements in traditional Japanese aesthetic philosophy. And although Kawakubo is the quintessential modernist designer, fashion scholar Harold Koda has suggested that she has been influenced by a thousand-year-old canon of aesthetics according to which there is a beauty in poverty and simplicity no less than in richness and ornamentation. Imperfection itself can add to an object's beauty, because it reminds us of the frailty and transitory nature of things—and beauty is most heartbreakingly beautiful when we perceive how quickly it passes. As Koda has observed, the aesthetic and conceptual meaning of the "rips" in Kawakubo's sweater differs significantly from the political and satiric meaning of the ripped and oversized "poor look" that simultaneously emerged as an element of London street fashion, which Vivienne Westwood made famous.[11]

LEFT: *Rei Kawakubo, Four-layered nylon milanese skirt, Spring/Summer 1990 collection. Photograph by Peter Lindbergh for* Six 5, *1990, published by Comme des Garçons Co., Ltd.*

The overwhelming inky *blackness* of Kawakubo's clothes seemed especially depressing or ominous to many fashion journalists. "I always felt very comfortable with the color black," Kawakubo said.[12] On another occasion, she noted, "I work in three shades of black."[13] In retrospect, this absence of color, initially indebted to bohemian black, seems to have heralded a decade-long international love affair with black clothes that is only now beginning to wind down.

In 1988, with the cryptic aplomb of a conceptual artist, Kawakubo declared that "red is black." And she showed black jackets slashed under the arms to reveal brilliant red blouses. In her 1989 collection, she showed sugar-pink, apple-green, and sky-blue chiffon and organdy blouses and trousers of extraordinary beauty.

Over the years her shapeless garments have given way to clothes that fall somewhat closer to the body or that juxtapose tailored and draped elements. Yet, as she told *Women's Wear Daily* in 1983, she still wants to make "clothes where the body can move freely."[14]

Kawakubo continues to explore the possibility of new forms, in conjunction with her team of pattern makers: Must a garment have only two sleeves, for example, or could it not have multiple openings? Her "Elastic" and "Wrapped" collections of 1983 suggested that clothing could be worn in a variety of ways.

"I start from zero," Kawakubo has said. Beginning with the thread itself and working outside the Western fashion tradition, she has rethought the entire appearance and construction of clothes. Kawakubo admires the pioneering modernists in design and architecture, people like Le Corbusier, and there is a similar purism in her approach to fashion. "The austerity of Kawakubo's fashion design puts her work firmly in the avant-garde camp," writes Deyan Sudjic, the author of a recent monograph on Kawakubo.[15]

Kawakubo's "delight . . . in the shock of the new" also embraces the most advanced textile and dyeing technology. As Sudjic points out, her close collaboration with textile manufacturers has resulted in such new fabrics as "the rayon crisscrossed with elastic that allowed Kawakubo to make the garments in the women's collection of 1984 bubble and boil as though they were melting." Her "Bonded" dress of 1986 bonds cotton, rayon and polyurethane to produce an abstract shape.

For those willing to explore her dramatically different approach to fashion, Kawakubo's clothes came with the force of revelation. Her supporters (and there have been more and more of them) believe that the Japanese look is "the supreme modern style" that finally succeeded in yanking fashion away from nostalgia.[16] Kawakubo has created a strong new image for the new woman of today.

The 1987 exhibition "Three Women," held at New York's Fashion Institute of Technology, presented Kawakubo, alone among contemporary women designers, in the company of fashion icons Madeleine Vionnet and Claire McCardell. "These women make clothes that make women," declared the catalogue text by curators Richard Martin, Harold Koda, and Laura Sinderbrand. "[They] make clothes that foster a new intelligence and new directions in apparel. Their analytical considerations of construction, of the body, and of the social role of women were and are brave and abiding ideas about fashion."[17] The curators gave Kawakubo carte blanche to design a large exhibition space devoted to her clothes for women.

Yet even this major exhibit did not encompass the totality of her work, since Kawakubo also designs clothes for men. And she is closely involved in the design of her stores around the world, her fashion photographs, and her publication-catalogue, *Six*. Moreover, unlike many designers, she is president of her own company of 450 employees and makes business as well as creative decisions.

Although her innovative designs were initially regarded as extremely weird and controversial, over the years she has come to be recognized as one of the most important creators in the field of fashion design — someone who gives the avant-garde a good name.

"I am not happy to be classified as another Japanese designer," Kawakubo told *Women's Wear Daily* in 1983. "There is no one characteristic that all Japanese designers have. . . . What I do is not influenced by what's happened before in fashion or by a community cultural influence."[18] Of course, she has a point: She is a unique individual and an international fashion power. But from the historian's point of view it is also significant that she is Japanese — and a Japanese woman, at that.

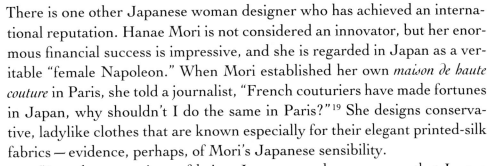

## HANAE MORI

There is one other Japanese woman designer who has achieved an international reputation. Hanae Mori is not considered an innovator, but her enormous financial success is impressive, and she is regarded in Japan as a veritable "female Napoleon." When Mori established her own *maison de haute couture* in Paris, she told a journalist, "French couturiers have made fortunes in Japan, why shouldn't I do the same in Paris?"[19] She designs conservative, ladylike clothes that are known especially for their elegant printed-silk fabrics — evidence, perhaps, of Mori's Japanese sensibility.

"I am less conscious of being Japanese and more aware that I am a woman," Mori told another Parisian journalist. "It helps me be in touch with other women and create dresses for those leading full and active lives.[20] There *is* a difference between the work of male and female designers," she says.[21] "Men create fashion to please their own eye, what they like to look at, how they like a woman to appear. A woman creates from what makes her feel good within. I am closer to a woman's sensibilities. I can relate to how she wants her clothes to make her feel, what is easy for her life-style." In the past, she admits, "women may have tended to follow men's opinions." But, she adds, "as it becomes easier for women in business, I think the number of female couturiers is increasing. I hope my career and life will tell that a woman can have a full, complete life — with work and with family."

Mori's independence was encouraged by her father, a doctor, who wanted her to study medicine. Most middle-class Japanese wives do not work, but after Hanae's marriage to Ken Mori he supported his wife's ambitions — and since he was in the textile business, his support has always been instrumental. "You know," she said, "my husband was the son of a remarkable and very feminist mother." Today Hanae Mori's sons, Kei and Akira, work in the family business, but mother and sons agree that Ken Mori is "our true boss — he talks to the bankers!"[22]

# 17
# NEW YORK: CLOSING THE GENDER GAP

"Increasingly, talented female designers are coming into their own — both in creative and marketing terms," declared fashion writer June Weir in a 1985 article, "Closing the Gender Gap." She went on to note that whereas "a decade ago there were only a handful [of women designers], now their ranks seem to be multiplying daily," and that "women designers are becoming successful and influential forces in the American fashion market."[1]

### PRIMA DONNA

ABOVE: *Donna Karan, Washed-silk chemise dress and "stuffed" swing coat, Spring 1990 collection, modeled by Paulina Porizkova. Photograph courtesy of Donna Karan.*

OPPOSITE: *Donna Karan for DKNY, Shawl-collared wool blanket coat, wool cardigan sweater, paisley wool-challis scarf, leather shoulder bag, and sunglasses, Autumn 1990 collection. Photograph by Peter Arnell, courtesy of Arnell/Bickford Associates and Donna Karan.*

Donna Karan is probably the most famous woman designer in America today — in the same league with men like Ralph Lauren and Calvin Klein. "A kid from Queens is now Queen of Seventh Avenue," boasted *Vogue* in 1989, adding that "Karan's professional rise has a lot to do with the current rise of 'fortysomething' female executives, like herself, who want to look pulled together but not prim."[2]

At a time when the strict, man-tailored Dress for Success look was getting tired, and when executive women no longer felt so much pressure to look like men, Karan developed a sophisticated, sensual alternative to the business suit. Based on her own experience, Karan suspected that women would appreciate a system of dressing that was as easy as menswear, while also retaining the comfort and sensuality of clothes to fit a woman's body.

"Yes, women's clothes should be almost like men's," Karan says, but they should be more "comfortable . . . sensual," and — a favorite word —

ABOVE: *Donna Karan, Silk body-blouse and wool crepe jersey skirt, Autumn 1988 collection. Photograph by Roxanne Lowit.*

RIGHT: *Donna Karan, Cashmere velour jacket and cashmere-and-Lycra turtleneck bodysuit, important belt, jewelry, and gloves, Autumn 1988 collection, modeled by Iman. Photograph by Roxanne Lowit.*

"womanly."[3] She is not referring to "femininity" or "*la vraie femme*," however, but rather something more in line with contemporary American attitudes.

"I'm a woman," Karan has said, in interview after interview. "I'm a female designer. I understand women."[4] She elaborates: "I'm a very busy working woman and mother. The last thing I have time to do is worry about my clothes."[5]

Behind Karan's meteoric rise is a long struggle. Both the struggle and the success say something about women's role in fashion. Her parents were involved in the fashion industry and, as a child, Karan was "bitter because my mother was one of the only working women."[6] She felt happier when,

at the age of fourteen, she began working part time herself, as a salesgirl in a boutique. She also began designing, using her own body to make the patterns.

Karan attended Parsons but dropped out to work as an assistant to Anne Klein, the influential sportswear designer who pioneered the concept of tailored separates. "Anne Klein was a woman who understood women," says Karan. "I was in awe of her, she was such an innovator."[7] Later, building on Klein's approach to classic sportswear, Karan would make her own mark.

But as an insecure teenage "gofer," Karan felt that she was never "good enough [to] please Anne."[8] After nine months, Klein fired her. According to Klein's widower, Karan was "distracted" by a romance with boutique owner Mark Karan and was "not pulling her weight."[9] The break was traumatic for Karan: "I never got over the blow of losing my job with Anne." Karan worked briefly with another sportswear designer, Patti Capalli.

But when they went on a business trip to Europe, Karan suddenly felt that "I saw my whole life ahead of me as a mad woman designer and I decided I had to have something else. Mark . . . came to the airport when I got home. We were married three days later."[10] Then she called Klein and asked for her job back. She was rehired in 1968, and by 1971 she was named associate designer at Anne Klein.

Nevertheless, Karan intended to leave her job in 1974, after she became pregnant. As she told one journalist, "Anne was a very demanding woman, and I didn't think I could work like that once I had a child. Being a working mother isn't exactly easy."[11] But Anne Klein became seriously ill, and Karan kept working.

Her colleague, Julius Stern, a veteran of the garment industry, recalls the day that Karan's daughter, Gaby, was born: "She called me up at five in the morning, and she said, 'Julie, I'm going into labor. Could you come over?' So I said, 'If you're going into labor, your husband is there, what do

you need me for?' But she said she wanted to give me notes for the office. So I got there at 6:00 a.m., and she was holding onto a chair timing her contractions. In between she was giving me notes about the clothes. I said to Donna, 'This is not for me. I wanna get out of here!'"[12]

According to Karan, the office kept calling. "They wanted to know when I was coming back to work. I said, 'You're kidding. There's no way. The doctor won't let me!'" Then, just five days after Karan gave birth, Klein died. Although she felt "terribly guilty about . . . leaving Gaby," the twenty-six-year-old Karan became head designer at the company, along with Louis Dell'Olio.[13]

Karan sometimes felt ambivalent about working under another woman's name, especially when people outside the industry assumed that *she* was Klein or asked, "Did Anne design it?"[14] This was especially ironic since Karan and Dell'Olio were changing the Anne Klein look, making it more sophisticated. "What happened to that suburban woman who used to be the Anne Klein customer?" asked Karan. "She moved to the city. She got a job." Indeed, soon the Anne Klein woman was "everywhere," and Karan felt she "didn't want to see everyone wearing my clothes. I was losing my identity."[15] "Donna aimed at a more personalized collection," agreed Dell'Olio.[16]

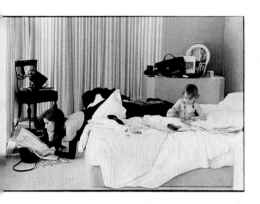

ABOVE: *Donna Karan, Lycra unitard, Autumn 1988 collection. Photograph by Dennis Piel, courtesy of Arnell/Bickford Associates and Donna Karan.*

In 1985 Karan launched her own company, designing what she described as a set of clothes "for myself and a few friends."[17] Since then, her success has been astronomical. By eschewing the design fantasies that characterize most feminine clothes, Karan created a sort of uniform that appealed strongly to successful working women. Not only is Karan a woman designing for other working women like herself, she's also "the size of more women than Carolyne Roehm or Carolina Herrera is," as the late Nina Hyde pointed out.[18] "I'm a woman with a rounded figure," admits Karan. "I'm not a model size 8. I won't design clothes that can't be worn by a woman who is a size 12 or 14."[19] This is another factor in Karan's success: "I'm dealing with the fallibility of a woman's body," she insists.[20] Industry professionals like Kal Ruttenstein of Bloomingdale's qualify this slightly: "You need a good body — not a perfect body — to wear [her clothes]."[21]

In 1989 she launched a less expensive line, DKNY (Donna Karan New York) which is aimed at a younger, less affluent market. She's "hot and getting hotter," crowed *Women's Wear Daily* in 1989.[22] In the 1970s Karan was "approached to write a book like *Dress for Success*." But as she said then,

I believe that a woman's professional clothes have to come from the *inside out*. The clothes are never going to make the woman. . . . But I guarantee you that if a woman's together, she's going to know enough about herself to look outta sight! . . . And when you have an assurance about yourself, honey, you can walk into any room and command anything. But you've got to work at it. It *doesn't* come easily.[23]

Karan has been called the archetypal New Yorker — fast, loud, funny, bright, egotistical.[24] But her frantic activity goes beyond the norm even for

New York's fast lane. And conflicts and compromises remain part of Karan's life. Interviews with her over the past fifteen years reveal a woman apparently obsessed with the mother-child relationship. "Until the day I die I will be a guilty mother," she told *Women's Wear Daily*, admitting that she spoiled daughter Gaby because she was so seldom at home with her.[25] Shortly before launching DKNY, Karan told her husband that she wanted to have another child. He said that she had to choose between a baby and a major new line. She was much too busy to do both, especially as she is also designing hosiery and jewelry and says that she is "dying to do menswear."

Yet even Karan's neuroses are in tune with those of her contemporaries. When her advertisements showed a successful executive woman in a cluttered bedroom with a baby about to scribble on her Filofax, millions of working women seemed to have felt a sense of identification. As fashion journalist Georgina Howell has observed, Karan's advertising campaign features an idealized version of the designer's life.[26]

## "Big-Time Femininity"

If Donna Karan is the Queen of Seventh Avenue, Carolyne Roehm epitomizes what might be called Uptown high-society fashion. "Feminism?" Karan says in response to a reporter's question. "I live it."[27] But Roehm admits to be annoyed by "this whole feminism thing — it's so 1970s."[28]

"Femininity was a big factor in my life," says Roehm, "and so I was attracted to Oscar de la Renta because he made very lovely, feminine clothes. Otherwise, I would have gone to Calvin Klein and learned about sportswear." During the ten years she worked as an assistant to the man *Women's Wear Daily* calls "Oscar de l'Amour,"[29] Roehm's innate fascination with "pretty, little-girl feminine things" developed into an understanding of what she calls "big-time femininity."

She was born plain Jane Caroline Smith, the only child of schoolteachers from Missouri. At age twenty-three, after studying fashion design at Washington University, she came to New York, and spent a year designing polyester sportswear for Sears. She had her first breakthrough when Oscar de la Renta hired her. "She had a good personality," he later told reporter Jesse Kornbluth. "She was a real woman."[30] Oscar and his wife, Françoise (the former editor in chief of French *Vogue*), became like Roehm's second parents, she says. They "taught me a more sophisticated, adult sense of luxury." A frequent dinner guest in their home, Roehm was introduced to a wealthy cosmopolitan style of life, which she herself now epitomizes.

Her own name also changed: From Caroline Smith to Carolyne Roehm. In 1978 she married Axel Roehm, heir to a German chemical fortune, and moved to Europe. Less than a year later, however, she called de la Renta to say that the marriage was not working. He offered her a job designing Miss O, his less expensive line, and she returned to New York to resume work.

In 1985, she was able to launch her own company, financed by more than $1 million from her fiancé, Wall Street financier Henry Kravis. "Henry

ABOVE: *Carolyne Roehm lives the kind of life for which she designs. Photograph courtesy of Carolyne Roehm.*

RIGHT: *Carolyne Roehm, Wedding dress, Autumn 1990 collection. Photograph by Roxanne Lowit.*

told me, 'Carolyne, I may be in love with you, but I'm not going to throw money away.'"[31]

Roehm learned a great deal during her years working with de la Renta. In style and attitude, however, she has asserted her independence. She recalls:

Oscar said to me once, "The trouble with women designers is that they are not objective. Women designers have a tendency to dress themselves." And that's absolutely true, but I think it's also a little oversimplified. Frankly, I'm enough of a businesswoman to know that I can't just dress myself, because not every woman in the world has my body.

I think women designers do personalize, and we may not have the objectivity of men, but I think we also have strong feelings about women's needs. As a female designer, comfort is very important to me. I've had women say to me, "I feel so much sexier in your clothes than in clothes designed by men." They've also said that my attention to detail inside the clothing seems feminine. And I think women designers may be more tactile: I would love to line everything in silk.

When I think of the adjectives I use to describe my clothes, they are always very female: flirty and kicky, sexy and sultry, elegant and feminine. Everything for me always has to do with this *persona* of a woman who is very feminine and sexy. I love coming in to the office and fighting my battles and then I love to go home and drop all of that. That's why I would *loathe* being a man and always wearing a gray suit or black tie.

ABOVE: *Carolyne Roehm, Evening dress, Autumn 1990 collection. Photograph by Roxanne Lowit.*

In an article on "Couture's Grand Ladies," fashion journalist Suzy Menkes describes Roehm as "a glamorous, dark-haired socialite" and "wife of the mega-rich financier" who is also "a dynamic and successful dress designer."[32] Carolyne Roehm is one of the best-known women designers working in the United States today, but media attention has tended to focus less on her clothes than on her social position — as the glamorous wife of leveraged-buy-out king Henry Kravis — and for this reason her image has sometimes been controversial.

As Kravis himself told *Vogue*, "I sometimes wonder if she's . . . not taken quite so seriously because she happens to be married to me." Even her own advertisements present her as a "a society princess dabbling in fashion," or as a friend told *Vogue*: "Those ads feature a concubine."[33]

This is, perhaps, the crux of the matter: Other "designing bluebloods," such as Jacqueline de Ribes and Carolina Herrera, also risk being dismissed as frivolous socialites, but only Roehm has been the subject of a lot of sniping that she "married money."[34] Issues of class *and sex* dominate the popular perception of her career.

A notorious article in *New York* magazine described her as "the very emblem of the Working Rich," or as they were called in the old days, "the nouveau riches."[35] More recently, she appeared on the cover of *Fortune*, illustrating an article on "The CEO's Second Wife" — the "trophy wife." This second wife, much younger than her husband and often taller as well, is not only beautiful but also accomplished, often with a successful career of her own. According to the article, many powerful, wealthy men seek to marry a glamorous consort, who "certifies her husband's status."[36] There is probably some sociological validity in these analyses, but they tend to ignore Roehm's own history of serious involvement in fashion.

"People seem to think that my husband is just humoring me by letting me have a little business," says Roehm with polite exasperation. "Women say to me, 'Now, when did you decide to do this? Why do you work so hard when you're married to a wealthy man?' Give me a break! I wanted to be a fashion designer all my life! I spent ten years working in the fashion industry. I designed polyester sportswear! Maybe twenty-five years from now

ABOVE: *Mary McFadden in a lavishly embroidered dress of her own design, 1990. Photograph courtesy of Mary McFadden.*

they'll admit, 'This woman really wanted to be a designer.'"

Although day clothes now make up some fifty percent of her collection, evening clothes are Roehm's strongest suit. As she has said, "I like women to be seductive and I'm not interested in career dressing. . . . The executive woman in a little grey suit was a thing of the 1980s."[37] Undeniably seductive and feminine, her evening dresses have also evolved since she began, becoming younger and more streamlined, less ruffly than those of her mentor, Oscar de la Renta. But femininity is always the keynote. According to Roehm,

Men often say to me, "I'm so glad that there's a good woman designer out there, because my wife has never looked sexier." And, of course, I love that kind of response from men, because I am very male-oriented in that respect. I think it's my own interest in men, and the relationship between men and women, that influences my clothing. Both the visual aspect of when a woman walks in a room, and also when a man, you know, dances with a woman, and puts his . . . how the fabric feels. If I were a man I would want to feel that.

## UPTOWN LADIES

Before Roehm, there was Mary McFadden, whom John Fairchild describes as "the first really big name from a top-drawer social family to become an important designer."[38] Standing five feet five and weighing barely a hundred pounds, with jet black hair and milky skin, McFadden is a striking and even exotic figure. But as her friend, financier Felix Rohatyn, says, "Underneath the tiny, frail exterior there beats the heart of a tycoon."[39]

When she achieved overnight success in 1973, she was one of a group of socialite designers, including Gloria Vanderbilt, Charlotte Ford, and Diane von Fürstenberg. Most press reports then and later mentioned her class background, although the emphasis varied: *New York* magazine made the subtle point that her mother was a Cutting, while the more proletarian *Daily News* observed simply that "Mary McFadden joins other rich girls designing for the working woman." But the really notable fact, as the *Daily News* put it, was that "the daughters of privilege" were now focusing less on marrying well than on trying "to make a bundle themselves just like daddy."[40] McFadden's role as a businesswoman — "a new type of tycoon"[41] — is, in fact, a major aspect of her image.

"In the past, women were considered dressmakers, and they couldn't get beyond that role," says McFadden. "They weren't supposed to be creative artists or have the discipline to create a financial empire. But sex barriers have broken down, and each year there are more and more good business women."[42]

According to a 1990 article, "Mary, Mary, Quite Contrary: The Life and Loves of Mary McFadden," by journalist Michael Gross, McFadden's longtime friend J. Patrick Lannan pushed her "to go into business for herself . . . and he offered her three suggestions: sell furniture and art . . . run

BELOW: *Mary McFadden, Pleated evening dress with bands of embroidery, Spring/ Summer 1989 collection. Photograph courtesy of Mary McFadden.*

a fast-food operation . . . or start a fashion label."[43] She chose fashion, and became particularly well-known for her Fortuny-pleated evening dresses.

Another aspect of her public persona is her image as an American exotic. This refers not only to her appearance (although reporters have described her as looking like Cleopatra) but more importantly to her clothes, which tend to evoke the costumes of long ago and far away.[44] Although she briefly studied fashion at the Traphagen School, her unique personal style really seems to have evolved during the course of her first two marriages in South Africa and Rhodesia. Returning to New York in 1970 at the age of thirty-two to work as a fashion editor at *Vogue*, McFadden impressed her colleagues with the exotic, African-inspired clothes she wore to the office.

McFadden insists that "it makes no difference whether a designer is a man or a woman. It's the individual vision that's important." This is also true elsewhere in the world of fashion, she adds. For example, "most of the people at *Vogue* have always been women. Even if men like Si Newhouse and Alex Liberman controlled the editorial division, they were very feminine-oriented. But there is no reason why men can't be *as* good as women at editing. Men like André Leon Talley and Paul Sinclair are as enthusiastic about fashion — and probably more knowledgeable — than any female editors. They live and dream and breathe it."

Venezuelan-born Carolina Herrera is always described as a "socialite-turned-designer." No one has ever disputed that she had great personal style: She was on the "Best-Dressed List" so often that she was finally ensconced in its "Hall of Fame." But many people were surprised when, in 1981, she began designing clothes professionally.

Ellin Saltzman of Macy's remembers thinking, "My God, another socialite designing a fly-by-night collection no one will ever buy or wear."[45] Herrera admits, "If I said I always wanted to be a designer, I'd be lying." At eighteen she was married and having babies. But she was always very interested in clothes. Moreover, like Roehm and McFadden, and like Jacqueline de Ribes in France and Anouska Hempel in Great Britain, Herrera lived the life for which she designed. Women like Jacqueline Onassis soon began buying her pretty, feminine clothes. Her wedding dresses, in particular, have been a success. Herrera explains:

My clothes are feminine. Maybe *feminine* is not the word. If you are a woman, then obviously you are feminine. What word can we use? Like a real woman, no? . . . showing a little bit of leg, showing a little décolletage . . . . Several years ago I think fashion was very much for men, but if Armani's kind of fashion is too masculine, another kind may be too sexy. I think that between women and men, the mind works in a different way. Men look at women with different eyes, they look at women in a very sexy way, maybe too sexy or too flashy or too . . . something. Women are more . . . we are more calm about everything.[46]

TOP: *Carolina Herrera, Suit, dress, and hats, Spring/ Summer 1991 collection. Photograph courtesy of Carolina Herrera.*

ABOVE: *Carolina Herrera, Evening dress, Autumn/ Winter 1986 collection. Photograph by Patrice Casanova, courtesy of Carolina Herrera.*

ABOVE: *Betsey Johnson,
Striped leotards and leggings,
Spring 1984 collection.
Photograph by Roxanne Lowit.*

TOP RIGHT: *Joan Vass for
Joan Vass USA, Cotton
hooded check jacket and
leggings, Autumn 1990
collection. Photograph courtesy
of Joan Vass USA.*

RIGHT: *Joan Vass, Collarless
three-button jacket and
paperbag pants, Autumn 1989
collection. Photograph courtesy
of Joan Vass.*

joan vass

8622 SUNSET BOULEVARD, WEST HOLLYWOOD
235 NEWPORT CENTER DRIVE, NEWPORT BEACH

Meanwhile, Downtown has its fashion leaders, too. A Youthquaker in the 1960s, Betsey Johnson is still a "Downtown girl." She still designs for herself, and believes that this is typical of women designers: "You truly have to believe in your work and feel that you'd wear absolutely everything you make. I know it's true for Norma [Kamali] and Donna [Karan] and the other women designers I can think of. They are their customer. Of course, my identity is very different from Norma's or Donna's, and at bigger companies like Liz Claiborne or Adrienne Vittadini—whoo! they've got stuff happening all over the place for different types of customers."[47]

If women are designing for themselves, what do male designers do? "I think men definitely pretend that they are women," says Johnson. "They've got to have that femininity in themselves, or they've got to have some woman—a mannequin or a dear friend—who to them epitomizes the feminine mystique."

Johnson believes that her own clothes also reflect "the left side of my brain—the frilly, feminine, romantic side." Her flower prints are feminine, of course, but more fundamentally, she says that much of her work comes from lingerie and notes that she "[hasn't] seen that very much in men's designs." If many of the "petite" details in her work reflect the ambiance of a "real *boudoir*," another major influence comes from leotards and dance costume. Here, "male or female doesn't matter," she says. "Rudi Gernreich [the American fashion innovator of the 1960s] was also a dancer, and he had a real understanding of body movement."

TOP: *Betsey Johnson, Caps, playsuits, and leggings in kaleidoscopic colors, Autumn/Winter 1989–1990 collection. Photograph by Maria Chandoha Valentino.*

ABOVE: *Betsey Johnson, Petticoat and corselette, Spring 1984 collection. Photograph by Roxanne Lowit.*

Although she loves "the Dada-ness and Dali-ness" of Schiaparelli, it is really Claire McCardell whom Johnson idolizes. "She is just the beginning and the end of a designer in terms of inspiration for me," says Johnson. "She would have had a heyday with all the stretch fabrics now; she really only had that black wool jersey, which was her stretch fabric. She was so inventive. Perry Ellis, Calvin Klein, they've all been influenced by Claire."

But whereas most designers have drawn on McCardell's clean-cut, all-American look, Johnson has been inspired by her "funny play clothes, her wide elastic belts, her bubble suits, the whole baby-doll, off-the-shoulder look." Says Johnson: "I think women love to look sexy—and there's nothing wrong with that." She admits that a few people complained about "a couple of [Johnson's fashion promotion] videotapes, taken out of context." But special clothes "can really make women feel better. I'm incredibly supportive of women, and I feel my clothes make women look terrific."

For some years after McCardell, there were relatively few famous women designers in America, but Johnson does not think there was "any male domination that kept them from getting into the career marketplace. They just didn't have the talent to get through." She adds that "there were some great designers who are unknown, because they were under labels, like Erica Allias, who was one of the great sixties' women designers, and Monica Tilley, who was one of the best swimwear designers of all time. And one of the best children's-wear designers, Betsy Daniels. I mean you don't think of a man as a children's-wear designer." It is also worth noting that

Johnson's longtime business partner is a woman, Chantal Bacon.

Has being a woman affected Johnson's career? "I have never felt that being anything but talented was important," says Johnson, seriously. "I have never felt discrimination." Pause: "I've just felt they were against me and my ideas," and she laughs. "I've had people just not believe in me period, because they thought I was too far out, too weird. But it was never because I was a woman. And the only way I got people to believe in me was to be good, to be professional, to be disciplined, and to have the work sell."

"Sex has nothing to do with designing. Sex is another activity,"[48] says Joan Vass in a gravelly New York voice that has been described as "a cross between Betty Boop and Grandma Moses." Vass describes herself as "an old woman who is crazy about clothes." She is certainly one of fashion's more unusual mavericks.

An intellectual with a career in art history, Vass did not enter the fashion business until age forty-nine, when in 1976 she organized "a sort of charity idea" whereby elderly and housebound individuals could earn extra money by hand-knitting mufflers and hats. Vass was persuaded to design the garments, which were snapped up by Bendel's and then Bergdorf Goodman, thus parlaying her hobby of knitting into what became a multi-million-dollar business.

A woman of strong opinions, Vass sees "no reason to adopt a sexist attitude towards clothing: Men are just as good at designing as women, and women are just as good as men. Probably male designers are different, but I think that we should look for differences, individuality, variety, rather than sameness."

When it comes to *wearing* clothes, women tend to be "more courageous, more willing to experiment," thinks Vass—although even many women have become more conformist in their dress, something she relates to the "right-wing drift in our politics." Nevertheless, she insists, "No one should dictate to others how to dress, any more than what to read. I'm certainly not here to tell people what to wear. I think it is more important that we don't lose Roe versus Wade."

Her premiere line, Joan Vass N.Y., consists of quirky classics, such as "couture" hand-knit sweaters that appeal to individualistic consumers. In 1984 Vass signed a license agreement with Signal Knitting Mills to produce a second, bread-and-butter line of less expensive mix-and-match separates. She also designs witty T-shirts, like one with the Latin expression *Amor vincet omnia* (Love conquers all).

She has created clothes inspired by iguanas, pantsuits in a silk moire wood-grain print, and wonderfully bizarre and funny hats. "Clothes are fun," she says. "Why shouldn't they be amusing?" She likes to do "crazy things," but her humor is always intelligent and intentional. "It's interesting to me that women don't make the absurdly ruffly clothes," she comments. "They may make very absurd clothes, but they tend not to make ultrafeminine, woman-who-looks-like- a-boudoir-lamp clothes. Carolyne Roehm is a little like Lacroix and Oscar de la Renta, but not quite, she's more hard edge. When I make a ruffle, it's funny."

In addition to fashion designers per se, there are also those who design accessories. Worldwide, there are many women in this field. One thinks of Maud Frizon's shoes, for example, or the jewelry of Paloma Picasso. Unlike shoemaking and jewelry design, however, which have traditionally been male crafts, millinery has long been associated with women. In fact, historically, the milliner was a very romantic figure in the popular imagination: the sexy "aristocrat" of working-class women.

ABOVE: *Patricia Underwood, Hat, Spring 1991 collection. Photograph courtesy of Patricia Underwood.*

"The other image of the milliner was that she was an independent woman," says designer Patricia Underwood. "A lover would set up his discarded mistress as a milliner. Once she has her own millinery shop, she's independent." (Think of Chanel.) "Millinery is a business that you can start with a very small outlay," says Underwood. "You can make a hat in the kitchen. It's not like going into the dress business."[49] In Underwood's case, "It was either be a milliner or a truck driver. Those were my two options, because I'd been fired from any job I ever had, and I suddenly needed to support myself and my child."

Today both men and women work as milliners. Still, Underwood believes that "when I see members of the general public, I have to be careful." When she sees someone wearing an outfit that she likes, "If I say, 'Oh, that looks great'—it's not received the same way as if a man says it." (Some women fashion designers, such as Isabel Toledo and Diane Pernet, have also said that some members of the public react differently to advice or compliments coming from another woman, as opposed to comments made by a man.)

Whether or not the millinery designer is male or female, however, "hats are *not* coming back," says Underwood. They are "an option," but no longer regarded as an essential accessory. Some of Philippe Model's hats for Karl Lagerfeld—such as the "Chair" hat—have recently been widely publicized. Underwood, though, eschews fantasy hats in favor of what she laughing describes as "sensible, practical hats."

## DESIGNING WOMEN

"Women designers are infinitely more practical than male designers because we've dressed ourselves since age nine," designer Patricia Clyne told *Vogue*. "We can be just as imaginative, but it's . . . probably a little more disciplined." Clyne was featured in an article that focused specifically on a new generation of women designers—who are about the same age (thirty), and who design smart clothes for other smart young women.[50]

ABOVE: *Adrienne Vittadini, Hand-knit wool turtleneck sweater and leggings, Autumn 1990 collection. Photograph courtesy of Adrienne Vittadini.*

Another young designer, Jennifer George, believes that being a woman "absolutely" influences her designs. "I always think about myself, what I need, what I would wear. I think that women designers, in general, think of themselves and their needs and their bodies." The fact that men designers do not have this intimate physical awareness "is at the root of the difference between male and female designers."[51]

"Men may have more creative freedom, suggests George: "If you see an outrageously kooky, whimsical dress, nine times out of ten it was designed by a man." On the other hand, the tendency toward practicality is "part of what makes women's designs so salable," she adds. "Look at Donna Karan, Liz Claiborne, Adrienne Vittadini."

The Hungarian-born Adrienne Vittadini has had a "phenomenal success" based on what *The New York Times* calls "her ability to catch the mood of the moment and interpret it for the woman who likes clothes but is not obsessive about them."[52] Best known for her knitwear and for her "happy" prints, Vittadini designs almost 1,000 pieces a season (compared to about 40 for Carolyne Roehm), although she freely credits the assistance of her team. When she began her company in the late 1970s, her husband recalls, "It was supposed to be a little business to keep Adrienne busy."[53] A decade later, it had grown to become a multi-million-dollar empire, embracing far more than sweaters.

Vittadini believes that as a woman designer, she has "an innate sense of what other women want.[54] I love being a woman," says Vittadini, whose advertising campaign tries to project "a real woman in a real situation, but with an undertone of glamour." She uses words like "instinctive" and "intuitive" to describe the female design experience, compared with the "more detached" male perspective. Both have advantages, she insists: women may flirt with male designers and identify with female designers, but they are really most concerned with the product. "The bottom line is the clothes. I know what my needs are — and my customer has the same needs."

The phrase "a Nicole Miller dress" is familiar to many American women and has been for almost a decade. Yet she held her first fashion show only in 1990. On her first foray into the fashion arena, she "scored a technical knockout," declared *The New York Times*'s Woody Hochswender: "Her clothes were among the best-made and most wearable of the New York

TOP: *Charlotte Neuville,
Cotton poplin tile-print
cardigan jacket and skirt,
Spring 1991 collection.
Photograph courtesy of
Charlotte Neuville.*

ABOVE: *Rebecca Moses,
Skirt and bustier, Resort 1990
collection. Photograph by L &
I, courtesy of Rebecca Moses.*

ABOVE LEFT: *Jennifer
George, Polka-dot dress,
Spring 1991 collection.
Photograph courtesy of
Jennifer George.*

collections — and will probably cost the least of any of them."[55]

"My mother was French," recalls Miller, "and she had a real feeling for clothing, which is where my interest in design comes from."[56] Miller herself attended the *Ecole de la Chambre Syndicale*, but she ultimately concluded that it was too "tough to break in [in France]," so she came back to the United States.

"The women who are big names in France aren't big commercial successes," argues Miller. "Someone who might be my counterpart, like Chantal Thomass, does things that are too funny to really be taken seriously. Some of her ideas are brilliant, but you don't want to spend a thousand dollars on something that's too funny. But the industry here in America is so huge, there is more room for women. It used to be the big names here were all men, too. But now there are a lot of real heavyweight women around, getting more press and recognition."

Nevertheless, Miller is not sure that women have achieved equality in the American design world. "When you look at people like Michael Kors who has been out of school eight years, or Michael Leva, or Marc Jacobs, all these guys are really aggressive and outgoing," muses Miller. "You don't see women being that aggressive. The men promote themselves more."

"Someone once asked me if I thought it was a disadvantage — business-wise — to be a woman," says Patricia Clyne, "because people seem to be

more willing to put money behind a man. But I think it's an advantage to be a woman. A lot of male designers have an ideal woman in mind, which might make fashion news, but when all is said and done, I think we're more than somebody's ideal. . . . I don't have a muse!"[57]

Fashion is a tough business, though, for young designers. Rebecca Moses had to fight her former business partner for the right to use her own name. Patricia Clyne has had financial problems. Diane Pernet, for several years a fixture in the downtown fashion scene, recently moved to Paris. But the young women keep coming — and coming back.

Charlotte Neuville's most successful style to date has been her "boyfriend" jacket, a big, boxy jacket designed to look as though it had been borrowed from "his" closet. She got the idea by going through her husband's closet, trying on everything. After she chose one of his sports jackets, she took it to work, tried it on a fitting model, and began modifying it, going through seven patterns before she got the right shape. The "ease and comfort" of menswear are really important to her, she says.[58]

"I really like to forget what I'm wearing," agrees Clyne. "For example, I've always been a pants person. I just work better in them, I feel more comfortable, I can walk faster." George, who is known for the loose, easy comfort of her big shirts, has a similar ethos: "My clothes don't wear you," she says. And she adds a final practical, female note: "All my friends were pregnant," says George, which led her to launch a maternity line, called Mother George.

Diane Pernet has always emphasized the sensual, focusing on evening clothes and elegant daywear, and more recently also lingerie. Her clothes are often "very body-conscious," but she insists that she is "not just dressing people with perfect bodies. Sensuality has to do with the way something *feels* on you."[59]

"I don't really understand why there are so many male designers," says Pernet. "No one understands a woman better than another woman. A man is often just playing out a lot of his fantasies, which may be very insensitive. I think a lot of women still like to be dressed by a man, though. I guess it's like in any other field: a battle between men and women, with women beginning to get an equal footing."

## HOLY TOLEDO!

Isabel Toledo is a cult figure in avant-garde fashion circles ("a raw talent," says one editor). When she first began designing professionally, in 1986, her clothes were almost immediately featured in *Harper's Bazaar* and *Vogue*. But now, several years later, she is still looking for reliable financial backing.

Whether or not Seventh Avenue appreciates homegrown innovators (as opposed to the ones abroad), downtown fashion observers love Toledo. "Best overall collection for our money was Isabel Toledo, who ignored the market and concentrated on a well-edited, very weird, internal vision," raved Walter S. in 1989 in the *Village Voice*.[60] Kim Hastreiter of *Paper* describes Toledo as a "great designer . . . traveling on that new American highway of fashion," along with more established talents like Isaac Mizrahi and Geoffrey Beene.[61]

Born in Cuba, Toledo designs clothes that are all-American in their adventurous modernism. Like Claire McCardell, Toledo works in materials such as denim and cotton flannel plaid. She emphasizes the element of shape: a circle skirt, a curved bra top, the sweeping arc of a coat.

"I'm not a fashion designer," insists Toledo. "I'm a *seamstress*. I really love the technique of sewing more than anything else. I've sewed ever since I was a kid. In Cuban society, sewing was something women do. I remember as a child being fascinated by my grandmother's sewing machine."[62] When it is tentatively suggested that some people say that in the past women were "only" seamstresses, whereas now they are "real" designers, Toledo interrupts, urgently, "But the seamstress is the one who knows fashion from the inside! That is an art form really, not fashion design, but the *technique* of how it's done."

"Maybe it's an oversimplification," she suggests, "but I think that male designers tend to work on paper, from the flat drawing, whereas women like Madame Grès knew how to put the garment together in three dimensions. If you don't know how to sew, how to drape the material and make the pattern, you're limited. Women designers like Vionnet and Madame Grès and Claire McCardell made amazing clothes, because they understood technique."

Why are there so many male designers? "Because women don't like other women telling them what to wear," claims Toledo. "They'd rather take fashion advice from a man." But she insists, "The fact is, I'm a woman and I know what's best for me."

According to her husband, the artist Ruben Toledo, who handles the business side of Isabel's career, the common idea that women make more "practical" clothes can actually work against a woman designer. "The buyers are weird," says Ruben. "They'll accept creative ideas from a man, whereas from a woman they'll expect a comfortable little skirt. If fashion were a restaurant, they'd be telling the woman, 'Just give me a bowl of soup' — but they'd ask the guy for a pastry or a stuffed chicken."

In one of his iconoclastic fashion illustrations, entitled "Fashion history goes on strike," Ruben portrayed the styles of the past from New Look to Mod parading across the page, begging: "Let us rest in peace! No more retro! Look forward, not backward!" As Ruben says, "Maybe because we are immigrants, America feels like the future to us. Some people confuse it with a young look, but Isabel's clothes are not necessarily young — just optimistic."

Isabel Toledo takes risks, exploring new directions for the future.

"People think that fashion is men's domain, because the major names are men — like Dior and Saint Laurent," says Patricia Clyne. Even when the fashion press focuses on "young designers," men seem to get the most attention. Because fashion thrives on novelty, the fashion press loves "the new kid on the block," observes Jennifer George. "And nine times out of ten,

TOP: *Diane Pernet, Evening coat, Autumn/Winter 1989–1990 collection. Photograph courtesy of Diane Pernet and J. Henry Fair.*

ABOVE: *Diane Pernet, Evening dress, Spring 1990 collection. Photograph courtesy of Diane Pernet.*

BELOW: *Designer Isabel Toledo with models in her denim and tartan fashions, 1988. Photograph courtesy of Isabel and Ruben Toledo.*

OVERLEAF: *Isabel Toledo, Linen "packing" skirt and linen jersey sweater with horseshoe neckline, Spring 1987 collection, worn by Naomi Campbell. Photograph courtesy of Michael O'Brien.*

that's a man." Not that fashion journalists are *biased* toward men, she hastens to add, but there does seem to be "a *mystique* about the male designer."

"The fashion designer is invariably male, young, and vanguard," at least in the popular imagination, agrees F.I.T. professor Richard Martin. The fashion press has "delighted in a suite of young design 'geniuses,' most often men, heralded as salvific creators." These "pernicious and unexamined assumptions of male creativity and female reception [give] an ascribed heroism to the male designer that evades the female designer." The fashion press also heralds female designers, of course, but usually for somewhat different reasons. As Martin notes, it is widely believed that "women designers design for themselves," motivated by their practical needs and "natural" good taste. While there is certainly some validity to this, "it can also be a further gender trap, assuming that women can only do for themselves, not for the generic population."[63] Yet as the women featured in this book clearly demonstrate, creativity and design intelligence are not the prerogative of only one sex. Indeed, one of the most encouraging aspects of the current fashion scene is the way a wide variety of individuals are free to make their own unique contributions.

OPPOSITE TOP: *Isabel Toledo, Silk jersey dress with satin underskirt, Autumn 1990 collection. Photograph courtesy of the photographer, Mark Contratto.*

OPPOSITE BOTTOM: *Isabel Toledo, Layered cotton net dress, Autumn 1989 collection. Photograph courtesy of the photographer, Mark Contratto.*

BELOW: *Isabel Toledo, Matte jersey wrap dress, executed for Woolite promotion, 1989. Photograph courtesy of the photographer, Stephen Gan.*

# POSTSCRIPT

According to a recent article in *The New York Times*, businessmen are increasingly "interested in investing in women." Unfortunately, this is not because they now recognize that women can also be creative but because the AIDS epidemic has devastated the fashion world.

Investors are now reluctant to back male designers, because "they don't want their money to drop dead." Designer Carmelo Pomodoro reports that a group of Japanese investors recently asked him for a list of five up-and-coming designers. "I gave them a list with three women and two men. . . . They said they were not interested in the men, because of the AIDS factor."[1] Other investors are insisting that designers take and pass AIDS tests, refusing to back those who cannot get "key-man" insurance policies. Redlining by insurance companies is only part of the problem, however.

There is also increasing discrimination within the fashion industry against homosexual men. Even before AIDS, prejudice against homosexuals existed, and one journalist reported that "the word 'fag' is being flung about the jealous jungle of Seventh Avenue as irresponsibly as 'pink' was in the McCarthy era."[2] Today, when most AIDS victims in the fashion industry have been homosexual men, backers increasingly ask of a designer, "Is he straight?"

According to a 1990 article in *The Advocate: The National Gay Newsmagazine*, the late designer Rudi Gernreich was quoted as saying that "everybody" in the fashion business was gay. When journalist Stuart Timmons asked if he really meant that all fashion designers were gay, Gernreich replied, "All the good ones. I mean the men. There are a few pretty good women designing these days who are heterosexuals." Why were gay designers "all in the closet?" asked Timmons. "To protect their jobs," replied Gernreich.[3]

No convincing theory has yet been advanced to explain why homosexual men have played such an important role in women's fashion (at least in the twentieth century). Back in the 1950s, the psychologist Edmund Bergler argued that a repressed fear and hatred of the female body lay behind the "dress absurdities" designed by the homosexual "czars of fashion creation."[6] Obviously, Bergler did not like contemporary fashions, and he seems to have felt fear and hatred toward homosexuals. His interpretation was also

wildly inaccurate just in terms of the way fashion operates: It is not a dictatorship, and designers, whether they are homosexual or heterosexual, try to create clothes that women will like — and buy.

Since most people outside New York City are apparently unaware that the fashion industry is heavily gay, their homophobia has had little impact — until recently. Now, however, many people in the garment industry are fearful that their product will be linked with AIDS.

When Perry Ellis died in 1986, his company initially denied that his death had anything to do with AIDS. As Ellis's former assistant Patricia Pastor explains, "a segment of the population [is] afraid they'll catch AIDS if they wear the clothes of a designer that had AIDS." But Anneliese Estrada, the widow of designer Angel Estrada, believes that the industry is underestimating the public — and shirking its responsibilities to sick people within the fashion community.

As some male designers die and others are refused backing, many observers predict greater opportunities for women to be stars. Success is not automatic, however: Patricia Pastor assumed design responsibilities when Ellis died, but after two collections were criticized in the press, she was replaced by Marc Jacobs. Nevertheless, the prevailing view is that women designers are more "reliable."

"Money is going to women," apparel-company consultant Alan Milstein told *Crain's New York Business*, citing designers Mary Anne Restivo and Rebecca Moses.[4] And designer Mary McFadden told John Fairchild, "People are dying like flies. I've lost two assistants. I'm sure in five years we will only be seeing women designers. You'll see. There won't be very many men left in fashion."[5]

If women are to succeed in fashion, it cannot be over the dead bodies of men. The death of creative males — like Angel Estrada, Perry Ellis, Halston, Willi Smith, Isaia Rankin, wedding-dress designer Frank Masandrea, makeup artist Way Bandy, and illustrator Antonio Lopez — hurts everyone in the world of fashion.

"I used to have Antonio do my illustrations," says Norma Kamali. "Now I don't use anyone." "Talented people are few and far between," agrees Louis Dell'Olio. "Yes, a job can always be filled. But there's no replacement for creativity."[7]

# Notes

## Introduction

1. Dianne T. Meranus, "Fashion Design: Men Do Dominate," *The F.I.T. Review* (Spring 1989), 18–21.
2. "Designers on Designers," *W* (November 27–December 4, 1989), 83.
3. See, for example, June Weir, "Closing the Gender Gap," *The New York Times Magazine* (June 30, 1985), 44.
4. Rebecca Voight, "Scene Dining," *Accent, The Magazine of Paris Style*, published in conjunction with *Paris Passion: The Magazine of the French Capital* (November/December 1987), 28.
5. Quoted in Meranus, "Fashion Design," 18–21.
6. Oscar de la Renta interview in Barbaralee Diamondstein, *Fashion: The Inside Story* (New York: Rizzoli, 1985), 61.
7. Sharon Lee Tate, *Inside Fashion Design* (New York: Harper and Row, 1984), 49.
8. Quoted in Meranus, "Fashion Design," 20.
9. Cecil Beaton, *The Glass of Fashion* (London: Weidenfeld & Nicolson, 1954), 161.
10. H. W. Yoxall, *A Fashion of Life*, (New York: Taplinger, 1967), 57.
11. See Caroline Evans and Minna Thornton, *Women and Fashion: A New Look* (London and New York: Quartet, 1989), 122–131.
12. "Women Designers Set New Fashions," *Life* (January 14, 1946), 87.

## Chapter 1

1. Annette B. Weiner and Jane Schneider, *Cloth and Human Experience* (Washington and London: Smithsonian Institution Press, 1989), 21–22.
2. Daniel Roche, *La Culture des apparences: Une histoire du vêtement xviie–xviiie siècle* (Paris: Fayard, 1989), 287.
3. Pierre Larousse, *Grand Dictionnaire universal du XIXe siècle* (Paris, 1865–1890), vol. 5, definition of "Couturier, -ière."
4. *Dictionnaire raisonné universal des Arts et Métiers* (Paris, 1773), vol. I, 571–3.
5. Roche, *La Culture des apparences*, 288.
6. *Dictionnaire raisonné universal des Arts et Métiers*, vol. I, 571–3.
7. Baroness H. L. D'Oberkirch, quoted in Emile L'Anglade, *Rose Bertin, the Creator of Fashion at the Court of Marie Antoinette* (London: John Long, 1913), 136, 140, 150.
8. D'Oberkirch, *Mémoires*, quoted in Nicole Pellegrin, *Les Vêtements de la Liberté* (Aix-en-Provence: Editions Alinea, 1989), 26.
9. Roche, *La Culture des apparences*, 277–293.
10. Amy Latour, *Kings of Fashion*, trans. Mervyn Savill (London: Weidenfeld & Nicolson, 1958), 46.
11. *Ibid.*, 50.
12. *Almanach des Modes* (1814), quoted in *Ibid.*, 51.
13. See note 3.
14. *Journal des Modes d'Hommes* (January 1869), n.p.
15. Charles Dickens, in *All the Year Round* (February 28, 1863), 9.
16. Hippolyte Taine, *La vie et les opinions de Thomas Graindorge*, quoted in Latour, *Kings of Fashion*, 92.
17. Quoted in *Ibid.*, 94.
18. Quoted in *Ibid.*, 94–95.
19. See Valerie Steele, *Paris Fashion: A Cultural History* (New York: Oxford University Press, 1988), 7, 11, 256–57.
20. Caroline Rennolds Milbank, *New York Fashion: The Evolution of American Style* (New York: Harry N. Abrams, 1989), 18.

## Chapter 2

1. *The Ladies' Home Journal* (September 1914), 58.
2. Jan Reeder, "Madame Jeanne Paquin," (M.A. thesis, Graduate Program in Museum Studies, Fashion Institute of Technology, New York, 1990).
3. A 1906 guidebook, quoted in Caroline Rennolds Milbank, *Couture* (New York: Stewart, Tabori & Chang, 1985), 42.
4. *Lady's Pictorial* (May 9, 1914), 759. See also *The Gentlewoman* (April 1914), 670. Both in *Paquin Publicité* file at the Costume Research Centre, Bath, England.
5. Maggy Rouff, *Ce que j'ai vu en chiffonnant la clientèle* (Paris: Librairie des Champs-Elysées, 1938), 17–21.
6. Robert Forrest Wilson, *Paris on Parade* (Indianapolis: The Bobbs-Merrill Company, 1924–25), 34.
7. Maggy Rouff, *Ce que j'ai vu . . .* , 10–21.
8. Mary Brooks Picken and Dora Loues Miller, *Dressmakers of France* (New York: Harper & Brothers, 1956), 63; Paul Poiret, *King of Fashion: The Autobiography of Paul Poiret*, trans. Stephen Hadden Guest (Philadelphia: J. B. Lippincott, 1931), 30.
9. Marcel Proust, *Within a Budding Grove*, in *Remembrance of Things Past*, trans. C. K. Scott Moncrieff and Frederick Blossom (New York: Random House, 1927–32), 675.
10. Lucille, Lady Duff-Gordon, *Discretions and Indiscretions* (London: Jarrolds, 1932), 65–66.
11. *Ibid.*, 87.
12. *Ibid.*, 65–66.
13. Quoted in the film *Chanel, Chanel*, RM Arts, 1986.
14. *Le Pavillon de l'Elégance*, special issue of the *Gazette du Bon Ton* (1925), 317.
15. Louise de Vilmorin, quoted in "Connaissez-vous Lanvin?" *Figaro* (January 24, 1986), in designer file, Union Français des Arts du Costume (UFAC).
16. Quoted in Milbank, *Couture*, 53.
17. *Le Pavillon de l'Élégance*, 317.
18. *Vogue* (February 1930), quoted in Musée de la Mode et du Costume, *Paris-Couture-Années trente*, text by Guillaume Garnier *et al.*, (Paris, 1987), 35.
19. Charlotte Aillaud, "A Lanvin Legacy: Embellishing a Family Tradition in Paris," *Architectural Digest* (September, 1988), 159.

## Chapter 3

1. Ernestine Carter, *Magic Names of Fashion* (Englewood Cliffs, NJ: Prentice-Hall, 1980), 54.
2. Axel Madsen, *Chanel: A Woman of Her Own* (New York: Henry Holt & Company, 1990), 3.
3. "Chanel Designs Again," *Vogue* (February 15, 1954), 83.
4. Marcel Haedrich, *Coco Chanel: Her Life, Her Secrets* (Boston: Little, Brown & Co., 1972), 49.
5. *Ibid.*, 62–63.
6. Georg Simmel, "Fashion," *International Quarterly* 10 (October 1904), 130–155.
7. Paul Morand, *L'Allure de Chanel*, quoted in Edmonde Charles-Roux, *Chanel and Her World* (London: Weidenfeld & Nicolson, 1982), 61.
8. Louis Octave Uzanne, *La Femme à Paris* (Paris, 1894), 290, 293–94.
9. Caroline Evans and Minna Thornton have a fascinating chapter on "Chanel: The New Woman as Dandy" in their book, *Women and Fashion: A New Look* (London and New York: Quartet, 1989).
10. Salvador Dali as told to André Parinaud, *The Unspeakable Confessions of Salvador Dali* (New York: Quill, 1981), 212.
11. Charles Baudelaire, "The Painter of Modern Life," in *The Painter of Modern Life and Other Essays*, trans. Jonathan Mayne (London: Phaidon Press, 1964), 27–28.
12. See "The Black Prince of Elegance" in Valerie Steele, *Paris Fashion: A Cultural History* (New York: Oxford University Press, 1988), 79–96.
13. Stuart Ewen, *All Consuming Images: The Politics of Style in Contemporary Culture* (New York: Basic Books, 1988), 129–130.
14. Quoted in Dali, *The Unspeakable Confessions*, 211.
15. Paul Morand, *L'Allure de Chanel* (Paris: Hermann, 1976), 45–46.
16. *Vogue* (November 1, 1916), 65; *Vogue* (August 1, 1916), 32, 39.
17. Francis Kennett, *Secrets of the Couturiers* (London: Orbis, 1984), 56.
18. Morand, *L'Allure de Chanel*, quoted in Charles-Roux, *Chanel and Her World*, 61.
19. Holly Brubach, "The School of Chanel," *The New Yorker* (February 27, 1989), 71–76.
20. Morand, *L'Allure de Chanel*, 52.
21. *Harper's Bazaar* (August 1922), in designer file, UFAC.
22. Edna Woolman Chase and Ivy Chase, *Always in Vogue* (Garden City, NY: Doubleday & Co., 1954), 239.
23. Robert Forrest Wilson, *Paris on Parade* (Indianapolis: The Bobbs-Merrill Company, 1924–5), 53.
24. From the film, *Chanel, Chanel.*
25. Chase and Chase, *Always in Vogue*, 182.
26. Helen Lawrenson, "The Madcap Who Made Women Young," *Cosmopolitan* (September 1961), 79.
27. Diana de Marly, *The History of Haute Couture* (New York: Holmes & Meier, 1980), 147.
28. Quoted in Madsen, *Chanel*, 110.
29. Cecil Beaton, *Self-Portrait with Friends*, ed. by Richard Buckles (London: Weidenfeld & Nicolson, 1979), 305.
30. Quoted in Madsen, *Chanel*, 150.
31. Phyllis Berman with Zina Sawaya, "The Billionaires Behind Chanel," *Forbes* (April 3, 1989), 104–108.
32. Loelia, Duchess of Westminster, *Grace and Favour* (London: Weidenfeld & Nicholson, 1961), 159.
33. Quoted in Madsen, *Chanel*, 217, and Edmonde Charles-Roux, *Chanel: Her Life, Her World, and the Woman Behind the Legend She Herself Created* (New York: Alfred A. Knopf, 1975), 299.
34. Horst P. Horst, *Salute to the Thirties* (New York: Viking, 1971), 176.
35. Gaia Servadio, *Luchino Visconti, A Biography*

(New York: Franklin Watts, 1983), 50.

36. Valentine Lawford, *Horst: His Work and His World* (New York: Alfred A. Knopf, 1984), 163.
37. Quoted in *Ibid.*, 192.
38. Madsen, *Chanel*, chapter 31.
39. Beaton, *Self-Portrait*, 154, 305, 307.
40. *Ibid.*, 307.
41. See the film *Chanel, Chanel*; also Karl Lagerfeld, in the *International Herald Tribune* (October 20, 1986), advertising section, iv.
42. *Vogue* (March 1, 1954), 101.
43. "What Chanel Storm Is About: She Takes a Chance on a Comeback," *Life* (March 1, 1954), 49.
44. Quoted in Madsen, *Chanel*, 289.
45. Charles-Roux, *Chanel and Her World*, 204.
46. Franco Zeffirelli, *Zeffirelli, An Autobiography* (New York: Weidenfeld & Nicolson, 1986), 100.
47. Beaton, *Self-Portrait*, 307.
48. Quoted in Judy Rumbold, "Hot Coco," *Elle*, (Great Britain; November, 1988), 105; and in Kennett, *Secrets of the Couturiers*, 57.
49. Quoted in Charles-Roux, *Chanel: Her Life, Her World*, 367.
50. Rumbold, "Hot Coco," 107.
51. Javier Arroyuello, "Fashion Royalty and the Couture Courts of Paris," *Vanity Fair* (March, 1986), 126.
52. *Ibid.*, 106–107.
53. Suzy Menkes, "An 80s Aristo for Coco," *The Times* (London; July 1, 1986), in designer file, UFAC.
54. *The New York Times* (February 14, 1967), 46.
55. Joseph Barry, "'I Am on the Side of Women,' Said My Friend Chanel," *Smithsonian* (May, 1971), 29.
56. Adelle-Marie Stan, "Four Designing Women," *Ms.* (November, 1986), 48.
57. Menkes, "An 80s aristo for Coco."

## CHAPTER 4

1. Ernestine Carter, *Magic Names of Fashion* (Englewood Cliffs, NJ: Prentice-Hall, 1980), 37.
2. Madeleine Chapsal, "Hommage à Madeleine Vionnet," *Vogue* (France; April 1975), 25–26.
3. *Ibid.*
4. Quoted in Madeleine Chapsal, *La Chair de la robe* (Paris: Fayard, 1989), 157.
5. From a film about Vionnet, quoted in *Figaro* (June 11, 1966), in designer file, UFAC.
6. Quoted in Musée de la Mode et du Costume, *Paris-Couture-Années trente*, text by Guillaume Garnier *et al.*, (Paris, 1987), 253.
7. Quoted in Musées de France, *L'Atelier Nadar et la mode*, text by Brigitte Scart and Yvonne Deslandres (exhibition catalogue; Nantes, n.d.), 83.
8. See the essay on Vionnet in Bruce Chatwin, *What Am I Doing Here?* (New York: Viking, 1989).
9. Quoted in Chapsal, *La Chair de la robe*, 159.
10. Chatwin, *What Am I Doing Here?*, 89.
11. Anne Hollander, *Seeing Through Clothes* (New York: Viking, 1978), 339.
12. Jeff Weinstein, "Vionnet, McCardell, Kawakubo: Why There Are Three Great Women Artists," *The Village Voice* (March 31, 1987), 39.
13. *Marie-Claire* (May, 1937), quoted in Jacqueline Demornex, *Vionnet* (Paris: Editions du Regard, 1990), 137.
14. Celia Bertin, *Paris á la Mode* (London: Victor Gollancz, 1956), 168.
15. Vionnet, quoted in Carter, *Magic Names of Fashion*, 45.
16. Chatwin, *What Am I Doing Here?*, 89.
17. Chapsal, *La Chair de la robe*, 159.
18. Chatwin, *What Am I Doing Here?*, 89.

19. Quoted in *Paris-Couture-Années trente*, 253.
20. Chatwin, *What Am I Doing Here?*, 90–91, and Carter, *Magic Names of Fashion*, 36.
21. Carter, *Magic Names of Fashion*, 37.
22. Quoted in *Paris-Couture-Années-Trente*, 14.
23. *Ibid.*
24. Vionnet, quoted in Irving Penn, *Inventive Paris Clothes, 1909–1939*, text by Diana Vreeland (New York: Viking, 1977), 36.
25. *Gazette du Bon Ton*, quoted in Caroline Evans and Minna Thornton, *Women and Fashion-Fashion*, 114.
26. Madeleine Ginsburg, "The Thirties," in Ruth Lynam, ed., *Couture: An Illustrated History of the Great Paris Designers and Their Creations* (Garden City, NY: Doubleday, 1972), 105.
27. Thérèse and Louise Bonney, *A Shopping Guide to Paris* (New York: Robert McBride, 1929), 27.
28. *Ibid.*
29. *Paris-Couture-Années trente*, 88–89.
30. Quoted in Chapsal, *La Chair de la robe*, 296–297.
31. Weinstein, "Vionnet, McCardell, Kawakubo," 41.
32. Quoted in Chapsal, *La Chair de la robe*, 156.
33. Latour, *Kings of Fashion*, 200.
34. Chatwin, *What Am I Doing Here?*, 90–91.

## CHAPTER 5

1. Quoted in Palmer White, *Schiaparelli, Empress of Paris Fashion* (New York: Rizzoli International, 1986), 44.
2. Elsa Schiaparelli, *Shocking Life* (New York: E. P. Dutton, 1954), 42–43; White, *Schiaparelli*, 49.
3. *Vogue* (October 15, 1931), in designer file, UFAC.
4. Quoted in White, *Schiaparelli*, 92.
5. Schiaparelli, *Shocking Life*, 75.
6. *Ibid.*, 46.
7. *Ibid.*
8. Salvadore Dali, quoted in White, *Schiaparelli*, 160.
9. Evans and Thornton, *Women and Fashion: A New Look* 139.
10. Quoted in White, *Schiaparelli*, 97.
11. Schiaparelli, *Shocking Life*, 53.
12. Billy Boy, photos by Robert Doisneau, "Hommage à Schiaparelli," *Femme* (June 1987), 50.
13. Quoted in Jody Shields, "Madcap Couturier," *Elle* (September 1988), 422, 424.
14. Jean Cocteau in *Harper's Bazaar* (April 1937), quoted in White, *Schiaparelli*, 176, 179.

## CHAPTER 6

1. H. W. Yoxall, *A Fashion of Life* (New York: Taplinger, 1967), 57.
2. Musée Richard Anacréon Grandville, *Femmes créatrices des années vingt* (Paris: Editions Arts et Culture, 1988), 41.
3. Quoted in *Ibid.*, 41.
4. Interview in *Harper's Bazaar*, quoted in Meredith Etherington-Smith, *Patou* (New York: St. Martin's, 1983), 71–72.
5. Thérèse and Louise Bonney, *A Shopping Guide to Paris* (New York: Robert McBride, 1929), 29–30.
6. *Paris-Couture-Années trente*, 252.
7. Bonney, *A Shopping Guide to Paris*, 9–12.
8. Jacques Damase, "La Mode Simultanée," *Pole Position* (December-January 1984–85), 74.
9. Sarah Mower, "Sonia Delaunay," *Vogue* (Great Britain; March 1991), 40–41.
10. Hélène Demoraine, "Sonia Delaunay," *Con-*

*naissance des Arts* (May 1966), in designer file, UFAC.
11. Quoted in Chatwin, *What Am I Doing Here?*, 155.
12. Quoted in Isabelle Anscombe, *A Woman's Touch: Women in Design from 1860 to the Present Day* (New York: Viking, 1984), 96.
13. *Ibid.*, 95.
14. *Ibid.*
15. *Ibid.*, 97.
16. Robert Forrest Wilson, *Paris on Parade* (Indianapolis: The Bobbs-Merrill Company, 1924–25), 37.
17. Amy Latour, *Kings of Fashion*, trans. Mervyn Savill (London: Weidenfeld & Nicolson, 1958), 206.
18. Maggy Rouff, *Ce que j'ai vue en chiffonnant la clientèle* (Paris: Librairie des Champs-Elysées, 1938), 30.
19. *Vogue* (April 1912), quoted in Musée de la Mode et du Costume, *Paul Poiret and Nicole Groult*, text by Guillaume Garnier et al. (Paris: Édition Paris Musées, 1986), 209, 35.
20. *Ibid.*, *Vogue* quoted, 211; Garnier, 35.
21. Quoted in Milbank, *Couture*, 156.
22. Quoted in *Ibid.*, 158.
23. Interview with Ingrid Bleichroder, quoted in Arlene Cooper, "How Madame Grès Sculpts with Fabric," *Threads* (April/May 1987), 51.
24. Personal communication to the author.
25. Quoted in Cooper, "How Madame Grès Sculpts With Fabric," 51. See also "Madame Grès, Hellene de Paris," *Jardin des Modes* (December 1980-January 1981), and Lucien François, *Comment un nom devient une griffe* (Paris: Gallimard, 1961).
26. "The Pulse of Fashion," *Harper's Bazaar* (July 1936), 27.
27. Anne Hollander, "A Sculptor in Fabric," *Connoisseur* (August 1982), 97.

## CHAPTER 7

1. "Valentina," in *Current Biography* (New York: The H. W. Wilson Co., 1946), 607–8.
2. Bettina Ballard, *In My Fashion* (New York: David McKay, 1962), 165.
3. "Vogue's Gallery of American Designers," *Vogue* (September 1, 1933).
4. Quoted in Bettina Berch, *Radical by Design: The Life and Style of Elizabeth Hawes* (New York: E. P. Dutton, 1988), 13.
5. Elizabeth Hawes, *Fashion Is Spinach* (New York: Random House, 1938), ix.
6. Edmund Wilson, *The Thirties* (New York: Farrar, Straus, and Giroux, 1980), 318–319.
7. Advertisement in Elizabeth Hawes File in the Brooklyn Museum.
8. *Vogue* (March 15, 1934).
9. *Harper's Bazaar* (October 1933), 28.
10. Hawes, *Fashion Is Spinach*, 181.
11. *Reader's Digest* (1938), quoted in Berch, *Radical By Design*, 1.
12. "Costume Designers" Scrapbook, Special Collections, Fashion Institute of Technology Library.
13. Berch, *Radical By Design*, 75.
14. "Fashion Show," *The New Yorker* (October 30, 1948), 18–19.
15. See "Can Ladies Wear Trousers?" and "Ruffles — If You Feel Like Them," from the *Pontiac Owners' Magazine*, in the designer file, Library of The Costume Institute, The Metropolitan Museum of Art.
16. I am grateful to Katie Valgenti for these observations, which she made in a presentation for my class in fashion history at the Fashion Institute of Technology.

17. Quoted in "Valentina," in *Current Biography* (1946), 607.
18. Ballard, *In My Fashion*, 164.
19. "Valentina, a Designer of Clothes for Stars in the Theatre, Dies at 90," *The New York Times* (September 15, 1989), B5.
20. *Vogue* (April 15, 1953), 72–73.
21. See note 19.
22. "Valentina Believes," *Harper's Bazaar* (January 1945), 68.
23. *Fortune* (December 1933), in Muriel King File, Special Collections, The Fashion Institute of Technology Library.
24. "Muriel King," in *Current Biography* (1943), 379–380.
25. *Ibid.*, 379.
26. *Harper's Bazaar* (December 1936), 62.
27. "Muriel King," in *Current Biography* (1943), 380. See also *Vogue* (July 1, 1943), 40.
28. Brendan Gill, *Here at The New Yorker* (New York: Random House, 1975), 203.
29. *Ibid.*, 206.
30. *The New Yorker* (April 4, 1936), 78.
31. *The New Yorker* (April 11, 1936), 72.
32. *The New Yorker* (May 9, 1936), 74, 76.
33. *The New Yorker* (April 19, 1947), 82.
34. *The New Yorker* (May 10, 1947), 72.
35. *The New Yorker* (February 6, 1960), 106.
36. Allan Keller, "Men Are Designing, Too," *World-Telegram* (no date, late 1930s), in "Costume Designers" Scrapbook, Special Collections, The Fashion Institute of Technology Library.

## CHAPTER 8

1. "Women Designers Set New Fashions," *Life* (January 14, 1946), 87.
2. *Vogue* (1941), quoted in Beryl Williams, *Fashion Is Our Business* (Philadelphia: J. B. Lippincott, 1945), 69.
3. *Harper's Bazaar* (October 1944), 89.
4. Claire McCardell, *What Shall I Wear?* (New York: Simon & Schuster, 1956), x.
5. Quoted in Williams, *Fashion Is Our Business*, 76.
6. Quoted in Sally Kirkland, "McCardell," in Sarah Tomerlin Lee, ed., *American Fashion* (New York: Quadrangle, 1975), 211.
7. Quoted in Phyllis Lee Levin, *The Wheels of Fashion* (Garden City, NY: Doubleday & Co., 1965), 224; Williams, *Fashion Is Our Business*, 90, 86.
8. Kirkland, "McCardell," 211.
9. Bettina Ballard, *In My Fashion* (New York: David McKay, 1967), 172.
10. Article from the *Knoxville News* (Fall 1944) in the Claire McCardell Files, Special Collections, The Fashion Institute of Technology Library.
11. McCardell, *What Shall I Wear?*, 14–15.
12. *Vogue* (January 1950), 93.
13. Quoted in "The American Look," *Time* (May 2, 1955), 85.
14. Ballard, *In My Fashion*, 172.
15. Quoted in Levin, *The Wheels of Fashion*, 108.
16. Milbank, *New York Fashion*, 162.
17. *Christian Science Monitor* (February 14, 1945), in the Tina Leser Scrapbooks, Special Collections, The Fashion Institute of Technology Library.
18. *New York Herald-Tribune* (October 19, 1955), in the Tina Leser Scrapbooks.
19. *Women's Wear Daily* (June 21, 1945), in the Tina Leser Scrapbooks.
20. Unidentified article (1945) by Catherine Roberts in the Tina Leser Scrapbooks.
21. "Global Fashions," *Holiday* (November 1949), in the Tina Leser Scrapbooks.
22. *Click* (July 1944), in the Tina Leser Scrapbooks.
23. Tina Leser advertisement from 1944, in the Tina Leser Scrapbooks.
24. "Male-Tested Fashions," *Cosmopolitan*

(January 1947), in the Tina Leser Scrapbooks.
25. Milbank, *New York Fashion*, 196.
26. "The American Look," 85.
27. Berch, *Radical By Design*, 75.
28. McCardell, *What Shall I Wear?*, 51.
29. *Ibid.*, 56.
30. "The American Look," 85.
31. Bernadine Morris, "Looking Back at McCardell: It's a Lot Like Looking at Today," *The New York Times* (May 24, 1972).
32. *Ibid.*
33. See note 10.
34. Adolph Klein quoted in *Time*, as quoted in McCardell, *What Shall I Wear?*, ix.
35. McCardell, *What Shall I Wear*, 5, 12, 4.
36. *Ibid.*, 18–19.

## CHAPTER 9

1. Hope Johnson, "Are Men Best Dress Designers?" *World-Telegram and Sun* (New York; January 18, 1954), in the designer file, Library of The Costume Institute, The Metropolitan Museum of Art. All quotations relating to the "Fath controversy" in the following paragraphs are from this source.
2. Louise Dahl-Wolfe, *A Photographer's Scrapbook*, (New York: Marek, 1984), 80.
3. Pieter Estersoh, "Louise Dahl-Wolfe," *Interview* (January 1981), 31.
4. Bridget Keenan, *Dior in Vogue* (New York: Harmony Books, 1981), 20.
5. Ballard, *In My Fashion*, 71–77.
6. See Steele, *Paris Fashion*, 275.
7. Johnson, "Are Men Best Dress Designers?"
8. See Isabelle Anscombe, *A Woman's Touch: Women in Design from 1860 to the Present Day* (New York: Viking Penguin, 1984), 11–12.
9. Quoted in Judy Rumbold, "Hot Coco," *Elle* (Great Britain; November 1988), 105; and in Frances Kennett, *Secrets of the Couturiers* (London: Orbis, 1984), 57.
10. Barbara Schreier, *Mystique and Identity: Women's Fashions of the 1950s* (Norfolk, VA: The Chrysler Museum, 1984), 9.
11. Christian Dior, *Christian Dior and I*, trans. Antonia Fraser (New York: E. P. Dutton, 1957), 35.
12. Anne Fogarty, *Wife-Dressing: The Fine Art of Being a Well-Dressed Wife* (New York: Julian Messer, 1959), 154.
13. Fogarty, quoted in Beryl Williams, *Young Faces in Fashion* (Philadelphia: J. B. Lippincott, 1956), 12.
14. Fogarty, *Wife-Dressing*, 10, 18, and dust jacket.
15. *Ibid.*, 25.
16. *Ibid.*, 45, 93, 9.
17. *Ibid.*, 145, 144.
18. Edith Head and Jane Kesmore Ardmore, *The Dress Doctor* (Boston: Little, Brown & Co., 1959), 193.
19. Sophie Gimbel, "Custom Order Clothes," in The Fashion Group, *Your Future in Fashion Design* (New York: Richard Rosen Press), 23.
20. Anne Klein, "Young Fashions," in *Ibid.*, 39–41.
21. Janey Ironside, *Fashion as a Career* (London: Museum Press, 1962), 55.
22. Quoted in Diamondstein, *Fashion: The Inside Story*, 9.
23. Pauline Trigère, quoted in *Ibid.*, 10.
24. Vicki Woods, "Talking Fashion," *Vogue* (October 1989), 454.

## CHAPTER 10

1. Quoted in Gigi Mahon, "Taking Off the White Gloves: S.I. Newhouse and Condé Nast," *The New York Times Magazine* (Sep-

tember 10, 1989), 50.
2. Horst P. Horst, *Salute to the Thirties* (New York: Viking, 1971), 13.
3. Ernestine Carter, *Magic Names of Fashion* (Englewood Cliffs, NJ: Prentice-Hall, 1980), 140.
4. Edna Woolman Chase and Ivy Chase, *Always In Vogue* (Garden City, NY: Doubleday & Co., 1954), 167–168.
5. Carmel Snow, with Mary Louise Aswell, *The World of Carmel Snow* (New York: McGraw-Hill, 1962), 36–37.
6. *Ibid.*, 44, 46.
7. Chase, *Always in Vogue*, 201–202.
8. *Ibid.*, 221–222.
9. Snow, *World of Carmel Snow*, 77–78.
10. Chase, *Always in Vogue*, 254.
11. Snow, *World of Carmel Snow*, 78.
12. Chase, *Always in Vogue*, 255.
13. Snow, *World of Carmel Snow*, 78, 75.
14. Quoted in Pieter Estersohn, "Louise Dahl-Wolfe," *Interview* (January 1981), 31.
15. Quoted in John Duka, "A Chronicler of Fashion, at 88, Reflects on Change," *The New York Times* (September 28, 1984), B6.
16. Louise Dahl-Wolfe, *A Photographer's Scrapbook* (New York: Marek, 1984), 39.
17. Snow, *World of Carmel Snow*, 99–100.
18. Duka, "A Chronicler of Fashion."
19. Snow, *World of Carmel Snow*, 99–100.
20. Estersohn, "Louise Dahl-Wolfe," 30.
21. Dahl-Wolfe, *A Photographer's Scrapbook*, 39.
22. *Ibid.*, 13. See also Duka, "A Chronicler of Fashion."
23. *Harper's Bazaar* (August 1936), 65.
24. Vreeland, quoted in Phyllis Lee Levin, *The Wheels of Fashion* (Garden City, NY: Doubleday & Co., 1965), 106, 99.
25. "Memos from Vreeland," *Mirabella* (October 1989), iv.
26. Quoted in Carter, *Magic Names of Fashion*, 163.
27. Diana Vreeland, with Christopher Hemphill, *Allure* (Garden City, NY: Doubleday & Co., 1980), 19.
28. Quoted in Levin, *The Wheels of Fashion*, 106.
29. Vreeland, *Allure*, 203.
30. Quoted in *The New York Times* (August 23, 1989), 1.
31. Richard Avedon, "Diana Vreeland: In Memoriam," *Vanity Fair* (January 1990), 158.
32. Quoted in Levin, *The Wheels of Fashion*, 116.
33. Diana Vreeland, *D.V.*, edited by George Plimpton and Christopher Hemphill (New York: Alfred A. Knopf, 1984), 149.
34. Vreeland, *Allure*, 134, 136.
35. Diane Rafferty, "Vreeland," *New York Woman* (November 1987), 60.
36. Vreeland, *Allure*, 56.
37. Christopher Cox, "Tall Girl Makes Good," *Soho News Style Supplement* (October 6, 1981), 21.
38. Nancy Axelrod Comer, "Women Photographers: Six Who Shoot Fashion," *Mademoiselle* (December 1986), 74–75.
39. Nancy Hall-Duncan, *The History of Fashion Photography* (New York: International Museum of Photography/Alpine Book Company, 1979), 217.
40. Comer, "Women Fashion Photographers," 75.

## CHAPTER 11

1. Clara Pierre, *Looking Good: The Liberation of Fashion* (New York: Reader's Digest Press, 1976), 248.
2. Quoted in Jane Mulvagh, *Vogue History of 20th Century Fashion* (New York: Viking, 1989), 239.
3. Barbara Hulanicki, *From A to Biba* (London: Hutchinson, 1983), 60, 62, 57.
4. Mary Quant, *Quant by Quant* (London: Cassel & Co., 1966), 21, 97, 48.
5. Quoted in Ruth Lynam, ed., *Couture: An Il-*

*lustrated History of the Great Paris Designers and Their Creations* (Garden City, NY: Doubleday & Co., 1972), 198.

6. Hulanicki, *From A to Biba*, 79, 82.
7. Quant, *Quant By Quant*, 79.
8. Sally Tuffin, quoted in Joel Lobenthal, *Radical Rags: Fashions of the Sixties* (New York: Abbeville Press, 1990), 15–16.
9. *Ibid.*, 15.
10. Betsey Johnson, quoted in *Ibid.*, 17.
11. Ashley, quoted in Amanda Greves, "Clothes Lines: Four Top British Designers Reveal their Visions and Methods," *Harper's and Queen* (April 1983), 160.
12. Author interview with Jacqueline Jacobson, January 1989. All quotations from Jacqueline Jacobson not otherwise attributed are from this interview.
13. Emmanuelle Khanh, quoted in Lobenthal, *Radical Rags*, 45–47.
14. *International Herald-Tribune*, quoted in Yvonne Deslandres and Florence Müller, *Histoire de la Mode au XXe siècle* (Paris: Somogy, 1986), 381.
15. "We Orbit Around . . . Betsey Johnson," *Mademoiselle* (August, 1966), 349.
16. Betsey Johnson, 1983, quoted in Jane Mulvagh, *Vogue History*, 238.
17. Kennedy Fraser, "On and Off the Avenue," *The New Yorker* (April 1, 1972), 97.
18. Author interview with Betsey Johnson, December 1988. All quotations from Betsey Johnson not otherwise attributed are from this interview.
19. Bill Cunningham, "Into the Woods," *Women's Wear Daily* (December 14, 1962), 8.
20. *The New York Times* (May 3, 1968), 56.
21. Bonnie Cashin Designer File, Special Collections, The Fashion Institute of Technology Library.
22. Beryl Williams, *Young Faces in Fashion* (Philadelphia: J. B. Lippincott, 1956), 142–143.
23. Bonnie Cashin Designer File.
24. Author interview with Bonnie Cashin, December 1990. All quotations from Bonnie Cashin not otherwise attributed are from this interview.
25. Alain Sorel, *The Creation of Fashion* (Paris: Stylists' Information Services, 1987), 54.
26. Jane Mulvagh, *Vogue History*, 298.
27. Norma Kamali, quoted in Lois Perschetz, ed., *W: The Designing Life* (New York: Clarkson N. Potter, Inc., 1987), 36.
28. June Weir, "Closing the Gender Gap," *The New York Times Magazine* (June 30, 1985), 45.

## CHAPTER 12

1. John Duka, "British Fashion: How It Shifted Into High Gear," *The New York Times* (March 24, 1984), 30.
2. Author interviw with Zandra Rhodes, June 1988. All quotations from Zandra Rhodes not otherwise attributed are from this interview.
3. Georgina Howell, "The Zandra Rhodes Dossier," *Vogue* (Great Britain; July 1978), 95.
4. Amanda Grieve, "Clothes Lines," *Harper's and Queen* (April 1983) 160.
5. Howell, "The Zandra Rhodes Dossier," 94.
6. Jean Muir, quoted in Mulvagh, *Vogue History of 20th Century Fashion*, 298.
7. Jean Muir, quoted in Ingrid Bleichroder, "Jean Muir: A Certain Style," *Vogue* (Great Britain; August 1985), 118.
8. Colin McDowell, *McDowell's Directory of Twentieth Century Fashion* (London: Frederick Muller, 1984), 210.
9. Iain Webb, "Secure with Miss Muir," *Harper's and Queen* (March 1991), 166–170.
10. Author telephone interview with Jean Muir, October 1989. All quotations from

Jean Muir not otherwise attributed are from this interview.
11. Quoted in Shane Adler Davis, "Jean Muir, Artist in Detail," *Costume: The Journal of the Costume Society* (1975), 32.
12. Author telephone interview with Vivienne Westwood, May 1989. All quotations from Vivienne Westwood not otherwise attributed are from this interview.
13. Liz Jobey, "Vivienne Westwood," *Vogue* (Great Britain; August 1987), 178.
14. Caryn Franklin, "Rule Britannia," interview with Vivienne Westwood, *i-D* (March 1987), 75.
15. Dick Hebdidge, *Subculture: The Meaning of Style* (New York: Methuen, 1979), 107–108.
16. Vivienne Westwood, quoted in Catherine McDermott, *Street Style: British Design in the 80s* (New York: Rizzoli International, 1987), 34.
17. Quoted in Jobey, "Vivienne Westwood," 178.
18. Grieve, "Clothes Lines," 161.
19. McDermott, *Street Style*, 33–34.
20. Grieve, "Clothes Lines," 160.
21. Jobey, "Vivienne Westwood," 178.
22. Grieve, "Clothes Lines," 160.
23. Franklin, "Rule Britannia," 74–75.
24. Jim Shelley, "Vivienne Westwood and Sarah Stockbridge," *Blitz* (March 1988), 47.
25. *Women's Wear Daily* (December 22, 1982), 7.
26. Michael Roberts, "From Punk to PM," *Tatler* (April 1989), 104.
27. "Royal Flush: Vivienne Westwood," *i-D* (August 1987), 57.
28. Franklin, "Rule Britannia," 74–75.
29. *Ibid.*
30. Richard Buckley, "Katharine the Great: Miss Hamnett Talks," *DNR: The Magazine* (February 1985), 41.
31. Caryn Franklin, "Power Dressing," interview with Katharine Hamnett, *i-D* (February 1987), 52.
32. Sarah Mower, "Katharine Hamnett: The Designer Star," *Vogue* (Great Britain; February 1987), 132.
33. Meredith Etherington Smith, "New Guard/Old Guard: Fashion Designers Katharine Hamnett and Jean Muir," *Ultra* (December 1984), 119.
34. Franklin, "Power Dressing," 52.
35. Paul Mathur, "Hamnett," *Blitz* (November 1989), 27.
36. *The New York Times* (March 24, 1984), 30.
37. "Katharine Hamnett Interview," *Art & Design* (December 1986), 41.

## CHAPTER 13

1. Liz Jobey, "Designing Women," *Vogue* (Great Britain; July 1987), 116.
2. "Sonia Rykiel," *Vogue* (Great Britain; May 1976), 130.
3. Author interview with Sonia Rykiel, November 1988. All quotations from Sonia Rykiel not otherwise attributed are from this interview.
4. Axel Madson, *Living for Design: The Yves Saint Laurent Story* (New York: Delacourt, 1979), 134–35.
5. *Women's Wear Daily* (January 17, 1978), 6–7.
6. Richard Actis-Grande, "Conversation avec Sonia Rykiel," reprinted from *Depêche-Mode*, n.p, n.d. Courtesy of Sonia Rykiel.
7. Sonia Rykiel, *Et je la voudrai nue . . .* (Paris: Bernard Grasset, 1979), 67–69.
8. Quoted in Madeleine Chapsal et al., *Rykiel* (Paris: Herscher, 1985), 44.
9. *Women's Wear Daily* (January 17, 1978), 6–7.

10. Lily Armon, "Un Style à part dans la mode actuelle — Sonia Rykiel," *Liberation* (August 1980), 10–12.
11. Rykiel, *Et je la voudrai nue . . .*, 70.
12. "Chantal Thomass: La Renouveau du froufrou," *Jardin des Modes* (October 1982), 26.
13. Gérard Depardieu, "Chantal Thomass," *La Mode en Peinture* (Winter 1982–83), n.p.
14. *Ibid.*
15. "Les Dessous de la mode," *Ena Mensuel* (February 1988), 13.
16. *Vogue* (Great Britain; October 1987), 152, 162.
17. Lisa Armstrong, "Myrène de Prémonville, the Designer Who Suits Herself," *Vogue* (Great Britain; March 1991), 208.
18. Joby, "Designing Women," 112.
19. Kim Hastreiter, "Mad Mollies," *Paper* (March 1989), 32.
20. Author telephone interview with Agnès de Fleurieu, July 1988. All quotations from Agnès de Fleurieu not otherwise attributed are from this interview.
21. Anne-Marie Beretta publicity materials, 1989.
22. Rebecca Voight, "Martine Sitbon: France's Best-Kept Fashion Secret," *i-D* (March 1989), 28.
23. Elise Maiberger, "Sitbon Pretty," *The Face* (June 1988), 18.
24. Voight, "Martine Sitbon," 29.

## CHAPTER 14

1. Daniela Petroff, "Women Designers," *The International Herald Tribune* (October 3–4, 1981), part of the special section, "Who's Who in Italian Fashion," 8S.
2. Laura Biagiotti, written responses to questions submitted by the author, January 1991. All quotations from Laura Biagiotti not otherwise attributed are from this personal communication.
3. Mariuccia Mandelli, written responses to questions submitted by the author, January 1989. All quotations from Mariuccia Mandelli not otherwise attributed are from this personal communication.
4. Grazietta Butazzi, ed. *Italian Fashion: The Origins of High Fashion and Knitwear* (Milan: Electa, 1987), 154.
5. See note 1.
6. Quoted in Silvia Giacomoni, *The Italian Look Reflected* (Milan: Mazzotta, 1984), 86–87.
7. *Ibid.*, 87.
8. McDowell, *McDowell's Directory of Twentieth-Century Fashion*, 188.
9. Quoted in Giacomoni, *The Italian Look Reflected*, 104.
10. *Ibid.*, 19–20.
11. Quoted in Marie-Ange Poyet, "Krizia et les Mariucci ou une femme et ses doubles," *Joyce* (Spring/Summer 1988), 118–119.

## CHAPTER 15

1. Author interview with Sybilla, June 1989. All quotations from Sybilla not otherwise attributed are from this interview.
2. "Deux Grands d'Espagne: Sybilla et Javier Valhonrat," *Jardin des Modes* (April 1–8, 1989), 16.
3. Michael Gross, "Ten to Watch," *The New York Times Magazine*, "Fashions of the Times" (August 23, 1987), 170.
4. "View," *Vogue* (September 1988), 158.
5. Ada de la Fuente, "El inevitable éxito de una nina salvaje," [The Inevitable Success of a Wild Girl], *Vogue* (Spain; August 1988), 120.

## CHAPTER 16

1. Ben Brantley, "Kawakubo Talks," *Women's Wear Daily* (1 March 1983), 48.
2. Suzy Menkes, "Feminist versus Sexist," *The Times* (London; March 22, 1983), 11.
3. *Vogue*, letters to the editor (July 1983), 70.
4. Holly Brubach, "The Truth in Fiction," *Atlantic Monthly* (May 1984), 96.
5. Geraldine Ranson, "Japan, the Shock of the New," in Brenda Polan, ed., *Fashion 84* (New York: St. Martin's Press, 1983), 53.
6. Nicholas Coleridge, *The Fashion Conspiracy* (London: Heinemann, 1988), 89.
7. Deyan Sudjic, *Rei Kawakubo and Comme des Garçons* (New York: Rizzoli, 1990), 42.
8. Quoted in Kennedy Fraser, *Scenes from the Fashionable World* (New York: Alfred A. Knopf, 1987), 80.
9. Mary Russell, "Japanese Fashion Now," *Vogue* (September 1982), 194.
10. Quoted in Leonard Koren, *New Fashion Japan* (Tokyo and New York: Kodansha, 1984), 117.
11. Harold Koda, "Rei Kawakubo and the Aesthetic of Poverty," *Dress* 11 (1985), 8.
12. Quoted in Koren, *New Fashion Japan*, 114.
13. Quoted in Evans and Thornton, *Women and Fashion*, 163.
14. Brantley, "Kawakubo Talks," 48.
15. Sudjic, *Rei Kawakubo*, 13.
16. Charlotte Du Cann, *Vogue Modern Style* (London: Century, 1988), 48.
17. Fashion Institute of Technology, *Three Women: Madeleine Vionnet, Claire McCardell, and Rei Kawakubo*, exhibition catalogue (New York, 1987), n.p.
18. Brantley, "Kawakubo Talks," 48.
19. Quoted in *L'Express* (January 10–16, 1977), in designer file, UFAC.
20. Carol Mongo, "Paris Style From A to Z," *Accent: The Magazine of Paris Style* (Winter 1987), 87.
21. Hanae Mori, written responses to questions submitted by the author, August 1988. All quotations from Hanae Mori not otherwise attributed are from this private communication.
22. Quoted in *Madame Figaro* (April 17, 1987), in designer file, UFAC.

## CHAPTER 17

1. June Weir, "Closing the Gender Gap," *The New York Times Magazine* (June 30, 1985), 44.
2. Stephanie Mansfield, "Prima Donna," *Vogue* (August 1989), 291, 293.
3. Quoted in "Karan About Women," *Self* (February 1989), 105.
4. Donna Karan, Guest Lecture at the Fashion Institute of Technology (February 10, 1986). Videotape.
5. Quoted in Susan Snell, "Donna Karan Bares Body Suit and Soul," *Dallas Apparel News, Holiday/Resort* (August 1985), 32.
6. Quoted in Mansfield, "Prima Donna," 293.
7. Snell, "Donna Karan Bares Body Suit and Soul," 32.
8. Mansfield, "Prima Donna," 370.
9. Lee Wohlfert-Wihlborg, "The Label Is Anne Klein, but the Name That Keeps It Going Belongs to Donna Karan," *People* (March 29, 1982), 93.
10. Quoted in Bernadine Morris, *The Fashion Makers: An Inside Look at America's Leading Designers* (New York: Random House, 1978), 135.
11. Quoted in Joan Lebow, "Designer Profile," *New York Apparel News* (October 1981), 132.
12. Quoted in Nina Darnton, "On Her Own,"

*The New York Times* (April 14, 1985), 75.
13. Wohlfert-Wihlborg, "The Label Is Anne Klein," 94.
14. Lebow, "Designer Profile," 132.
15. Quoted in Darnton, "On Her Own," 70.
16. Quoted in "Split Personalities," *Women's Wear Daily* (October 31, 1984), 40.
17. Quoted in Liz Jobey, "Designing Women," *Vogue* (Great Britain; July 1987), 110.
18. Quoted in Mansfield, "Prima Donna," 370.
19. Jobey, "Designing Women," 110.
20. *Ibid.*
21. Susan Alai, "Donna Karan Takes the Lead," *Women's Wear Daily* (July 10, 1985), 6.
22. "Donna Karan: Hot and Getting Hotter," *Women's Wear Daily* (April 3, 1989), 6.
23. "Donna Karan, Designing Woman," in Catherine Milinaire and Carol Troy, *Cheap Chic* (New York: Crown Publishers, 1978), 100.
24. Lois Perschetz, *W: The Designing Life* (New York: Clarkson N. Potter, 1987), 201.
25. Quoted in *Ibid.*
26. Georgina Howell, "The Attitude Sell," *Vogue* (March 1989), 370. See also Susan Smith, "Whatever Happened to Donna Karan's Working Woman?" *Vogue* (Great Britain; November 1988), 21.
27. Jobey, "Designing Women," 110.
28. Author interview with Carolyne Roehm, February 1989. All quotations from Carolyne Roehm not otherwise attributed are from this interview.
29. "Oscar de la Renta: Fashion's Gentle Lothario," in Pershetz, *W: The Designing Life*, 42.
30. Jesse Kornbluth, "The Working Rich," *New York* (November 24, 1986), 33.
31. "Designing Woman," *Savvy* (January 1986), 26.
32. Suzy Menkes, "Couture's Grand Ladies," *The Illustrated London News* (Spring 1990), 68.
33. Georgina Howell, "Roehm's Empire," *Vogue* (August 1990), 354, 358.
34. Jennet Conant, "The Social Sewing Circle: Those Designing Blue Bloods Get Ever So Haute," *Newsweek* (June 30, 1986), 56–57.
35. Kornbluth, "The Working Rich," 31.
36. Julie Connelly, "The CEO's Second Wife," *Fortune* (August 28, 1989), 53, 60.
37. Menkes, "Couture's Grand Ladies," 68.
38. John Fairchild, *Chic Savages* (New York: Simon & Schuster, 1989), 167.
39. Quoted in *Women's Wear Daily* (May 22, 1978), 4.
40. Priscilla Tucker, "Mary Had a Little Dress," *Daily News* (April 6, 1980), in designer files, Special Collections, The Fashion Institute of Technology Library.
41. Bridget Foley, "Mary McFadden: A New Type of Tycoon," *New York Apparel News* (March 1983), 20.
42. Author interview with Mary McFadden, December 1988. All quotations from Mary McFadden not otherwise attributed are from this interview.
43. Michael Gross, "Mary, Mary Quite Contrary: The Life and Loves of Mary McFadden," *New York* (March 26, 1990), 44.
44. Diane Rafferty, "Beyond Fashion," *Connoisseur* (October 1988), 148–152.
45. Ellin Saltzman quoted in Harriet Shapiro, "From Venezuela to Seventh Avenue, Carolina Herrera's Fashions Cast a Long Shadow," *People* (May 3, 1982), 121.
46. Author interview with Carolina Herrera, February 1989. All quotations from Carolina Herrera not otherwise attributed are from this interview.
47. Author interview with Betsey Johnson, May 1989. All quotations from Betsey Johnson not otherwise attributed come from this interview.

48. Author interview with Joan Vass, August 1989. All quotations from Joan Vass not otherwise attributed come from this interview.
49. Author interview with Patricia Underwood, January 1989. All quotations from Patricia Underwood not otherwise attributed are from this interview.
50. Page Hill Starzinger, "Smart Women, Smart Clothes," *Vogue* (September 1988), 641.
51. Author telephone interview with Jennifer George, December 1990. All quotations from Jennifer George not otherwise attributed are from this interview.
52. Anne-Marie Shiro, "For Fall, Fashions That Make One Statement: Wearability," *The New York Times* (April 8, 1990), 48.
53. Anne-Marie Schiro, "Adrienne Vittadini: From Sweaters To an Empire," *The New York Times* (July 19, 1988), B20.
54. Author telephone interview with Adrienne Vittadini, December 1990. All quotations from Adrienne Vittadini not otherwise attributed are from this interview.
55. Woody Hochswender, "A First Show With the Right Flare," *The New York Times* (November 3, 1990), 31.
56. Author interview with Nicole Miller, March 1989. All quotations from Nicole Miller not otherwise attributed are from this interview.
57. Author interview with Patricia Clyne, September 1988. All quotations from Patricia Clyne not otherwise attributed are from this interview.
58. Vicky Woods, "Designing Woman: Charlotte Neuville," *Vogue* (September 1989), 156–157.
59. Author interview with Diane Pernet, January 1989. All quotations from Diane Pernet not otherwise attributed are from this interview.
60. Walter S., "Showboat," *The Village Voice* (May 2, 1989), 38.
61. Kim Hastreiter, "The New York Collections," *Paper* (January 1990), 30.
62. Author interview with Isabel Toledo, January 1989. All quotations from Isabel Toledo not otherwise attributed are from this interview.
63. Richard Martin, "The Emperors of New Clothes," *Textile and Text*, 12:4 (1990), 31 (emphasis added).

## POSTSCRIPT

1. Woody Hochswender, "AIDS and the Fashion World: Industry Fears for Its Health," *The New York Times* (February 11, 1990), 1, 42. See also Christopher Canatsey, "AIDS Phobia on Seventh Avenue," *The Advocate* (September 25, 1990), 38–43.
2. Quoted in Katie Kelly, *The Wonderful World of Women's Wear Daily* (New York: Saturday Review Press, 1972), 242.
3. Stuart Timmons, "Designer Rudi Gernreich Stayed In the Fashion Closet," *The Advocate* (September 25, 1990), 45.
4. Phyllis Furman and Linda Moss, "A Requiem for Fashion," *Crain's New York Business* (April 9, 1990), 36–37.
5. John Fairchild, *Chic Savages* (New York: Simon and Schuster, 1989), 167–170.
6. Edmund Bergler, *Fashion and the Unconscious* (New York: Brunner, 1953), vii–viii.
7. Furman and Moss, "A Requiem for Fashion," 4–5.

217

# BIBLIOGRAPHY

## ARTICLES AND BOOKS

Aillaud, Charlotte. "Legend: Madame Grès, Timeless Style of the Parisian Couturière." *Architectural Digest* (September 1988).

Alai, Susan. "Donna Karan Takes the Lead." *Women's Wear Daily* (July 10, 1985).

———. "The Rich Life of Carolyne & Henry." *W* (June 16–23, 1986).

Andriotakis, Pamela. "The Heir to the House of Lanvin Married a Model Who's Now a Designing Wife." *People* (May 17, 1982).

L'Anglade, Emile. *Rose Bertin, The Creator of Fashion at the Court of Marie Antoinette* (London: John Long, 1913).

"Anne-Marie Beretta: La Volonté d' épurer." *Jardin des Modes* (October 1982).

Anscombe, Isabelle. *A Woman's Touch: Women in Design from 1860 to the Present Day* (New York: Viking, 1984).

Armstrong, Lisa. "Myrène de Prémonville, the Designer Who Suits Herself." *Vogue* (Great Britain; March 1991).

Arroyuelo, Javier. "Fashion Royalty and the Couture Courts of Paris." *Vanity Fair* (March 1986).

Avedon, Richard. "Diana Vreeland: In Memorium." *Vanity Fair* (January 1990).

Aveline, Michel, ed. *Chanel, Overture pour la mode à Marseille* (Marseille: Musées de Marseille, 1989).

Ballard, Bettina. *In My Fashion* (New York: David McKay, 1967).

Barry, Joseph. "'I Am On the Side of Women,' Said My Friend Chanel." *Smithsonian* (May 1971).

Beaton, Cecil. *Self-Portrait With Friends*, ed. by Richard Buckles (London: Weidenfeld & Nicolson, 1979).

Benaïm, Laurence. *L'Année de la mode 1987–88* (Lyon: La Manufacture, 1988).

———. *L'Année de la mode 1988–89* (Lyon: La Manufacture, 1989).

Bender, Marylin. *The Beautiful People* (New York: Coward-McCann, 1967).

Berch, Bettina. *Radical By Design: The Life and Style of Elizabeth Hawes* (New York: E. P. Dutton, 1988).

Berman, Phyllis, and Zina Sawaya. "The Billionaires Behind Chanel." *Forbes* (April 3, 1989).

Bertin, Celia. *Paris à la Mode* (London: Victor Gollancz, 1956).

Bleichroder, Ingrid. "Jean Muir: A Certain Style." *Vogue* (Great Britain; August 1985).

Bloomfield, Judy. "Happy Partners Bacon & Johnson." *Women's Wear Daily* (September 7, 1988).

"Body Worship." *Newsweek* (January 28, 1974).

Bogart, Anne. "Regal Air: La Comtesse de Ribes' Chic Fashions Are More Than a Case of Noblesse Oblige." *Harper's Bazaar* (September 1989).

Bonney, Thérèse, and Louise Bonney. *A Shopping Guide to Paris* (New York: Robert McBride, 1929).

Boy, Billy, with photos by Robert Doisneau. "Hommage à Schiaparelli." *Femme* (June 1987).

Brady, James. *Superchic* (Boston: Little, Brown & Co., 1974).

Brantley, Ben. "All Dressed Up." *Women's Wear Daily* (February 24, 1982).

———. "Kawakubo Talks." *Women's Wear Daily* (March 1, 1983).

———. "Spain's New Flame." *Vanity Fair* (November 1989).

Brubach, Holly. "Quoting Chanel." *The Atlantic* (January 1984).

———. "School of Chanel." *The New Yorker* (February 27, 1989).

Buckley, Richard. "Katherine the Great: Miss Hamnett Talks." *DNR: The Magazine* (February 1985).

Bumiller, Elisabeth. "Japanese Style." *Vogue* (December 1990).

Butazzi, Grazietta, ed. *Italian Fashion* (Milan: Edizion Electa, 1987).

Byers, Margaretta. *Help Wanted—Female* (New York: Julian Messner, 1941).

Canatsey, Christopher. "AIDS Phobia on Seventh Avenue." *The Advocate* (September 25, 1990).

Carter, Ernestine. *Magic Names of Fashion* (Englewood Cliffs, NJ: Prentice-Hall, 1980).

Chadwick, Whitney. "The Muse as Artist: Women in the Surrealist Movement." *Art in America* (July 1985).

Chamberlin, Anne. "The Fabulous Coco Chanel." *Ladies Home Journal* (October 1963).

"Chanel Designs Again." *Vogue* (February 15, 1954).

"Chanel #1." *Time* (January 25, 1971).

"Chanel No. 1." *Look* (October 23, 1962).

"Chanel Show Jan. 26; House's Future in Doubt." *Women's Wear Daily* (January 12, 1971).

"Chantal Thomass: La Renouveau du froufrou." *Jardin des Modes* (October 1982).

Chapsal, Madeleine. "Chanel au travail." *L'Express* (August 11, 1960).

———. "La Grande Mademoiselle." *Mademoiselle* (March 1961).

———. "Hommage à Madeleine Vionnet." *Vogue* (France; April, 1975).

——— et al. *Rykiel* (Paris: Herscher, 1985).

———. *La Chair de la robe* (Paris: Fayard, 1989).

Charles-Roux, Edmonde. *Chanel: Her Life, Her World, and the Woman Behind the Legend She Herself Created* (New York: Alfred A. Knopf, 1975).

———. *Chanel and Her World* (London: Weidenfeld & Nicolson, 1982).

Chase, Edna Woolman, and Ivy Chase. *Always in Vogue* (Garden City, NY: Doubleday & Co., 1954).

Chatwin, Bruce. *What Am I Doing Here?* (New York: Viking, 1989).

Cocteau, Jean. "Mademoiselle Chanel." *Harper's Bazaar* (March 1954).

Coffin, David Page. "Rei Kawakubo: This Designer is Reinventing Fashion." *Threads* (February/March 1988).

Coleridge, Nicholas. *The Fashion Conspiracy* (London: Heinemann, 1988).

Comer, Nancy Axelrod. "Betsey Johnson." *Mademoiselle* (August 1972).

———. "Women Photographers: Six Who Shoot Fashion." *Mademoiselle* (December 1986).

Conant, Jennet. "The Social Sewing Circle: Those Designing Blue Bloods Get Ever So Haute." *Newsweek* (June 30, 1986).

———. "The Norma Conquests." *Manhattan Inc.* (December 1987).

"Connaissez-vous Lanvin?" *Figaro* (January 24, 1986).

Cooper, Arlene. "How Madame Grès Sculpts with Fabric." *Threads* (April-May 1987).

Cox, Christopher. "Tall Girl Makes Good." *Soho News Style Supplement* (October 6, 1981).

Cuadrado, John. "The Fashion Image: Louise Dahl-Wolfe." *Architectural Digest* (September 1988).

Cunningham, Bill. "Into the Woods." *Women's Wear Daily* (December 14, 1962).

———. "The Collections." *Details* (September 1987).

Daché, Lilly. *Talking Through My Hats* (New York: Coward-McCann, 1946).

Dahl-Wolfe, Louise. *A Photographer's Scrapbook* (New York: Marek, 1984).

Daria, Irene. "Carolina Herrera: A Personal Evolution." *Women's Wear Daily* (March 2, 1987).

———. *The Fashion Cycle* (New York: Simon & Schuster, 1990).

Darnton, Nina. "On Her Own." *The New York Times* (April 14, 1985).

Daves, Jessica. *Ready-Made Miracle* (New York: G. P. Putnam's Sons, 1967).

Davis, Shane Adler. "Jean Muir, Artist in Detail." *Costume: The Journal of the Costume Society* (1975).

Delmar, Michael. "Avec Rei Kawakubo." *Jardin des Modes* (September 1987).

Demasse, Jacques. *Sonia Delaunay: Fashion and Fabrics* (London: Thames & Hudson, 1991).

Demoraine, Hélène. "Sonia Delaunay." *Connaissance des Arts* (May 1966).

Demornex, Jacqueline. *Madeleine Vionnet* (Paris: Editions du Regard, 1990).

Denys, Jean. "Chanel Aujourd'hui." *Elle* (November 17, 1958).

Depardieu, Gérard. "Chantal Thomass." *La Mode en Peinture* (Winter 1982–83).

"Designing Women." *Savvy* (January 1986).

"Designing Women." *Harper's Bazaar* (September 1989).

Deslandres, Yvonne, and Florence Müller. *Histoire de la Mode au XXᵉ siècle* (Paris: Somogy, 1986).

"Deux Grands d'Espagne: Sybilla et Javier Valhonrat." *Jardin des Modes* (April 1–8, 1989).

Diamondstein, Barbaralee. *Fashion: The Inside Story* (New York: Rizzoli International, 1985).

"Diana Vreeland." *Vogue* (December, 1989).

Dreier, Deborah. "Designing Women." *Art in America* (May 1987).

Duka, John. "British Fashion: How It Shifted Into High Gear." *The New York Times* (March 24, 1984).

———. "A Chronicler of Fashion, at 88, Reflects on Change." *The New York Times* (September 28, 1984).

Estersohn, Pieter. "Louise Dahl-Wolfe." *Interview* (January 1981).

Etherington-Smith, Meredith. "New Guard/Old Guard: Fashion Designers Katharine Hamnett and Jean Muir." *Ultra* (December 1984).

Evans, Caroline, and Minna Thornton. *Women and Fashion: A New Look* (London and New York: Quartet, 1989).

Fairchild, John. *The Fashionable Savages* (New York: Doubleday & Co., 1965).

———. *Chic Savages* (New York: Simon & Schuster, 1989).

The Fashion Group. *Your Future in Fashion Design* (New York: Richard Rosen Press, 1966).

Fashion Institute of Technology, *Three Women: Madeleine Vionnet, Claire McCardell, and Rei Kawakubo*. Exhibition catalogue (New York, 1987).

"Fashion: The American Look." *Time* (May 2, 1955).

"Femme de la semaine: Chanel." *L'Express* (August 17, 1956).

Fitzgerald, Sheryl. "The Enduring Appeal of Coco Chanel." *Newsday* (July 19, 1984).

Fogarty, Anne. *Wife-Dressing: The Fine Art of Being a Well-Dressed Wife* (New York: Julian Messer, 1959).

Foley, Bridget. "Mary McFadden: A New Type of Tycoon." *New York Apparel News* (March 1983).

François, Lucien. *Comment un nom devient une griffe* (Paris: Gallimard, 1961).

Franklin, Carny. "Power Dressing," Interview with Katharine Hamnett. *i-D* (February 1987).

———. "Rule Britannia," Interview with Vivienne Westwood. *i-D* (March 1987).

Fraser, Kennedy. "On and Off the Avenue." *The New Yorker* (April 1, 1972).

———. *The Fashionable Mind* (New York: Alfred A. Knopf, 1981).

de la Fuente, Ada. "El inevitable éxito de una nina salvaje" [The Inevitable Success of a Wild Girl]. *Vogue* (Spain; August 1988).

Furman, Phyllis, and Linda Moss. "A Requiem for Fashion." *Crain's New York Business* (April 9, 1990).

Gandee, Charles. "Norma Kamali Comes Home." *House and Garden* (December 1988).

Giacomoni, Silvia. *The Italian Look Reflected* (Milan: Mazzotta, 1984).

Gold, Arthur, and Robert Fitzgerald. *Misia: The Life of Misia Sert* (New York: Alfred A. Knopf, 1980).

Grieve, Amanda. "Clothes Lines: Four Top British Designers Reveal Their Visions and Methods." *Harper's and Queen* (April 1983).

Gross, Michael. "The Cutting Edge." *New York* (May 15, 1985).

———. "Chanel Today." *The New York Times Magazine* (July 28, 1985).

———. "Four Women in Fashion: True to Their Vision." *The New York Times* (April 16, 1987).

———. "Mary, Mary, Quite Contrary: The Life and Loves of Mary McFadden." *New York* (March 26, 1990).

Haedrich, Marcel. *Coco Chanel: Her Life, Her Secrets* (Boston: Little, Brown & Co., 1972).

Hall-Duncan, Nancy. *The History of Fashion Photography* (New York: International Museum of Photography/The Alpine Book Company, Inc., 1979).

Hastreiter, Kim. "Vass Appeal." *Mirabella* (January 1991).

Hawes, Elizabeth. *Fashion is Spinach* (New York: Random House, 1938).

———. *Men Can Take It* (New York: Random House, 1939).

———. *Why Is a Dress?* (New York: The Viking Press, 1942).

———. *Why Women Cry, or Wenches with Wrenches* (New York: Reynal & Hitchcock, 1943).

———. *It's Still Spinach* (Boston: Little, Brown & Co., 1954).

Head, Edith, and Jane Kesmore Ardmore. *The Dress Doctor* (Boston: Little, Brown & Co., 1959).

———, with Joe Hyams. *How To Dress for Success* (New York: Random House, 1967).

Hebdidge, Dick. *Subculture: The Meaning of Style* (New York: Methuen, 1979).

Hochswender, Woody. "AIDS and the Fashion World: Industry Fears for its Health." *The New York Times* (February 11, 1990).

———. "A First Show with the Right Flair." *The New York Times* (November 3, 1990).

Hollander, Anne. "A Sculptor in Fabric." *Connoisseur* (August 1982).

———. "The Great Emancipator, Chanel." *Connoisseur* (February 1983).

Horst, Horst P. *Salute to the Thirties* (New York: Viking, 1971).

"The House of Schiaparelli." *Vogue* (April 15, 1931).

Howell, Georgina. "The Zandra Rhodes Dossier." *Vogue* (Great Britain; July 1978).

———. "Anouska Who?" *Vanity Fair* (November 1988).

———. "The Attitude Sell." *Vogue* (March 1989).

———. "Roehm's Empire." *Vogue* (August 1990).

Hulanicki, Barbara. *From A to Biba* (London: Hutchinson, 1983).

Ironside, Janey. *Fashion as a Career* (London: Museum Press, 1962).

Jobey, Liz. "Designing Women." *Vogue* (Great Britain; July 1987).

———. "Vivienne Westwood." *Vogue* (Great Britain; August 1987).

Johnson, Hope. "Are Men Best Dress Designers?" *World-Telegram and Sun* (New York; January 18, 1954).

"Just a Simple Little Dressmaker." *Life* (August 19, 1957).

Keller, Allan. "Men are Designing, Too." *World-Telegram* (n.d., late 1930s), in "Costume Designers" Scrapbook in Special Collections, Fashion Institute of Technology Library.

Kelly, Katie. *The Wonderful World of Women's World Daily* (New York: Saturday Review Press, 1972).

Kennett, Frances. *Secrets of the Couturiers* (London: Orbis, 1984).

Kidd, J. D. "Comme des Garçons: The Woman Behind the Boys." *Daily News Record* (May 9, 1983).

Kirke, Betty. "A Dressmaker Extraordinaire: Discovering the Secrets of Madeleine Vionnet's Celebrity" *Threads* (February/March 1989).

Kirkland, Sally. "McCardell," in Sarah Tomerlin Lee, ed. *American Fashion* (New York: Quadrangle, 1975).

Klensch, Elsa. "Rei Kawakubo." *Vogue* (August 1987).

Koda, Harold. "Rei Kawakubo and the Aesthetic of Poverty." *Dress* 11 (1985).

Koren, Leonard. *New Fashion Japan* (Tokyo and New York: Kodansha, 1984).

Kornbluth, Jesse. "The Empress of Clothes." *New York* (November 29, 1982).

———. "The Working Rich." *New York* (November 24, 1986).

Latour, Amy. *Kings of Fashion*, trans. Mervyn Savill (London: Weidenfeld & Nicolson, 1958).

Lavrentier, Alexander. *Varvara Stepanova: The Complete Work* (Cambridge: The M.I.T. Press, 1988).

Lawrenson, Helen. "The Madcap Who Made Women Young." *Cosmopolitan* (September 1961).

Le Moy, Pascale Villiers. "The Timeless Fashions of Madame Grès." *Connoisseur* (August 1982).

Lebow, Joan. "Designer Profile." *Women's Wear Daily* (October 31, 1981).

Leusse, Claude de. "Timeless Chanel." *Women's Wear Daily* (January 17, 1971).

Leser, Tina. *Scrapbooks* (unpublished). Special Collections, Fashion Institute of Technology Library.

Levin, Phyllis Lee. *The Wheels of Fashion* (Garden City, NY: Doubleday and Co., 1965).

Leymarie, Jean. *Chanel* (New York: Rizzoli International, 1987).

Lobenthal, Joel. *Radical Rags: Fashions of the Sixties* (New York: Abbeville Press, 1990).

The London Museum. *Mary Quant's London*, with an introduction by Ernestine Carter (London, 1973).

Long, Lois. "On and Off the Avenue." *The New Yorker* (various issues, 1920s–1970).

Lucille, Lady Duff Gordon. *Private Collection Scrapbooks* (unpublished). Special Collections, Fashion Institute of Technology Library.

———. *Discretions and Indiscretions* (London: Jarrolds, 1932).

Lynam, Ruth, ed. *Couture: An Illustrated History of the Great Paris Designers and Their Creations* (Garden City, NY: Doubleday & Co., 1972).

"Madame Grès for the People." *Connoisseur* (January 1985).

"Madame Grès, Helene de Paris." *Jardin des Modes* (December 1980-January 1981).

Madson, Axel. *Living for Design: The Yves Saint Laurent Story* (New York: Delacourt, 1979).

———. *Chanel* (New York: Henry Holt & Co., 1990).

Mahon, Gigi. "Taking Off the White Gloves: S. I. Newhouse and Condé Nast." *The New York Times Magazine* (September 10, 1989).

Maiberger, Elise. "Sitbon Pretty." *The Face* (June 1988).

Mansfield, Stephanie. "Prima Donna." *Vogue* (August 1989).

———. "Rebecca Moses." *Vogue* (December 1989).

Marquand, Lilou. *Chanel m'a dit* (Paris: Editions Jean-Claude Clattès, 1990).

Martin, Richard. "The Emperors of New Clothes" *Textile and Text* 12:4 (1990).

Mathur, Paul. "Hamnett." *Blitz* (November 1989).

Mattera, Jeanne. "Louise Dahl-Wolfe: Still Snappy." *Women's Wear Daily* (October 31, 1984).

Mazzoli, Rita. "Une femme et les villes: Agnès B, l'art et la manière." *Murs, Murs* (June 1987).

McCardell, Claire. *Notebooks* (unpublished). Parsons School of Design.

———. *What Shall I Wear?* (New York: Simon & Schuster, 1956).

McDermott, Catherine. *Street Style: British Design in the 80s* (New York: Rizzoli International, 1987).

McDowell, Colin. *McDowell's Directory of 20th Century Fashion* (London: Frederick Mullen, 1984).

———. "Krizia—Tough and Witty." *Country Life* (March 19, 1987).

McRobbie, Angela, ed. *Zoot Suits and Second-Hand Dresses* (Boston: Unwin Hyman, 1988).

Melinkoff, Ellin. *What We Wore: An Offbeat Social History of Women's Clothing, 1950-1980* (New York: Quill, 1984).

Melly, George. *Revolt Into Style* (London: Allen Lane, 1970).

Menkes, Suzy. "Feminist versus Sexist." *The Times* (March 22, 1983).

———. "An Eighties Aristo for Coco." *The Times* (July 1, 1986).

———. "Chanel's Toy Boy." *The Times* (April 15, 1986).

———. "Couture's Grand Ladies." *The Illustrated London News* (Spring 1990).

———. "Who's Avant-Garde Now?" *International Herald Tribune* (March 15, 1991).

Meranus, Dianne T. "Fashion Design: Men Do Dominate." *F.I.T. Review* (Spring 1989).

Merkin, Daphne. "Prima Donna." *Mirabella* (September 1990).

Milbank, Caroline Rennolds. *Couture* (New York: Stewart, Tabori & Chang, 1985).

———. *New York Fashion: The Evolution of American Style* (New York: Harry N. Abrams, 1989).

Milinaire, Caterine, and Carol Troy. *Cheap Chic* (New York: Harmony Books, 1975).

Morand, Paul. *L'Allure de Chanel* (Paris: Hermann, 1976).

Moreno, Elizabeth. *Sonia Delaunay: Art Into Fashion* (New York: George Braziller, 1986).

Morieux, François. "Inès de la Fressange, mannequin-star." *Jours de France* (December 12-18, 1987).

———. "Le Mythe Chanel." *Tours de France* (August 23-29, 1988).

Morris, Bernadine. "Fashion Catches Up with Cashin." *The New York Times* (May 3, 1968).

———. "Looking Back at McCardell: It's a Lot Like Looking At Today." *The New York Times* (May 24, 1972).

———, with photographs by Barbara Walz. *The Fashion Makers: An Inside Look at America's Leading Designers* (New York: Random House, 1978).

———. "Zoran and Kamali: Success With the Offbeat." *The New York Times* (January 4, 1983).

———. "Jacqueline de Ribes had a Design Suited to Success." *The New York Times* (September 30, 1985).

———. "Valentina, A Designer of Clothes for Stars in the Theater, Dies." *The New York Times* (September 15, 1989).

Mower, Sarah. "Katharine Hamnett." *Vogue* (Great Britain; February 1987).

———. "Sonia Delaunay." *Vogue* (Great Britain; March 1991).

Mulvagh, Jane. *Vogue History of 20th-Century Fashion* (New York: Viking, 1989).

Musée de la Mode et du Costume. *Hommage à Elsa Schiaparelli* (Paris, 1974).

———. *Paul Poiret and Nicole Groult.* Text by Guillaume Garnier, et al. (Paris: Edition Paris Musées, 1986).

———. *Paris-Couture-Années trente.* Text by Guillaume Garnier, et al. (Paris, 1987).

Musée Historique des Tissus. *Paquin: Une retrospective de 60 ans de haute couture* (Lyons, 1989).

Musée Richard-Anacréon Grandville. *Femmes créatrices des années vingt* (Paris: Editions Arts et Culture, 1988).

Nemy, Enid. "Fashion was Her Pulpit." *The New York Times* (January 11, 1971).

Neville, Bernard. "Madame Vionnet," in Josephine Ross, ed., *The Vogue Bedtime Book II* (London: Century Hutchinson, 1986).

Osaki, Amy Boyce. "A 'Truly Feminine Employment': Sewing and the Early Nineteenth-Century Woman." *Winterthur Portfolio* 23:4 (Winter 1988).

Paquin, Jeanne. *Design and Publicité* (unpublished). Costume Research Centre, Bath, England.

Parker, Rozsika. *The Subversive Stitch: Embroidery and the Making of the Feminine* (New York: Routledge, 1989).

Pellegrin, Nicole. *Les Vêtements de la Liberté* (Aixen-Provence, Editions Alinea, 1989).

Penn, Irving. *Inventive Paris Clothes, 1909-1939*, with text by Diana Vreeland (New York: The Viking Press, 1977).

Perlingieri, Ilya Sandra. "Born to Shock." *Threads* (April/May 1988).

Perrot, Philippe. *Les Dessus et les dessous de la bourgeoisie: Une histoire du vêtement au xixe siècle* (Paris: Fayard, 1981).

———. *Le Travail des apparences, ou les transformations du corps féminin xviiie - xixe siècle* (Paris: Éditions du Seuil, 1984).

Perschetz, Lois, ed. *W: The Designing Life* (New York: Clarkson N. Potter, Inc., 1987).

Petroff, Daniela. "Women Designers." *The International Herald Tribune*, Special section, "Who's Who in Italian Fashion" (October 3-4, 1981).

Picken, Mary Brooks, and Dora Loues Miller. *Dressmakers of France* (New York: Harper & Brothers, 1956).

Pierre, Clara. *Looking Good: The Liberation of Fashion* (New York: Reader's Digest Press, 1976).

van der Post, Lucia. "The Queen of Simple Chic." *Financial Times Weekend* (March 9-19, 1991).

Poyet, Marie-Ange. "Krizia et les Mariucci ou une femme et ses doubles." *Joyce* (Spring-Summer 1988).

Quant, Mary. *Quant on Quant* (London: Cassel & Co., 1966).

Radakovitch, Anka. "Hot Kamali's Kicky Clothes." *New York Apparel News* (April 1984).

Rafferty, Diane. "Beyond Fashion: Mary McFadden Ransacks the Past for Her Timeless Evening Dresses." *Connoisseur* (October 1988).

Reed, Ruth Brown. "These Designing Young Americans." *Vogue* (September 1935).

Reed, Julia, "Talking Fashion: Carolina Herrera Is the Undisputed Queen of Seventh Avenue." *Vogue* (June 1990).

———. "DKNY." *Vogue* (December 1990).

Reeder, Jan. "The House of Paquin." *Textile and Text* 12:14 (1990).

Rhodes, Zandra, and Anne Knight. *The Art of Zandra Rhodes* (Boston: Houghton Mifflin Co., 1984).

Roberts, Michael. "From Punk to PM." *Tatler* (April 1989).

Roche, Daniel. *La Culture des apparences: Une histoire du vêtement xviie–xviiie siècle* (Paris: Fayard, 1989).

Roger-Milès, L. *Les Créateurs de la mode* (Paris: Eggimann, 1910).

Rouff, Maggy. *Ce que j'ai vu en chiffonnant la clientèle* (Paris: Librairie des Champs-Élysées, 1938).

———. *L'Philosophie d'élégance* (Paris: Éditions Littéraires de France, 1942).

"Royal Flush: Vivienne Westwood." *i-D* (August 1987).

Rumbold, Judy. "Hot Coco." *Elle* (Great Britain; November, 1988).

Russell, Mary. "New Japanese Fashions." *Vogue* (September 1982).

Rykiel, Sonia. *Et je la voudrai nue . . .* (Paris: Bernard Grasset, 1979).

Sarlin, Bob. "Chanel: A Show That Ran for 87 Years." *The New York Times* (January 11, 1971).

Schiaparelli, Elsa. *Shocking Life* (New York: E. P. Dutton, 1954).

Schifres, Alain. "La vie en B." *Le Nouvel Observateur* (March 7–13, 1986).

Schiro, Anne-Marie. "Adrienne Vittadini: From Sweaters to an Empire." *The New York Times* (July 19, 1988).

———. "For Fall, Fashions That Make One Statement: Wearability." *The New York Times* (April 8, 1990).

———. "To Sleep? Chances Are, To Dream." *The New York Times* (August 21, 1990).

Schreier, Barbara. *Mystique and Identity: Women's Fashions of the 1950s* (Norfolk, VA: The Chrysler Museum, 1984).

Scott-James, Anne. *In the Mink* (London: Michael Joseph, 1952).

Shapiro, Harriott. "From Venezuela to 7th Avenue." *People* (May 3, 1982).

Shelley, Jim. "Vivienne Westwood and Sarah Stockbridge." *Blitz* (March 1988).

Shields, Jody. "Madcap Couturier." *Elle* (September 1988).

Sirop, Dominique. *Paquin* (Paris: Adam Biro, 1989).

Snow, Carmel, with Mary Louise Aswell. *The World of Carmel Snow* (New York: McGraw-Hill, 1962).

Stan, Adelle-Marie. "Four Designing Women." *Ms.* (November 1986).

Starzinger, Page Hill. "Smart Women, Smart Clothes." *Vogue* (September 1988).

Steele, Valerie. *Paris Fashion: A Cultural History* (New York: Oxford University Press, 1988).

———. "Dressing for Work," in Claudia Kidwell and Valerie Steele, eds. *Men and Women: Dressing the Part* (Washington: Smithsonian Institution Press, 1989).

Stegemeyer, Anne. *Who's Who in Fashion* (New York: Fairchild, 1980).

Sudjic, Deyan. *Rei Kawakubo and Comme des Garçons* (New York: Rizzoli International, 1990).

Szabo, Julia. "Diane Von Furstenberg." *Vogue* (January 1991).

Tamerlin, Jane. "New York's Hot New Designer." *World Journal Tribune* (September 23, 1966).

Tate, Sharon Lee. *Inside Fashion Design* (New York: Harper & Row, 1984).

"Tête d'affiche: Inès de la Fressange." *Ena Mensuel* 179 (1988).

Thurman, Judith. "'Power Gives You an Aura,' Says Mary McFadden." *Mirabella* (September 1989).

"The Timeless Style of Madame Grès." *The New York Times* (October 10, 1979).

Timmons, Stuart. "Designer Rudi Gernreich Stayed In the Fashion Closet." *The Advocate* (September 25, 1990).

Treglia, Marie-Claude. "Agnès B.: L'Art de vivre les yeux ouverts." *Marie Claire* (November 1987).

Troy, Carol. "Like the Boys." *The Village Voice* (February 14, 1984).

Turbeville, Deborah. *Wallflower* (New York: Quartet, 1978).

———. *Les Amoureuses du temps passé* (Tokyo: Parco, 1985).

Vionnet, Madeleine. *Photograph Albums* (unpublished). Union Française des Arts du Costume (Paris).

Valentina. "Valentina Believes." *Harper's Bazaar* (January 1945).

———. "Designing for Life and Theatre." *Theatre Arts* (February 1945).

Vecchio, Robert, with text by Robert Riley. *The Fashion Makers/A Photographic Record* (New York: Crown Publishers, 1967).

Veillon, Dominique. *La Mode sous l'occupation* (Paris: Editions Payot, 1990).

"Vivienne Westwood." *The Face* (May 1987).

Voight, Rebecca. "Martine Sitbon: France's Best-Kept Fashion Secret." *i-D* (March 1989).

Vreeland, Diana. *American Women of Style* (New York: Costume Institute, Metropolitan Museum of Art, 1975).

———. *Allure* (Garden City, NY: Doubleday & Co., 1980).

———. *D.V.* George Plimpton and Christopher Hemphill, eds. (New York: Alfred A. Knopf, 1984).

Walkley, Christina. *The Ghost in the Looking Glass: The Victorian Seamstress* (London: Peter Owen, 1981).

"We Orbit Around . . . Betsey Johnson." *Mademoiselle* (August 1966).

Webb, Iain. "Secure With Miss Muir." *Harper's & Queen* (March 1991).

Weiner, Annette B., and Jane Schneider. *Cloth and Human Experience* (Washington and London: Smithsonian Institution Press, 1989).

Weinstein, Jeff. "Vionnet, McCardell, Kawakubo: Why There Are Three Great Women Artists." *The Village Voice* (March 31, 1987).

Weir, June. "Closing the Gender Gap." *The New York Times Magazine* (June 30, 1985).

"What Chanel Storm is About: She Takes Chance on a Comeback." *Life* (March 1, 1954).

White, Palmer. *Schiaparelli, Empress of Paris Fashion* (New York: Rizzoli International, 1986).

Williams, Beryl. *Fashion is Our Business* (Philadelphia: J. B. Lippincott, 1945).

———. *Young Faces in Fashion* (Philadelphia: J. B. Lippincott, 1956).

Wilson, Elizabeth. *Adorned in Dreams* (London: Virago Press, 1985).

Wilson, Robert Forrest. *Paris On Parade* (Indianapolis: The Bobbs-Merrill Company, 1924–25).

Wizman, Ariel. "Martine Sitbon: Un tumultueux repertoire." *Jardin des Modes* (June 1989).

Wohlfert-Wihlborg, Lee. "The Label Is Anne Klein, But the Name That Keeps It Going Belongs to Donna Karan." *People* (March 29, 1982).

"Women Designers Set New Fashions." *Life* (January 14, 1946).

Woods, Vicky. "Designing Woman: Charlotte Neuville." *Vogue* (September 1989).

———. "Talking Fashion: Pauline Trigère." *Vogue* (October 1989).

Yoxall, H. W. *A Fashion of Life* (New York: Taplinger, 1967).

Zaletova, Lidya, et al. *Revolutionary Costume: Soviet Clothing and Textiles of the 1920s* (New York: Rizzoli International, 1989).

Zerbib, Chantal. "'La femme n'est pas un clown, ou la mode vue par Madame Grès." *Lire* (May 1986).

## PERIODICALS

*Accent; American Fashions and Fabrics; l'Art et la Mode; Art, Goût, Beauté; Blitz; Connoisseur; Costume: The Journal of the Costume Society; Daily News Record; Details; Dress; Elle* (American, British, French); *The Face; Femina; Figaro* (including *Figaro-Modes* and *Madame Figaro*); *Gazette du Bon Ton; Harper's and Queen; Harper's Bazaar; i.-D.; International Herald Tribune; Interview; Jardin des Modes; Life; Look; Mademoiselle; Mirabella; La Mode en Peinture; Les Modes; New York; New York Apparel News; The New York Times; The New York Times Magazine; The New Yorker; L'Officiel de la Couture; Paper; Threads; Vanity Fair; The Village Voice; Vogue* (American, British, French, Italian, Spanish); *W; Woman's Wear Daily.*

## FILM

*Chanel, Chanel,* A film by Eila Hershon and Roberto Guerra, RM Arts, 1986

# INDEX

Abbott, Bernice 129
Adrian 101
Dr. Agha 128
Agnès 75
Agnès B. 166
Agnoga 177
AIDS 212
Albertina 171
Albini, Roberto 168
Alix, see Mme Grès
Allias, Erica 201
Amiot, Félix 48
Anger, Kenneth 167
*Anna and the King of Siam* 143
Ant, Adam 156
Antonelli, Maria 171, 172, 173
Apollinaire, Guillaume 74
  "On Her Dress She Wears Her Body" 74
Armani, Giorgio 53, 171, 176
Arnell, Peter 8, 191
Arno, Peter 100
Arrowsmith, Clive 150, 151
Arroyello, Javier 50
Art Deco 29, 35, 36, 175
Ascoli, Marc 168
Ashley, Laura 137, 138, 139
Atkinson, Brooks 96
Augustabernard 70, 80, 83
Avedon, Richard 130, 189

Bacon, Chantal 202
Bailey, David 126
Bailly, Christiane 138, 139
Balenciaga, Cristóbal 37, 49, 116, 138, 167, 175, 178
Ballard, Bettina 92, 106, 108, 117
Ballarian, Dick 173
Ballerino, Louella 103
Balsan, Etienne 40, 42
Bandy, Way 212
Banton, Travis 122
Bara, Clementine 27
Barbier, Georges 29, 30
*Barefoot Contessa* 172
Barnes, Jhane 16
Baron de Meyer 7 2
Baroness d'Oberkirch 20
Barton, Germaine, see Mme Grès
Baudelaire, Charles 41
Bauer, Britta 133
M Baulard 20
Beaton, Cecil 11, 45, 49, 50, 61
Beatty, Warren 138
Bechoff-David 73
Beckers, Jeanne Marie Charlotte, see Paquin, Jeanne
Beeche, Robyn 154
Beene, Geoffrey 207
Bendel's 202
Bérard, Bébé 48, 66
Béraud, Jean 28
Berch, Bettina 94, 112
Beretta, Anne Marie 166, 167
Bergdorf Goodman 173, 202
Bergler, Edmund 212
Bertall 23
Bertin, Rose 20, 21
Bettina 114
Biagiotti, Laura 144, 170, 173, 174, 176
Biba 17, 133, 134, 136
Biki 173
Billy Boy 69
Bird, J. 19
Blass, Bill 98
Bloomingdale's 101, 194
*Blow-Up* 124, 126
Bocher, Main Rousseau 80

Boiven, Jeanne 79
Bongard, Germaine 79
Mme Bonneau 21
Borea, Vera 173
Boucher, Françios 18
Mme Bourgueil 57
Bourke-White, Margaret 91, 99, 129
Boussac, Marcel 116
Bouvard, Palmyre 62
Boyer, Paul 27
Breton, André 68
Bricard, Mizza 116, 117, 118
Brigance, Tom 106
Brigman, Anne 128
Brissand, Pierre 30
Brodovitch, Alexey 92, 128
Brock, Jean 30
Brokaw, Lucille 128

Cale, John 141
Callas, Maria 173
Callot sisters 25, 31, 32, 33, 43, 70, 77
Callot, Joséphine 31
Callot, Marie 31
Callot, Marthe 31
Callot, Régina 31
Mme Camille 23
Campbell, Jeanne 133
Campbell, Mary 124
Campbell, Naomi 208–209
Capalli, Patti 193
Capel, Arthur "Boy" 42
Capezio 108
Cardin, Pierre 133, 138
Carnegie, Hattie 101, 103, 105, 122, 123
Carpentier, Susie 84, 86
Carter, Ernestine 39, 126, 128
Carven, House of 84, 88
Casanova, Patrice 199
Cashin, Bonnie 103, 142, 143, 144
Cassat, Mary
  *The Fitting* 24
Castillo 84
*Chambre Syndicale de la Haute Couture* 29, 83
Chanel, Gabrielle "Coco" 9, 11, 13, 14, 16, 27, 31, 34, 38–53, 54, 63, 66, 70, 72, 87, 100, 114, 117, 118, 137, 149, 152, 153, 175, 203
Chanel, House of 52, 63, 67, 74, 80, 143, 160
"Chanel Number 5" 46, 48
Chanel, Parfums 46, 48
Chapman, Ceil 103, 114
Chase, Edna Woolman 44, 126, 127
Chatwin, Bruce 63
Chaumont, Marcelle 84, 85
Mme Cheruit 30, 31, 70
Chloé 167
Churchill, Winston 48
*Ciao Manhattan* 142
Claiborne, Liz 133, 144, 201, 204
Clyne, Patricia 203, 205, 206, 207
Cobson, Corinne 166
Cocteau, Jean 66, 68, 69
Comme des Garçons 10, 182, 183, 184, 185, 186, 187
Contratto, Mark 210
Cooper, Arlene 83
Copeland, Jo 103
Corsaint-Dorvyne 65
Mme Cosme 73
Courrèges, André 50, 133, 134, 135, 138, 139
Cubism 76
Cunningham, Bill 142, 143

Dahl-Wolfe, Louise 52, 89, 102, 105, 106, 107, 109, 111, 114, 116, 117, 118, 125, 126, 127, 128, 129
d'Alençon, Emilienne 40

Dali, Salvador 41, 47, 64, 66, 67, 68
Daniels, Betsy 201
D'Annunzio, Gabriele 173
Davelli, Marthe 45
de Beauvoir, Simone 119
  *The Second Sex* 119
de Fleurieu, Agnès 166
Degas, Edgar
  *The Millinery Shop* 23
de Hoz, Martinez 59
de la Falaise, Maxime 133
de la Fressange, Inès 52, 53
de la Renta, Franciose 195
de la Renta, Oscar 9, 10, 195, 196, 198, 202
  Miss O line 195
Delaunay, Robert 74
Delaunay, Sonia 11, 70, 74, 75, 78
  *Robes-Poèmes* 74
Demaria, Simone 78
Demorest, Ellen Curtis 25
de Musset, Alfred 23
de Pougy, Liane 29
de Prémonville, Myrène 166
de Rauch, Madeleine 70, 73
de Ribes, Jacqueline 72, 197, 199
de Vilmorin, Louise 35
Dew, Diana 142
de Wagner, M and Mme 70, 76, 77
de Wagner, Maggy Besançon, see Rouff, Maggy
Diaghilev
  Ballets Russes 47
Dickens, Charles 24
Dior, Christian 9, 11, 49, 101, 108, 116, 119, 167, 207
Dmitri, Grand Duke 45
Dolci, Flora 174
Domenici, Anna 176
DKNY 8, 191, 194, 195
Dorothée bis 138, 140
Doucet, House of 31, 57, 58, 59
Doucet, Jacques 25, 57
Drecoll, Agnès 74
Drécoll, House of 70, 76, 77
Duchess Elizabeth de Gramont, 61, 82
Duchess of Windsor 68
Duchessa Simonetta Colonna di Cesaro, see Simonetta
Duff-Gordon, Sir Cosimo 32
Duke of Westminster 45, 46, 48, 52, 66

*Ecole de la Chambre Syndicale* 205
Elliot, Osborne 112
Ellis, Perry 201, 212
Elsie, Lilie
  *The Merry Widow* 34
Empress Eugènie 22
Empress Josephine 22
Erté 175
Estrada, Angel 212
Evans, Caroline 68
Evans, Lee 113
Exter, Alexandra 75, 76

Fabiani, Alberto 173
Fairchild, John 198, 212
Farly, Lilian 80
Fashion Institute of Technology 63, 112, 211
  "Three Women" exhibition 188
Fath, Genevieve 116
Fath, Jacques 15, 115, 116, 118, 119, 120
Fellowes, Mrs Reginald "Daisy" 82, 117
Fendi sisters 144, 171, 174, 175
Fendi, Adele 174
Fendi, Alda 174, 175
Fendi, Anna 174, 175
Fendi, Carla 174, 175

Fendi, Edoardo 174
Fendi, Franca 174, 175
Fendi, House of 176
Fendi, Paola 174, 175
Ferré 176
Feurer, Hans 183
Feydeau, Ernest
   L'Art de plaire 25
Fini, Leonor 68
Fisher, Lillian 75
Foale, Marion 134, 135, 137, 138
Fogarty, Anne 109, 112, 114, 119, 120, 121
Fontaine, Lynn 96
Fontana sisters 171, 172, 173
Fontana, Giovanna 172
Fontana, Micol 172
Fontana, Zoe 172
Ford, Charlotte 198
Forman, Edwin 110
Francis, Kay 100
Fraser, Kennedy 142
Freud, Sigmund 67, 68
Fribourg, Chantal 60
Friedan, Betty 119
   The Feminine Mystique 119
Frissell, Toni 129
Frizon, Maud 203
Frohman, Jesse 130
Funny Face 124
Futurism 76

Gan, Stephen 211
Garbo, Greta 98
Gardner, Ava 172
Garnier, Guillaume 61, 62, 79
Gaudry Eugènie 27
Gaultier, Jean-Paul 69, 157, 167
George, Jennifer 203, 204, 205, 206, 207
   "Mother George" line 206
Mme Gerber 57
Mme Germond 22
Gernreich, Rudi 201, 212
Gervex
   Pauquin at 5 o'clock 28
Giacomoni, Silvia 177
Gibo 181
Gill, Brendan 100
Gimbel, Sophie 103, 122
Ginsburg, Madeleine 62
Glaviano, Marco 174
Gluehom, Emma 123
Glyn, Elinor 32
   Three Weeks 32
Goddard, Paulett 96
Graham, Martha 108
Grateaux, Muriel 176
Gravenites, Linda 142
Greene, Joshua 12, 85
Gremela 37
Mme Grès Frontispiece, 11, 14, 70, 82, 83, 84,
   87, 89, 98, 116
Maison Grès 84
Griffin, Brian 10
Mme Gropius 74
Gross, Michael 198
Groult, Nicole 65, 70, 79, 80, 81, 82, 92

Haedrich, Marcel 39
Halston 212
Hamnett, Katharine 15, 152, 159, 160, 161, 169
   "Power Dressing" collection 160
Hardwick, Cathy 133
Harp, Holly 133, 142
Hastreiter, Kim 166, 206
Hawes, Elizabeth 90, 92, 93, 94, 95, 96, 99,
   100, 112
   "Amazon" evening dress 93
   "Alimony" evening dress 93, 95
   "Five Year Plan" dress 93
   "Foot Gloves" shoes 94
   "Ganges" evening dress 93
   "King of Hearts" suit 93
   "Limpopo" evening dress 93
   "Mad Hatter" coat 93
   "Misadventure" cape 93, 95
   "Nazi" dress 93

"People's Choice" dress 93
"Prosperity is Just Around the Corner" dress
   93
"Pussyfoot" shoes 94
"Revolt of the Masses" dress 93
"Rubicon" evening dress 93
"Volga" evening dress 93
"Yellow Peril" dress 93
Head, Edith 120
Hearst, William Randolph 126
Hebdige, Dick 153
Heim, Jacques 74
Hempel, Anouska 199
Hepburn, Katharine 91, 96, 99, 166
Hermès 37
Herrera, Carolina 72, 194, 197, 199
Hirokawa Taishi 145
Hochswender, Woody 204
Hollander, Anne 58, 87
Hoover, J. Edgar 94
Horn, Carol 133
Horst 47, 48, 126, 129
Howell, Georgina 195
Howley, James 110
Hoyningen-Huene, George 75, 78, 80, 83, 129
Hulanicki, Barbara 17, 132, 133, 134, 136, 137
Hyde, Nina 194

Iman 192
"Intimate Architecture" exhibition 176
Iribe, Paul 27, 29, 35
Ironside, Janey 122
Issermann, Dominique 131

Jacobs, Marc 205, 212
Jacobson, Jacqueline 138, 139, 140
Mme Jacquet 74
Janin, Jules 23
Mme Jenny 70, 72, 73, 84
Jenny, House of 73
Johnson, Betsey 133, 135, 141, 142, 200, 201,
   202
Joplin, Janis 142
Joyce, Emmett 101

Kahlo, Frida 15
Kaleidoscope 137, 138
Kamali, Norma 144, 145, 201, 212
Karan, Donna 8, 108, 133, 190, 192, 193, 194,
   201, 204
Karan, Gaby 194, 195
Karan, Mark 193
Kawakubo, Rei 9, 10, 68, 182, 183, 184, 185,
   186, 187, 188
   "Bonded" dress 188
Kellett, Caroline 51
Kennedy, Lucy, see Lucille
Comte de Kerlor 65
Khanh, Emmanuelle 138, 139, 141
Khudjakova, Elena 76
King, Muriel 90, 91, 92, 99, 100
   "Flying Fortress Fashions" 100
Kirkland, Sally 104
Klein, Adolphe 113
Klein, Anne 122, 144, 193, 194
Klein, Calvin 9, 190, 201
Koda, Harold 186, 188
Kornbluth, Jesse 195
Kors, Michael 205
Kozasu, Atsuko 186
Kravis, Henry 195, 196, 197
Krizia 16, 171, 174, 176, 177

La Belle Otéro 29
Lacroix, Christian 69, 157, 172, 202
Lagerfeld, Karl 9, 11, 34, 37, 44, 49, 50, 52, 53,
   167, 174, 203
Lalique 37
Lannan, J. Patrick 198
Lantelme 59, 61
Lanvin, Bernard 37
Lanvin, House of 35, 37, 75, 84
   "Arpège" 37
   "My Sin" perfume 37
Lanvin, Jeanne 11, 34, 35, 36, 37, 62, 70, 79,
   117

Lanvin, Marie-Blanche 35, 36
Lanvin, Maryll 37
Laura 143
Lauren, Ralph 190
Laurencin, Marie 79
Lavallière, Eve 59
Lecca, Dan 204
Le Corbusier 87, 188
Lelong 116
Leonardi, Elvira, see Biki
Lepape, Georges 35
Leroy, Louis Hippolyte 21, 22
Lesage 67
Leser, Curtin 109
Leser, Tina 14, 103, 106, 107, 109, 110, 111,
   114, 144
Let It Rock shop 156
Leva, Michael 205
Liberman, Alexander 131, 199
Lifar, Serge 51
Lindbergh, Peter 182, 184, 185, 186, 187
Lipman, Pearl Alexander 101
Logan, Jonathan 144
Long, Lois 100, 101
Loos, Adolf 41
Lopez, Antonio 212
Lord & Taylor 92, 93, 99, 106, 107, 108, 112,
   121
Loren, Sophia 173
Louis XIV 19
Louiseboulanger 31, 70, 71, 80, 82, 84
Lowit, Roxanne 1, 130, 131, 160, 161, 163,
   165, 168, 169, 192, 193, 196, 197, 201
Luba 133
Luce, Clare Booth 96
Lucille 32, 33, 34, 35
   "Do you love me?" dress 33
   "Gap in the hedge" dress 33
   "Garden of Love" dress 33
   "Gown of emotion" 35
   "I paid the price" dress 33, 35
   "Kiss me again" dress 33, 35
   "Sighing sound of lips unsatisfied" dress 33
Lumley, Joanna 149
Luther, Marylou 164

McCardell, Claire 12, 14, 99, 102–113, 116,
   122, 129, 188, 201, 207
   "Baby-doll" dress 106
   "Diaper Bathing Suit" 108
   "Kitchen Dinner Dress" 108
   "Monastic" dress 104, 105
   "Popover" dress 107
Machine Age 35
McClaren, Malcolm 153, 156
McDowell, Colin 175
McFadden, Mary 133, 198, 199, 212
McGowan, Cathy 137
Macy's 199
Mad Carpentier 84, 86
Mlle Madeleine 70, 76
Mainbocher 48, 80, 101, 116
Maltezos, Mad 84, 86
Mandelli, Mariuccia 16, 171, 172, 174, 175,
   176, 177
Man Ray 71
Mardon, Jeanne 63
Mme Marguerite 116
Marie-Antionette 20, 21
Marquise de Paris 80
Martin, Richard 188, 211
Masandrea, Frank 212
Massei, Enrica 176
Mauri, Rosella 176
Maxwell, Vera 103
Meisel, Steven 184
Mendes, Valerie 156
Menkes, Suzy 183, 197
Meranus, Dianne T. 10
Metzner, Sheila 130, 131
Meyer, Marcelle 79
Milbank, Caroline 25, 109, 112
Miller, Nicole 204, 205
Milstein, Alan 212
Mirabella, Grace 130

Missoni, Rosita 171, 176
Mitford, Unity 129, 130
Mizrahi, Isaac 207
Mod 207
Model, Philippe 203
    "Chair" hat 203
Monroe, Marilyn 165
Montana, Claude 37
Moon, Sarah 131
Morand, Paul 40, 43
Mori, Akira 189
Mori, Hanae 133, 189
Mori, Kei 189
Mori, Ken 189
Moriceau, Norma 152
Morris, Alice 109
Moscow Fashion Studio 76
Moses, Rebecca 205, 206, 212
Muir, Jean 15, 131, 137, 144, 149, 151, 152
Mulvagh, Jane 144
Munkacsi 128

Nast, Condé 126, 127
Natalie 89
Naylor, Genevieve 129
Netchvolodoff, Dmitri 63
Neuville, Charlotte 205
Newhouse, Si 199
New Look 49, 50, 101, 108, 119, 207
1925 Paris Exhibition 74
Noguchi, Isamu 99
Norell, Norman 101, 104
Novick, Elizabeth 131

Dell'Olio, Louis 194, 212
Onassis, Jacqueline 199
"Operation Modellhut" 48
Orrick, Mildred 109, 127

Mme Palmyre 22, 23, 24
"The Panther Woman of the Needle Trades" 92
Paquin, House of 43, 77
Paquin, Isadore Rene Jacob dit Paquin 28
Paquin, Jeanne 25, 26, 27, 28, 29, 30, 31, 34, 43
Paquin, Joseph 28
Paraphernalia 142
Paray, Lucile 70, 74, 78
Paris Exhibition of 1867 24
Paris Universal Exhibition of 1900 27, 28
Parisite, see Groult, Nicole
Parnis, Mollie 103
Parsons School of Design 104, 193
Pascali, Antonio 171, 173
Pastor, Patricia 212
Patou, Jean 43, 44, 49, 50, 72, 73
Patrick, Gail 99
Peck & Peck 111
Pernet, Diane 203, 206, 207
Petroff, Daniela 171, 173
Phelps 108
Picasso, Paloma 203
Piel, Dennis 193, 194
Pierre, Clara 133
Pinto, Aldo 176
Poiret, Denise 79
Poiret, House of 65, 66
Poiret, Paul 11, 27, 29, 31, 34, 37, 43, 44, 46,
    57, 62, 68, 79, 80
Pomodoro, Carmelo 212
Ponsonby, Loelia 46
Popova, Liubov 75, 76
Potter, Claire 101, 103, 111
Potter, Pauline 123
Porizkova, Paulina 170, 190
Premet 44
Princess Irene Galitzine 173
Princess Jean Louis "Baba" de Fraucigny-
    Lucinge 171
Prost, Rosalie 27
Proust, Marcel 31
Pucci 109
Punk 68

Quant, Mary 133, 134, 135, 138, 141

Raban, Paco 138

Mme Raimbault 21
Rankin, Isaia 212
Ranson, Geraldine 184
Raudnitz 31
Mme Raymonde 116
Redfern 14
Reeder, Jan 27
Régny, Jane 44, 70, 72, 73, 75
Reims, Bettine 131
Restivo, Mary Anne 212
Retama, Juan Carlos 178
Rhodes, Zandra 15, 146, 147, 148, 149, 150,
    151, 157
    "Butterfly No. 93" dress 148
    "Dinosaur" coat 148
Ricci, Louis 77
Ricci, Nina 11, 70, 77, 80
Ricci, Robert 77
Roberts, Catherine 110
Roche, Daniel 20, 21
Rodchenko, Alexander 78
Roehm, Axel 195
Roehm, Carolyne 1, 194, 195, 196, 197, 198,
    199, 202, 204
Rogers, Ginger 91, 99
Rohatyn, Felix 198
Rosenstein, Nettie 101, 103, 109
Rosier, Michèle 138, 139
Rotten, Johnny 153
Rouff, Maggy 29, 31, 65, 77, 80
Rouff, Maison 28
Ruggeri, Cinzia 176
Russell, Bertrand 153
Russell, Rosalind 96
Ruttenstein, Kal 194
Rykiel, Sonia 16, 138, 140, 144, 149, 162, 164,
    165, 186

S., Walter 206
Sacerdote, Jenny, see Mme Jenny
Saint Laurent, Yves 9, 16, 50, 133, 135, 138,
    166, 184, 207
Saks Fifth Avenue 100, 110, 114
Saltzman, Ellin 199
Sanina, Valentina Nicholaevna, see Valentina
Sanlorenzo sisters 176
Schiaparelli, Elsa 9, 11, 14, 37, 46, 47, 64-69,
    70, 72, 80, 100, 103, 148, 149, 167, 173,
    175, 201
    "Lamb-chop Hat" 68
    "Shoe Hat" 64, 68
    "Shocking" perfume 68
    "Tear Dress" 68
Schlee, George 96, 98
Schnurer, Carolyn 14-15, 103, 110, 111, 113, 114
    "Hakama" dress 112
Schön, Mila 171
Schreier, Barbara 119
Scorpio Rising 167
Sears 15
Sedgwick, Edie 142
Sem 42
Sert, Misia 40, 63
Sèvres 37
Sex Pistols 153
Shaver, Dorothy 106
Shearer, Norma 96
Shillard-Smith, Christine, see Leser, Tina
Shrimpton, Jean 137
Sider, Frances 103
Signal Knitting Mills 202
Simmel, George 40
Simonetta 171, 173
Sims, Naomi 130
Sinclair, Paul 199
Sinderbrand, Laura 188
Sitbon, Martine 163, 168, 169
    "Cinderella" collection 167
Smith, Jane Caroline, see Roehm, Carolyne
Smith, Willi 212
Snow, Carmel 126, 127, 128, 129
Snow, Palen 126
Snow, Tom 127
Sophie 114
Sorel, Alain 144
Stendhal 23

Stepanova, Varvara 75, 76, 78
Stern, Bert 129
Stern, Julius 193
Stone, Elisa 142
Streisand, Barbra 130
Studio Berçot 167
Sudjic, Deyan 188
Surrealism 67
Swanson, Gloria 96
Sybilla 178, 179, 180, 181

Tagore, Rabindranath 109
Taine, Hippolyte, 24
Talbot, Suzanne 35
Talley, André Leon 164, 199
Tapie, Bernard 84
Tate, Sharon 11
Thatcher, Margaret 157, 158, 159, 160
Thomass, Chantal 165, 166, 205
Thompson, Kay 124
Thornton, Minna 68
Thurber, James 90
Tierney, Gene 143
Tilley, Monica 201
Timmons, Stuart 212
Toledo, Isabel 203, 206, 207, 208-209, 210
Toledo, Ruben 207
Townley Frocks 104, 105, 109
Traphagen School 199
Trigère, Pauline 103, 122, 123
Tuffin, Sally 134, 135, 137, 138
Turbeville, Deborah 131
Turner, Jessie Franklin 101
Twiggy 130, 137, 167

Underwood, Patricia 203

Valentina 90, 92, 96, 97, 98, 99, 103
Valentino, Maria Chandoha 53, 201
Vallhonrat, Javier 178, 180, 181
Vanderbilt, Gloria 198
Van Dongen 73-74
Valois, Rose 83
Vass, Joan 200, 202
Velvet Underground 141, 167
Versace, Gianni 171, 176
Vertès 66
Victoria & Albert Museum 186
Mme Victorine 23
Vionnet, House of, Biarritz 57
Vionnet, Madeleine 9, 11, 13, 14, 31, 37, 42,
    44, 54-65, 67, 70, 77, 82, 83, 84, 93, 98,
    100, 101, 114, 129, 149, 188
Vittadini, Adrienne 16, 201, 203, 204
von Fürstenberg, Diane 133, 144, 198
von Horn, Baroness Toni 129
von Unworth, Ellen 131
Vreeland, Diana 11, 54, 57, 98, 109, 116, 124,
    129, 130, 131, 173

Weinstein, Jeff 63
Weir, June 190
Wertheimer, Pierre 46, 48
Westwood, Vivienne 6, 9, 15, 68, 152, 153,
    154, 155, 156, 157, 158, 159, 166, 186
    "Buffalo Girls" collection 156, 157
    "Hobos" collection 156
    "Pirates" collection 154, 156
    "Savages" collection 154, 156
    "Witches" collection 156, 157
White, Carmel 126
Williamns, Beryl 142
Wilson, Edmund 92
Wilson, Robert Forrest
    Paris on Parade 31
Woolf, Virginia 16
Worth, Charles Frederick 11, 22, 23, 24, 27,
    31, 32, 34, 37, 118
Worth, House of 25, 28, 43, 148
Wright, Frank Lloyd 87

York, Susannah 137, 138
Youthquakers 129

Zeffirelli, Franco 50